Other Books and Series by Jeff Bowen

Applications for Enrollment of Chickasaw Newborn Act of 1905
Volumes I thru VII

Cherokee Intermarried White 1906 Volume I, II & III

Visit our website at **www.nativestudy.com** to learn more about these
and other books and series by Jeff Bowen

I0222594

CHEROKEE
INTERMARRIED WHITE
1906
VOLUME IV

TRANSCRIBED BY
JEFF BOWEN

NATIVE STUDY
Gallipolis, Ohio
USA

Other Books and Series by Jeff Bowen

1901-1907 Native American Census Seneca, Eastern Shawnee, Miami, Modoc, Ottawa, Peoria, Quapaw, and Wyandotte Indians (Under Seneca School, Indian Territory)

1932 Census of The Standing Rock Sioux Reservation with Births And Deaths 1924-1932

Census of The Blackfeet, Montana, 1897- 1901 Expanded Edition

Eastern Cherokee by Blood, 1906-1910, Volumes I thru XIII

Choctaw of Mississippi Indian Census 1929-1932 with Births and Deaths 1924-1931   Volume I
Choctaw of Mississippi Indian Census 1933, 1934 & 1937, Supplemental Rolls to 1934 & 1935 with Births and Deaths 1932-1938, and Marriages 1936-1938 Volume II

Eastern Cherokee Census Cherokee, North Carolina 1930-1939
Census 1930-1931 with Births And Deaths 1924-1931 Taken By Agent L. W. Page Volume I
Eastern Cherokee Census Cherokee, North Carolina 1930-1939
Census 1932-1933 with Births And Deaths 1930-1932 Taken By Agent R. L. Spalsbury   Volume II
Eastern Cherokee Census Cherokee, North Carolina 1930-1939
Census 1934-1937 with Births and Deaths 1925-1938 and Marriages 1936 & 1938 Taken by Agents R. L. Spalsbury And Harold W. Foght Volume III

Seminole of Florida Indian Census, 1930-1940 with Birth and Death Records, 1930-1938

Texas Cherokees 1820-1839 A Document For Litigation 1921

Choctaw By Blood Enrollment Cards 1898-1914 Volumes I thru XVII

Starr Roll 1894 (Cherokee Payment Rolls) Districts: Canadian, Cooweescoowee, and Delaware Volume One
Starr Roll 1894 (Cherokee Payment Rolls) Districts: Flint, Going Snake, and Illinois Volume Two
Starr Roll 1894 (Cherokee Payment Rolls) Districts: Saline, Sequoyah, and Tahlequah; Including Orphan Roll Volume Three

Cherokee Intruder Cases Dockets of Hearings 1901-1909 Volumes I & II

Indian Wills, 1911-1921 Records of the Bureau of Indian Affairs
Books One thru Seven;
Native American Wills & Probate Records 1911-1921

Other Books and Series by Jeff Bowen

Turtle Mountain Reservation Chippewa Indians 1932 Census with Births & Deaths, 1924-1932

Chickasaw By Blood Enrollment Cards 1898-1914 Volume I thru V

Cherokee Descendants East An Index to the Guion Miller Applications Volume I
Cherokee Descendants West An Index to the Guion Miller Applications Volume II (A-M)
Cherokee Descendants West An Index to the Guion Miller Applications Volume III (N-Z)

Applications for Enrollment of Seminole Newborn Freedmen, Act of 1905

Eastern Cherokee Census, Cherokee, North Carolina, 1915-1922, Taken by Agent James E. Henderson   *Volume I (1915-1916)*
Volume II (1917-1918)
Volume III (1919-1920)
Volume IV (1921-1922)

Complete Delaware Roll of 1898

Eastern Cherokee Census, Cherokee, North Carolina, 1923-1929, Taken by Agent James E. Henderson   *Volume I (1923-1924)*
Volume II (1925-1926)
Volume III (1927-1929)

Applications for Enrollment of Seminole Newborn Act of 1905 Volumes I & II

North Carolina Eastern Cherokee Indian Census 1898-1899, 1904, 1906, 1909-1912, 1914 Revised and Expanded Edition

1932 Hopi and Navajo Native American Census with Birth & Death Rolls (1925-1931) Volume 1 - Hopi
1932 Hopi and Navajo Native American Census with Birth & Death Rolls (1930-1932) Volume 2 - Navajo

Western Navajo Reservation Navajo, Hopi and Paiute 1933 Census with Birth & Death Rolls 1925-1933

Cherokee Citizenship Commission Dockets 1880-1884 and 1887-1889 Volumes I thru V

Copyright © 2014
by Jeff Bowen

ALL RIGHTS RESERVED
No part of this publication may be reproduced
or used in any form or manner whatsoever
without previous written permission from the
copyright holder or publisher.

Originally published:
Baltimore, Maryland
2014

Reprinted by:

Native Study LLC
Gallipolis, OH
www.nativestudy.com
2020

Library of Congress Control Number: 2020917307

ISBN: 978-1-64968-073-0

Made in the United States of America.

This series is dedicated to
Jerry Bowen
the Brave and the Strong.

DEPARTMENT OF THE INTERIOR

Commissioner to the Five Civilized Tribes

Muskogee, Indian Territory, March 9, 1907.

NOTICE IS HEREBY GIVEN that the undersigned, the Commissioner to the Five Civilized Tribes, has been designated by the Secretary of the Interior, as the official to make and approve appraisals of the value of improvements upon land in the Cherokee Nation which were made prior to November 5, 1906, by white persons who intermarried with Cherokee citizens prior to December 16, 1895, and who have the right under the Act of Congress approved March 2, 1907 (Public 180), to sell improvements.

NOTICE IS FURTHER GIVEN that former claimants to citizenship by intermarriage who have made permanent and valuable improvements on lands of the Cherokee Nation and who claim the right to sell the same under and by virtue of said Act of Congress of March 2, 1907 (Public 180), must appear before the Commissioner to the Five Civilized Tribes prior to April 1, 1907, and designate the land upon which are located the improvements which they claim the right to sell by virtue of said Act; and if any such intermarried citizen shall fail to appear before the Commissioner to the Five Civilized Tribes prior to April 1, 1907, it will be considered that he makes no claim to the benefits conferred by said Act. Such appearance and designation of improvements must be made before the Commissioner at his office in Muskogee, Indian Territory, at any time between Monday, March 11th, 1907, and Saturday, March 30th, 1907, inclusive, or at any of the following named places between the dates named at which places the Commissioner will have a representative to receive said designations and hear testimony relative thereto:

Bartlesville, Ind. Ter., Monday March 18th, 1907, to Saturday March 23rd, 1907, inclusive.

Tulsa, Ind. Ter., Monday March 25th, 1907, to Saturday March 30th, 1907, inclusive.

Claremore, Ind. Ter., Monday March 18th, 1907, to Saturday March 23rd, 1907, inclusive.

Nowata, Ind. Ter., Monday March 25th, 1907, to Saturday March 30th, 1907, inclusive.

Vinita, Ind. Ter., Monday March 18th, 1907, to Saturday March 23rd, 1907, inclusive.

Pryor Creek, Ind. Ter., Monday March 25th, 1907, to Saturday March 30th, 1907, inclusive.

Tahlequah, Ind. Ter., Monday March 18, 1907, to Saturday March 23rd, 1907, inclusive.

Sallisaw, Ind. Ter., Monday March 25th, 1907, to Saturday March 30th, 1907, inclusive.

Designations must be made in person by the intermarried white claimant, or in case proper proof is made that he is physically unable to appear, by some adult member of his immediate family, or in case proper proof is made of the fact that the intermarried white claimant is physically unable to appear and has no adult member of his immediate family, by a person holding a properly executed power of attorney; provided, that in every case the designation must be made by a party familiar with the character, ownership, location and value of the improvements to be designated. At the time of said designation the testimony of any competent person will be taken by the Commissioner as to the location, character and value of said improvements.

No former intermarried white claimant will be permitted to designate improvements upon more land than he would have been entitled to take in allotment for himself had he been admitted to citizenship. If any intermarried white claimant has made a tentative selection of a full allotment he will not be allowed to designate improvements upon other land.

NOTICE IS FURTHER GIVEN that if any citizen of the Cherokee Nation entitled to select an allotment shall claim that the improvements on land tentatively selected by a former intermarried white claimant, or held by him, do not belong to said intermarried white claimant, or makes any adverse claim to said improvements, or to the right of the intermarried white claimant to sell said improvements under the Act approved March 2, 1907 (Public 180), said citizen must appear before the Commissioner to the Five Civilized Tribes either at Muskogee, Indian Territory, prior to April 1, 1907, or at one of the places above designated and within the dates above designated and make formal complaint before the Commissioner to the Five Civilized Tribes of his contention. At Muskogee, Indian Territory, between March 11th and March 30th, 1907, inclusive, and at the other places herein named during the hearings at said places as herein fixed, plats will be open for inspection showing the location of tentative allotments made by former claimants to citizenship by intermarriage and all other land on which such claimants claim improvements, so far as indicated by the records of this office.

All persons interested should take careful note of the limitation of time herein provided for, within which designations and complaints may be made, and that they must be made by appearance before the Commissioner.

TAMS BIXBY,
Commissioner.

This particular notice concerns the appraisals of improvements on properties held by Cherokee intermarried whites. You would have found notices like this throughout the Nation to bring in people to finalize the allotment question, of who belonged and who did not.

DEPARTMENT OF THE INTERIOR,

COMMISSIONER TO THE FIVE CIVILIZED TRIBES.

In the matter of the application for the enrollment of
ALBERTIN HAMPTON as a citizen by intermarriage of the Cherokee
Nation.

D E C I S I O N

THE RECORDS OF THIS OFFICE SHOW: That at Fairland, Indian
Territory, July 9, 1900, Albertin Hampton appeared before the Commission to the Five Civilized Tribes, and made application for the
enrollment of himself as a citizen by intermarriage, and for the
enrollment of his wife, Jane E. Hampton, et al. as citizens by
blood of the Cherokee Nation. The application for the enrollment of
the said Jane E. Hampton et al. as citizens by blood of the Cherokee
Nation has been heretofore disposed of, and their rights to enrollment will not be considered in this decision. Further proceedings
in the matter of said application were had at Muskogee, Indian
Territory, September 3, 1902, October 14, 1902, and January 2, 1907.

THE EVIDENCE IN THIS CASE SHOWS: That the applicant herein,
Albertin Hampton, a white man, was married, in accordance with
Cherokee law, January 20, 1874, to his wife, Jane E. Hampton, nee
Thomas, who was at the time of said marriage a recognized citizen
by blood of the Cherokee Nation, and whose name appears on the approved partial roll of citizens by blood of the Cherokee Nation,
opposite No. 195; that since said marriage the said Albertin Hampton
and Jane E. Hampton have resided together as husband and wife, and
have continuously lived in the Cherokee Nation. Said Albertin
Hampton is identified on the Cherokee authenticated tribal roll of
1880, and the Cherokee census roll of 1896, as "Bert Hampton", an
intermarried citizen of the Cherokee Nation.

IT IS, THEREFORE, ORDERED AND ADJUDGED: That in accordance with
the decision of the Supreme Court of the United States, dated November
5, 1906, in the case of Daniel Red Bird et al. vs. the United States,

under the provisions of Section twenty-one, of the Act of Congress
approved June 28, 1898 (30 Stat., 495), Albertin Hampton is entitled to enrollment as a citizen by intermarriage of the Cherokee
Nation, and his application for enrollment as such is accordingly
granted.

_____
                                         Commissioner.

Dated at Muskogee, Indian Territory,
this___JAN 18 1907_____

The above is an accepted decision of the Commissioner to the Five
Civilized Tribes. The Attorney for the Cherokee Nation had fifteen days
after the date of Commissioner's decision in which to protest.

W.W. HASTINGS.
ATTORNEY

OFFICE OF

H. M. VANCE.
SECRETARY.

Attorney for the Cherokee Nation,

MUSKOGEE, I.T.   January 18, 1907.

The Commissioner to the Five Civilized Tribes,

Muskogee, Indian Territory.

Sir:

Receipt is acknowledged of the testimony and of your decision enrolling Albertin Hampton, as a citizen by intermarriage of the Cherokee Nation. Time for protesting said decision is waived and I consent that said person may be placed upon the schedule immediately.

Yours very truly,

W. M. Hastings

Attorney for Cherokee Nation.

The above is a notice of the Attorney waiving the time for protesting the Commissioner's decision (on the two previous pages) concerning Albertin Hampton's application and consenting to place the applicant upon schedule immediately.

INTRODUCTION

The *Cherokee Intermarried White*, National Archive film M-1301, Rolls 305-307, are found under the heading of Applications for Enrollment of the Commission to the Five Civilized Tribes. The genealogical value of this series concerning the relationships between many Cherokee tribesman and their marriages among another race is very important and virtually a treasure trove of information long sought after. While on the other hand what these cases are really about are the efforts of many to attain Cherokee land allotments. Referenced from the Supreme Court Decision, Cherokee Intermarriage Cases – 203 U.S. 76 (1906).

This collection of Intermarried claims involves two hundred and eighty-eight separate cases with a variety of scenarios from the divorced to the widowed to the deserving to the deceptive. During these times there were many that wanted what was rightfully only the Cherokees. You will see each case will be headed by the title from the first folder as an example: *Intermarried White I, Trans from Cher. 34*, the transfer number is the Dawes Commission number from the claimants spouse.

These cases are fascinating because of the generational bloodlines that can be verified by documentation rather than just word of mouth. From Kent Carter's book, *The Dawes Commission*, "The tribe also, continued to oppose the enrollment of whites who had married into the Cherokee tribe. That controversy dragged through the U.S. Court of Claims and then the Supreme Court, which finally ruled in favor of the tribe on November 05, 1906. The court upheld the Cherokee citizenship laws that denied rights to any white who had married into the tribe after November 1, 1877. It also upheld an 1839 law which stated that anyone who moved out of the nation lost their citizenship unless they were readmitted. The applications of 3,341 persons were rejected as a result of this ruling, and the allotment clerks were forced to undo a great deal of their work. With the issue finally settled by the courts, the commission was able to send the first schedule of Cherokees by intermarriage, containing fifty-five names, to the secretary of interior on June 10, 1907. Eventually only 286 people were enrolled as intermarried whites----far fewer than the number put on the rolls of the Choctaw and Chickasaw tribes, which had much more liberal laws on rights based on marriage." [1]

---

[1] The Dawes Commission and the Allotment of the Five Civilized Tribes, 1893-1914 by Kent Carter, pg. 121

In Cohen's Handbook of Federal Indian Law he states, "In the *Cherokee Intermarriage Cases,* the Supreme Court considered the claims of certain white persons, intermarried with Cherokee Indians, who wanted to participate in the common property of the Cherokee Nation. Such persons were permitted by tribal law to be tribal citizens with limited rights in tribal property. The tribe had also provided for the revocation of citizenship rights of a white person who intermarried with a Cherokee if the Cherokee spouse were abandoned or if a widower or widow married a non-Cherokee. The Court found that the Cherokee Nation had authority to qualify the rights of citizenship which it offered to its "naturalized citizens. Such tribal action defeated the claims of the plaintiffs:

The laws and usages of the Cherokees, their earliest history, the fundamental principles of their national policy, their constitution and statutes, all show that citizenship rested on blood or marriage; that the man who would assert citizenship must establish marriage; that when marriage ceased (with a special reservation in favor of widows or widowers) citizenship ceased; that when an intermarried white married a person having no rights of Cherokee citizenship by blood it was conclusive evidence that the tie which bound him to the Cherokee people was severed and the very basis of his citizenship obliterated."[2]

An important footnote that Cohen published within his pages for the above paragraph also needs to be studied. He noted, "Under Cherokee law white persons intermarrying with Cherokees before 1875 were tribal citizens for most purposes, including allotment of tribal land, but had no interest in tribal funds except those funds derived from tribal lands. A Cherokee law that became effective in 1875 provided that whites marrying Cherokees had no rights to tribal property but could obtain full citizenship by the payment of $500 to the tribe. In 1877 the tribe provided that no intermarried citizen could obtain any rights to tribal land or funds."[3]

During many years of study this author has found cases that should have been accepted, especially with the particular documentation presented. All in all the outcome of the decision made should have rendered a different result. Also there have been many that numb the mind as to how they their cases were even considered. The years have given many the hopes that their ancestors were one of those that had a decent claim and an honest consideration. Like any time in history there are political struggles

---

[2] Felix S. Cohen's Handbook of FEDERAL INDIAN LAW 1982 ED. pgs 20-21.
[3] Felix S. Cohen's Handbook of FEDERAL INDIAN LAW 1982 ED. pg 21 footnote16.

and the human factor that points out man is not perfect. These pages were transcribed with the wish that another person somewhere along the line will find their relation from the past and give them the answers long hoped for.

Jeff Bowen
Gallipolis, Ohio
NativeStudy.com

Cherokee Intermarried White 1906
Volume IV

Cher IW 103

◇◇◇◇◇

E.C.M.

DEPARTMENT OF THE INTERIOR,

COMMISSIONER TO THE FIVE CIVILIZED TRIBES.

In the matter of the application for the enrollment of

EDWARD BYRD

As a citizen by intermarriage of the Cherokee Nation.

CHEROKEE NO. 5432.

◇◇◇◇◇

Department of the Interior,
Commission to the Five Civilized Tribes,
Chelsea, I. T. November, 1900   .

In the matter of the application of Edward Byrd for the enrollment of himself, wife and children as Cherokee citizens.   He being sworn testified beofre[sic] Commissioner Needles as follows:

Q What is your name? A. Edward Byrd.
Q What is your age? A. About 57.
Q What is your post office address? A. Chelsea.
Q What district do you live in? A+ Cooweescoowee.
Q Are you a recognized citizen of the Cherokee Nation? A. Yes sir.
Q By blood or intermarriage? A. Intermarriage.
Q For whom do you apply for enrollment? A. Myself, wife and one child
Q What is your wifes[sic] name? A. Jane
Q How old is she? A. 45
Q What year were you married to her? A. 10th day of April 1876.
Q What is this childs[sic] name? A. Daisy D.
Q What is her age? A. 20 years.
Q Have you lived continuously with your wife ever since you were married to her?
A. Yes sir.

1880 roll, page 72, No 338, Ed. W. Byrd, Cooweescoowee. Adpt. white

1

1880	72	339 Jane Byrd	"	N. C.
1880	72	341 Daisy D. Byrd,	"	
1896	297	162 Edward Byrd,	"	
1896	115	511 Jane Byrd	"	
1896	115	513 Daisy D. Byrd,	"	

The name of Edward Byrd appears on the authenticated 1880 roll as Ed. W. Byrd, and on the 1896 roll as Edward Byrd. He appears as an inter-married white. The name of his wife Jane appears on the authenticated 1880 roll and also on the census roll of 1896, and the name of his daughter Daisy appears on the authenticated roll of 1880 as Daisy D. Byrd and on the census roll of 1896 as Daisy D. Byrd. They all being duly identified and having made satisfactory proof as to residence the said Edward Byrd will be listed for enrollment as a Cherokee by inter-marriage and his wife and daughter as Cherokee citizens by blood.

* *

Chas. von Wise[sic] being sworn states that as stenographer to the Commission to the Five Civilized Tribes he reported in full all the proceedings in the above entitled cause and that the foregoing is a full, true and correct transcript of his stenographic notes in said proceedings

Chas von Weise

Subscribed and sworn to before me this the 16th of November, 1900

TB Needles
Commissioner.

◇◇◇◇◇

Cherokee 5432.

Department of the Interior,
Commission to the Five Civilized Tribes,
Muskogee, I. T., September 27, 1902.

In the matter of the application of Edward Byrd for the enrollment of himself as a citizen by intermarriage, and for the enrollment of his wife, Jane Byrd, and child Daisy D. Byrd, as citizens by blood of the Cherokee Nation.

La Fayette A. Byrd, being sworn and examined by the Commission, testified as follows:

Q What is your name? A La Fayette A. Byrd.
Q How old are you? A The 15th day of next February I will be 66.
Q What is your postoffice? A Chelsea.
Q Are you acquainted with Edward Byrd, the applicant in this case? A Yes sir.

Q Are you related to him in any way? A He is my brother.

Q Is he the same Edward Byrd for whom application was made as an intermarried citizen of the Cherokee Nation on November 15, 1900? A Yes sir.

Q What is his wife's name? A Jane.

Q What was her maiden name prior to her marriage? A Nelums.

Q Is she a sister of your wife? A Yes sir.

Q Had your brother ever been married prior to his marriage to his present wife, Jane? A Yes sir.

Q What was her name? A Her maiden name was Nicholson. I don't remember her given name.

Q Was she living or dead when your brother married his wife, Jane? A She was dead.

Q How long has your brother and his present wife Jane, been married? A As well as I remember about 21 or 2 years.

Q Has your brother and his wife Jane, lived together as husband and wife cntinuously[sic] from the time of their marriage up until the present time? A Yes sir.

Q Never have been separated? A No sir.

Q He never has married any other woman since his marriage to her? A No sir.

Q They were living together on the first day of September, 1902? A Yes sir.

Q How long has your brother resided in the Cherokee Nation? A He has been here I think he told me something like 33 or 4 years.

Q Of your knowledge? A Yes, to my knowledge because he was here when I came here and I have been here twenty-nine years.

Q To your knwoledge[sic] he has been here twenty-nine years? A Yes sir.

Q And he has resided continuously with his wife Jane, in the Cherokee Nation since his marriage? A Yes sir, with the exception that he went on the strip once. He went to St. Louis and returned back, he was on a visit.

Q I am talking about living here? A Yes sir, this has been his home.

Q Is his wife Jane, and his daughter Daisy D. living at this time? A Yes sir.

Q And they live in the Cherokee Nation near Chelsea? A Yes sir, in Chelsea.

The undersigned, being duly sworn, states that as stenographer to the Commission to the Five Civilized Tribes he correctly recorded the testimony and proceedings in this case, and that the foregoing is a true and complete transcript of his stenographic notes thereof.

E.G. Rothenberger

Subscribed and sworn to before me this 13th day of October, 1902.

BC Jones
Notary Public.

◇◇◇◇◇

Cherokee Intermarried White 1906
Volume IV

Cher -5432

Department of the Interior,
Commission to the Five Civilized Tribes,
Vinita, I. T., January 5, 1903.

In the matter of the application of EDWARD BYRD, for the enrollment of himself as a citizen by intermarriage, and his wife JANE BYRD, and his daughter DAISY D. BYRD, as citizen by blood, of the Cherokee Nation:

EDWARD BYRD, being first duly sworn, testified as follows:

Examined by the Commission:

Q What is your name ? A Edward Byrd.
Q What is your post office ? A Chelsea, Indian Territory.
Q You are a white man, are you ? A Yes sir, I am a white man.
Q Claiming as a citizen by intermarriage of the Cherokee Nation ? A Yes sir.
Q What is the name of the wife through whom you claim ? A Jane Byrd.
Q When were you married to her ?
A I was married to her in 1876, to the best of my memory. I think it was 1876.
Q She was your wife in 1880 ? A Yes sir.
Q You and your wife are down together on the roll of 1880 ? A Yes sir.
Q Was she your wife in 1880 ? A Yes sir.
Q Have you ever been separated ? A No sir.
Q How long have you lived in the Cherokee Nation ?
A Since 1868; in August I think I come.
Q From 1868 up to the present time ? A Yes sir.
Q Has your wife been living with you ever since you were married ? A Yes sir.
Q How many children have you ? A Daisy D. Byrd, one of them is married.
Q Daisy D. Byrd is the one living with you ? A Yes sir.
Q She has lived in the Cherokee Nation all her live ? A Yes sir.
Q Living there now ? A Yes sir, living there now at Chelsea.
Q Your wife is living now ? A Yes sir, was when I left home; when I left yesterday evening, but she was sick, however.

I, E. C. Bagwell, a stenographer to the Commission to the Five Civilized Tribes, on oath state that the foregoing is a correct transcript of the stenographic notes of the testimony and proceedings had in the above entitled cause, as the same were taken by Jesse O. Carr, stenographer, and by him read to me.

F. C. Bagwell

Subscribed and sworn to before me this the 5th day of February, A. D., 1903.

Samuel Foreman
Notary Public.

◇◇◇◇◇

(The testimony below typed as given.)

DEPARTMENT OF THE INTERIOR
COMMISSIONER TO THE FIVE CIVILIZED TRIBES
MUSKOGEE, IND. TER.
JAN. 4 1907

IN THE MATTER OF THE APPLICATION FOR THE
ENROLLMENT OF EDWARD BYRD AS A CITIZEN
BY INTERMARRIAGE OF THE CHEROKEE NATION.

CENSUS CARD NO. 5432.

EDWARD BYRD BEING FIRST DULY SWORN TESTIFIED AS FOLLOWS:

EXAMINATION BY THE COMMISSIONER:

Q State your name. A Edward Byrd.
Q How old are you. A I was born the 6th of May in '43.
Q What is your post office address? A Chelsea Indian Territory
Q You claim to be a citizen by intermarriage of the Cherokee Nation. A Yes sir.
Q Thru whom do you claim your intermarried rights.
A Why I claim my intermarried rights under my marriage to Liza Ann Nicholson.
Q When were you married to Liza Ann Nicholson
A That is she is a Cherokee by blood; I was married to her on the 11th day of December if my mem'ry serves me right in Sixty-eight according to the laws of the Cherokee Nation
Q Have you got your license. A I dont know where my license is; I had a license and had seven signers at that time; and I've got a man here that I married at his house and I really dont know what became of the license; them times they didn't keep a full record before Maj. Lack come in; and I've got any amount of people in the country that know me.
Q Were you ever married before you married Liza Ann Nicholson
A No sir
Q Was she ever married before she married you? A No sir not that I know of; no she never was married.

Cherokee Intermarried White 1906
Volume IV

Q Was Liza Ann Nicholson a recognized citizen of the Cherokee Nation at the time she married you. A Yes sir.

Q Is she living or dead. A She's dead.

Q When did she die.

A I can't tell you about when.

Q Just about when. A I as married in '68 and I think she died in seventy two; I think she died in seventy one or two, I won't be positive.

Q What was the name of Liza Ann Nicholson's father and mother. A Her father was named Brack Nicholson; he was a white man and her mother was Pauline.

Q Was she a recognized citizen by blood of the Cherokee Nation

A She was a recognized citizen by blood of the Cherokee Nation

Q Is she living at this time? A No sir she's dead.

Q Did Eliza Ann Nicholson have any brothers or sisters.

A Yes sir she had one brother they called Joseph Nicholson I think that was his full name and one called Richard and then she had some half brothers.

Q Is Joseph Nicholson and Richard Nicholson living at this time? A No, both dead.

Q Have they got any families

A No sir they have got no families; I dont think they ever married.

Q When did they die. A They died, let me see if I can tell; they must have died in, I think Joseph Nicholson died in about seventy five, I think; I really cant[sic] tell you but that's my judgment.

Q When did Richard Nicholson die. A He died before that some time; I dont know just what time he died; before his brother Joseph died

Q When were you married to your present wife - how many times have you been married. A Twice.

Q When were you married to your present wife. A I was married to her in April '76 I think it was.

Q Is she a citizen of the Cherokee Nation. A Yes sir she's a Cherokee by blood; she's got certificates of her land; she hasn't got her deeds yet.

Q Was she married before she married you? A No sir.

Q Where was you married to her. A I was married out near Alluwe at Parson Adams' he was a Delaware.

Q Were you married under Cherokee license the second time

A Yes we got license to marry but there wasn't any petition or anything; they didn't require that.

Q Have you got your license with you which you married under the second time. A Yes I believe I've got that license.

Q Do you desire to offer this certificate in evidence.

A I believe I will not put it in.

It will be necessary for you to furnish the Commissioner with evidence showing that you was married to Eliza Ann Nicholson according to the Cherokee Law prior to November 1 1875 and that Eliza Ann Nicholson was a recognized citizen by blood of the Cherokee Nation at the time you married her, before you can be enrolled.

The applicant is identified on the 1880 Cherokee roll of Coo-wee-scoo-wee District opposite No. 338; his present wife is identified on said district opposite No. 339; the present wife is also identified on the final roll of citizens by blood of the Cherokee Nation opposite No. 24962.

ooOoo

M.W. COUCH BEING FIRST DULY SWORN TESTIFIED AS FOLLOWS:

EXAMINATION BY THE COMMISSIONER

Q What is your name. A M.W. Couch

Q How old are you. A Sixty four.

Q What is your post office address. A Chelsea.

Q Are you a citizen of the Cherokee Nation. A I am.

Q By blood or intermarriage. A Intermarriage.

Q Are you acquainted with Edward Byrd. A I am

Q How long have you known him. A Since 1868.

Q Did you know his first wife. A I did.

Q What was her name. A Eliza Nicholson.

Q How long did you know Eliza Nicholson. A From the time she was five years old to the time she died.

Q Was she a citizen of the Cherokee Nation. A Yes.

Q Citizen by blood. A Yes sir.

Q How do you know that fact. A Understood it that way all the time.

Q Was she generally considered a citizen. A Yes

Q Were her people citizens. A Yes.

Q Was she on any of the Cherokee rolls or do you know.

A I dont know.

Q Was her father and mother both citizens or just her mother

A Her mother; her father was a white man like myself.

Q Her father was a white man and her mother a citizen. A Yes

Q Full blood or missed blood. A Mixed blood.

Q Are you any relation to Eliza Ann Nicholson. A Only by marriage.

Q What relation are you to Eliza Nicholson. A I married her cousin.

Q First cousin. A Eliza Nicholson was my first wife's own cousin.

Q Was your first wife a citizen by blood of the Cherokee Nation. A Yes.

Q What was your first wife's name. A Mary Wright.

Q Was you present when Edward Byrd was married to Eliza Nicholson. A I was

Q Was he married under Cherokee license? A He was

Q Did you see the license. A I did

Q Who signed the license. I cant[sic] tell.

Q You are sure he was married under Cherokee license. A Yes

Q And you are sure you saw the license. A Yes.

Q Was it signed by the clerk of Coo-wee-scoo-wee District A Yes

Q Did you see the signature. A Yes; I'm satisfied.

Q What is it; guess work, or do you think it was signed by the clerk of Coo-wee-scoo-wee District.

Q Just like you pick up a piece of writing and dont know whose name it was; it was forty years ago and I'm satisfied it was signed.

ooOoo

ALECK LANDRUM BEING FIRST DULY SWORN TESTIFIED AS FOLLOWS:

EXAMINATION BY THE COMMISSIONER:

Q What is your name. A Aleck Landrum.

Q How old are you. A Forty six

Q What is your post office address? A Pryor Creek.

Q Are you a citizen of the Cherokee Nation? A Yes sir.

Q Citizen by blood A Yes sir

Q Do you know Edward Byrd

A Yes sir

Q Did you know his first wife Eliza Ann Nicholson. A Yes sir.

Q What relation was Eliza Ann Nicholson to yourself. A Half sister.

Q Same father or same mother. A Same mother.

Q Thru whom do you get your Cherokee blood, father or mother.

A Mother.

Q Was your father a citizen by blood. A Yes sir; citizenship on both sides; my father and mother were both Cherokees.

Q When did your mother die. A I disremember; I haven't got a family record of her death.

Q About when was it. A It must have been about seventy.

Q About when. [sic] It must have been about 1870 that my mother died.

Q Did Eliza Nicholson have any brothers. Full brothers.

A Yes sir.

Q What were their names. A Dick and Joe.

Q Are they living or dead. A They are dead

Q When did they die. A Dick Nicholson died when I was pretty small and Joe he must have died along about 1876 somewhere along there.

Q Do you know when Edward Byrd and Eliza Nicholson were married/ A I wasn't present when they married but I lived with them shortly after they married.

Q Do you know whether they were married according to the Cherokee law or not. A I do not; I never saw the license.

Q Was Edward Byrd recognized as a citizen of the Cherokee Nation after his marriage to Eliza Nicholson. A Yes sir

Q So recognized in the community in which he lived? A Yes sir

Q Were you present when he married his second wife? A No sir I was not.

Q Do you know whether she was a citizen by blood of the Cherokee Nation or not.

A She is a citizen by blood.

Cherokee Intermarried White 1906
Volume IV

ooOoo

Clara Mitchell Wood being first duly sworn upon her oath states that as stenographer for the Commissioner to the Five Civilized Tribes she reported the above and foregoing proceedings and that this is a correct transcript of her stenographic notes.

Clara Mitchell Wood

Subscribed and sworn to before me this 8th day of January 1907.

(No Signature Given.)
Notary Public.

◇◇◇◇◇

CHEROKEE-5432.

DEPARTMENT OF THE INTERIOR,
COMMISSIONER TO THE FIVE CIVILIZED TRIBES.
Muskogee, Indian Territory, January 5, 1907.

Supplemental testimony--
In the matter of making proof of the marriage of Edward Byrd to his Cherokee wife, prior to November 1, 1875.

John R. Price, being sworn by B. P. Rasmus, a Notary Public, testified as follows:

COMMISSIONER:

Q What is your name? A. John R. Price.
Q. How old are you? A. 61.
Q. What is your post office address? A. Tahlequah.
Q. Do you know Edward Byrd? A. I do.
Q. Do you know Eliza Ann Nicholson? A. I do.
Q. Do you know whether or not they were ever married? A. They were.
Q. When? A. In December, 1868.
Q. Where they married in accordance with the Cherokee law? A. I suppose so. I signed the petition for him.
Q. Did you ever see the license? A. I saw the petition.
Q. You didn't see the license? A. I did not.
Q. What District was that in? A. Cooweescoowee District.
Q. Who was the Clerk? A. It might have been Charley Rogers or Daniel Hicks.

9

Cherokee Intermarried White 1906
Volume IV

Q. Has Edward Byrd always been recognized as a citizen of the Cherokee Nation since 1868? A. Yes sir, ever since I have known him.

Q. His rights as a citizen have never been questioned since that time? A. No sir.

Q. Do you know his present wife? A. Yes sir.

Q. Do you know when he was married to his present wife? A. It must have been in '75 or '76 -- '76 I guess.

Q. Is she a citizen by blood of the Cherokee Nation? A. She is.

Q. Were they married in the Cherokee Nation? A. I suppose so. He never went out.

Witness excused.

Eula Jeanes Branson, being sworn, states that she correctly reported the proceedings had in the above and foregoing on the 5th. day of January, 1907.

Eula Jeanes Branson

Subscribed and sworn to before me, the 9th. day of January, 1907.

Walter W. Chappell
Notary Public.

◇◇◇◇◇

C. F. B. Cherokee 5432.

DEPARTMENT OF THE INTERIOR,
COMMISSION TO THE FIVE CIVILIZED TRIBES.
Muskogee, Indian Territory, January 12, 1907.

Supplemental proceedings in the matter of the application for the enrollment of Edward Byrd as a citizen by intermarriage of the Cherokee Nation.

D. W. Rider being first duly sworn by C. E. Webster, Notary Public, testified as follows:

Q What is our name? A D. W. Rider.

Q What is your age? A 59 years.

Q What is your post office address?
A Chelsea.

Q Do you know a person in the Cherokee Nation by the name of Edward Byrd?
A Yes sir.

Q How long have you known him? A Ever since '68.

Q Did you know him before he was married?
A Yes sir.

Q What was the name of his first wife?
A Nicholson, - Eliza Nicholson.

10

Q Did you know her before her marriage to Edward Byrd?
A Yes sir.

Q Was she a Cherokee by blood?   A Yes sir.
Q Was she a recognized citizen of the Cherokee Nation by blood at the time of their marriage?
A Yes sir.
Q Edward Byrd is a white man?   A Yes sir; supposed to be.
Q He claims the right to enrollment as a citizen of the Cherokee Nation by virtue of his marriage to Eliza Nicholson?
A Yes sir.
Q When were they married?
A Either in '68 or '69 in December.
Q Did Edward Byrd secure a license and marry his wife in accordance with the law of the Cherokee Nation?
A I suppose he did; he got his signers. The law required so many signers.
Q Do you know of any person who signed that petition?
A I signed it for one.
Q You are one of the signers to his petition?
A Yes sir.
Q You did not see them married?   A No sir.
Q You did not see his license?   A No sir.
Q But you understand and have every reason to believe that he did secure a license after he got that petition and that he married his wife in accordance with the law of the Cherokee Nation?
A That has always been my understanding. He has lived right there by me ever since.
Q That was the understanding of all the people who knew the parties?
A Yes sir.
Q Since that marriage has Edward Byrd been recognized as a citizen of the Cherokee Nation by intermarriage?
A Yes sir; so far as I know.
Q So far as you know, he has always exercised the rights and enjoyed the privileges of that class of citizens?
A Yes sir.
Q When did his first wife die?
A I don't remember the date of her death.
Q Did she and Edward Byrd live together as husband and wife until the time of her death?
A Yes sir.
Q Since her death, has Edward Byrd re-married?
A Yes sir.
Q Is his present wife a Cherokee by blood:
A Yes sir.
Q She is living at this time?   A Yes sir.
Q Was Edward Bird[sic] ever married except to these two women?
A Not that I know of.

Cherokee Intermarried White 1906
Volume IV

The undersigned being first duly sworn states that as stenographer to the Commission to the Five Civilized Tribes, she recorded the testimony taken in this case and that the foregoing is a full, true and correct transcript of her stenographic notes thereof.

Myrtle Hill

Subscribed and sworn to before me this the 14th day of January, 1907.

John E. Tidwell
Notary Public.

◇◇◇◇◇

E.C.M.   Cherokee 3432

DEPARTMENT OF THE INTERIOR,
COMMISSIONER TO THE FIVE CIVILIZED TRIBES.

In the matter of the application for the enrollment of Edward Byrd as a citizen by intermarriage of the Cherokee Nation.

D E C I S I O N .

THE RECORDS OF THIS OFFICE SHOW: That in November 1900 application was received by the Commission to the Five Civilized Tribes for the enrollment of Edward Byrd as a citizen by intermarriage of the Cherokee Nation. Further proceedings in the matter of said application were had at Muskogee, Indian Territory, September 27, 1902, January 5, 1903, January 4, 1907 and January 5, 1907.

THE EVIDENCE IN THIS CASE SHOWS: That the applicant herein, Edward Byrd, a white man, was married in accordance with Cherokee law in December 1868, to his wife, Eliza Ann Byrd, nee Nicholson, since deceased, who was at the time of said marriage a recognized citizen by blood of the Cherokee Nation; that from the time of said marriage until the death of said Eliza Ann Byrd, which occured[sic] about the year 1872, the said Edward Byrd and Eliza Ann Byrd resided together as husband and wife; that on April 10, 1876 the said Edward Byrd was married to one Jane Byrd, nee Nelums, who was at the time of said marriage a recognized citizen by blood of the Cherokee Nation, who is identified on the Cherokee authenticated tribal roll of 1880, Cooweescoowee District No. 339 as a native Cherokee, and whose name appears upon the approved partial roll of citizens by blood of the Cherokee Nation, opposite No. 24961. It is further shown that from the time of said marriage, the said Edward Byrd and Jane Byrd resided together as husband and wife and continuously lived in the Cherokee Nation, and that from the date of his first marriage in December 1868, the said Edward Byrd has continuously lived

12

in the Cherokee Nation up to and including September 1, 1902. Said applicant is identified on the Cherokee authenticated tribal roll of 1880 and the Cherokee census roll of 1896 as an intermarried citizen of the Cherokee Nation.

IT IS THEREFORE ORDERED AND ADJUDGED: That in accordance with the decision of the Supreme Court of the United States, dated November 5, 1906 in the case of Daniel Red Bird et al. vs. the United States Nos. 125, 126, 127 and 128, the applicant, Edward Byrd, is entitled, under the provisions of Section 21, of the Act of Congress approved June 28, 1898 (30th. Stats. 495), to enrollment as a citizen by intermarriage of the Cherokee Nation, and his application for enrollment as such is accordingly granted.

Tams Bixby
Commissioner.

Dated Muskogee, Indian Territory,
this   JAN 23 1907

◇◇◇◇◇

Cherokee
5432

Muskogee, Indian Territory, January 23, 1907.

W. W. Hastings,
     Attorney for the Cherokee Nation,
         Muskogee, Indian Territory.

Dear Sir:

     There is enclosed herewith a copy of the decision of the Commissioner to the Five Civilized Tribes, dated January 23, 1907, granting the application for the enrollment of Edward Byrd as a citizen by intermarriage of the Cherokee Nation.

Respectfully,

Encl. H-58   Commissioner.
   JMH

◇◇◇◇◇

Cherokee 5432   W.W.HASTINGS.   OFFICE OF   H.M. VANCE.
                 ATTORNEY.   SECRETARY.

Attorney for the Cherokee Nation,
MUSKOGEE, I. T.   January 23, 1907.

The Commissioner to the Five Civilized Tribes,
     Muskogee, Indian Territory.

Sir:

13

Receipt is acknowledged of the testimony and of your decision enrolling Edward Byrd as a citizen by intermarriage of the Cherokee Nation. Time for protesting said decision is waived and I consent that said person may be placed upon the schedule immediately.

Respectfully,

W. W. Hastings
Attorney for Cherokee Nation.

◇◇◇◇◇

Cherokee
5432

Muskogee, Indian Territory. January 23, 1907.

Edward Byrd,
    Chelsea, Indian Territory.

Dear Sir:

There is enclosed herewith a copy of the decision of the Commissioner to the Five Civilized Tribes, dated January 23, 1907, granting your application for enrollment as a citizen by intermarriage of the Cherokee Nation.

Respectfully,

E.R.C.   Commissioner.
Enc. E.C. 83

◇◇◇◇◇

OK CFB
Cherokee 3432
I W
Granted

Cher IW 104

◇◇◇◇◇

C.E.W.

DEPARTMENT OF THE INTERIOR,

COMMISSIONER TO THE FIVE CIVILIZED TRIBES.

In the matter of the application for the enrollment of

CHARLES BARNEY

AS a citizen by intermarriage of the Cherokee Nation.

CHEROKEE NO. 5552.

◇◇◇◇◇

DEPARTMENT OF THE INTERIOR
COMMISSION TO THE FIVE CIVILIZED TRIBES.
Chelsea, I.T.   November 17th, 1900.

IN THE MATTER OF THE APPLICATION OF CHARLES BARNEY FOR THE ENROLLMENT OF HIMSELF AS A CHEROKEE CITIZEN.

The said Charles Barney being sworn and examined by Commissioner T. B. Needles, testified as follows:

Q What is your name? A Charles Barney.
Q How old are you? A Sixty one years old.
Q What is your post office address? A Chelsea.
Q What district do you live in? A Cooweesdoowee[sic].
Q Are you a recognized citizen of the Cherokee Nation? A Yes, sir.
Q By blood or intermarriage? A By intermarriage.
Q Who do you want to enroll? A Just myself.
Q Is your wife living? A No, sir; she is dead.
Q What was her name? A Catherine.
Q What was her name before you married her? A Her name was Marcum.
Q When did you marry her? A In 1869. She has been dead ever since 1883.
Q Have you married since? A Yes, sir.
Q Is your present wife a white woman? A No, sir. She is a Cherokee.
Q What was your present wife's name? A None at all.
Q Your last wife is dead? A Yes, sir.
Q You are not married now? A No, sir.
Q And never married but twice? A No, sir; that is all.
Q Both of your wives were Cherokee? A Yes, sir.

Cherokee Intermarried White 1906
Volume IV

1880 Roll, page 74, No. 375, Charles Barney, Cooweescoowee District. Adopted White.

1896 Roll, page 295, No. 103, Charles Barney, Cooweescoowee District.

THE COMMISSIONER: The name of Charles Barney appears upon the authenticated roll of 1880 as an intermarried white. His name is also found upon the census roll of 1896? He is identified and makes satisfactory proof as to his residence, consequently he will be duly listed for enrollment as a Cherokee citizen by intermarriage.

The undersigned, being sworn, states that as stenographer to the Commission to the Five Civilized Tribes he correctly recorded the testimony and other proceedings in this application for enrollment and that the foregoing is a correct and complete transcript of his stenographic notes thereof.

Wm S Meeshean

Subscribed and sworn to before me this 19th day of November 1900.

CR Breckinridge

Commissioner.

◇◇◇◇◇

Cherokee 5552.

DEPARTMENT OF THE INTERIOR,
COMMISSION TO THE FIVE CIVILIZED TRIBES.
Muskogee, I. T., October 11, 1902.

In the matter of the application of Charles Barney for the enrollment of himself as a citizen by intermarriage of the Cherokee Nation.

SUPPLEMENTAL PROCEEDINGS.

CHARLES BARNEY, being sworn, testified as follows:

By the Commission,

Q What is your name? A Charles Barney.
Q What's your age at this time, Mr. Barney? A Sixty-two.
Q What is your postoffice address? A Chelsea.
Q What is your wife's name? A Catherine, that is, my first wife.
Q Your first wife? A She's dead.
Q Was your first wife, Catherine, a Cherokee or white woman?
A A Cherokee by blood.
Q When were you married to her? A Sometime in January.
Q January of what year? A I think it was in '68.
Q January, '68? A Yes, sir, as nigh as I can recollect.

Q When did you say she died? A She died the ninth day of April, '83.

Q She was living then in 1880, was she? A Yes, sir.

Q Well, did you and your wife, Catherine, live together from 1880 to the time of her death as husband and wife? A Yes, sir.

Q Well, after her death in '83 you married again, did you? A Yes, sir.

Q What was your second wife's name? A Her name was Lucy Williams.

Q Lucy Williams? A Yes, sir.

Q Is she living? A She's dead.

Q Is she a citizen by blood or a white woman? A She is a citizen by Cherokee blood.

Q A Cherokee by blood? A Yes, sir.

Q When did your wife, Lucy, die? A In '87.

Q In 1887? A No, 1888, I made a mistake.

Q Did you and she live together from the time of your marriage up to the time of her death as husband and wife? A Yes, sir.

Q Never were separated? A No, sir.

Q After the death of your wife, Lucy, did you marry again?
A No, sir.

Q Never married any more? A No, sir.

Q Just had the two wives? A Yes, sir.

Q You have lived single from 1888 up to the present time have you, since the death of your second wife? A Yes, sir.

Q You were a widower and single man on the first day of September 1902.[sic]
A Yes, sir.

Q Have you lived in the Cherokee Nation all the time since 1880 up to the present time?
A Yes, sir.

Retta Chick, being first duly sworn, states that, as stenographer to the Commission to the Five Civilized Tribes, she recorded the testimony and proceedings in the matter of the foregoing application, and that the above is a true and complete transcript of her stenographic notes thereof.

Retta Chick

Subscribed and sworn to before me this 22nd day of October, 1902.

BC Jones
Notary Public.

◇◇◇◇◇

Cherokee No.
5552.

DEPARTMENT OF THE INTERIOR,

COMMISSIONER TO THE FIVE CIVILIZED TRIBES,

MUSKOGEE, INDIAN TERRITORY, JANUARY 5, 1907.

IN THE MATTER OF THE APPLICATION for the enrollment of Charles Barney as a citizen by intermarriage of the Cherokee Nation.

CHARLES BARNEY, being first duly sworn by B. P. Rasmus, Notary Public, testified as follows:

EXAMINATION

ON BEHALF OF THE COMMISSIONER:

Q What is your name? A Charles Barney.
Q What is your age? A My age is 67 years old.
Q Your postoffice address? A Foil[sic].
Q Are you an applicant for enrollment as a citizen by intermarriage of the Cherokee Nation? A I guess I am.
Q You have no Cherokee blood? A Not a bit.
Q Your only claim to the right to enrollment as a citizen of the Cherokee Nation is by virtue of your marriage to a citizen by blood, is it? A Yes sir.
Q What is the name of the citizen through whom you claim your right to enrollment?
A She was a Ward. Old man War's[sic] last child he had, - she was a girl.
Q Is she living or dead? A Dead.
Q When did she die? A She died in April 1883, the 9th day.
Q When did you marry her? A Married her, - I don't know exactly whether it was 71 or 72, - it was a little before Christmas.
Q A little while before Christmas in 1871 or 1872?
A Yes, it was in my bible, but my bible aint at home.
Q Was she a recognized citizen of the Cherokee nation at the time you married her?
A Born and raised here in the Cherokee Nation.
Q Was she living in the Cherokee country when you married her?
A Born and raised in the Cherokee Nation.
Q I asked you if she was living in the Cherokee Nation at the time you married her?
A Yes, living here.
Q Did you marry her in accordance with the laws of the Cherokee Nation?
A Yes sir.
Q Did you secure a license? A Yes sir.
Q In what district was that license issued? A Delaware District.
Q In 1871 or 1872? A Yes, I was married to her before that by a preacher.

Q Where were you married the first time? A In Delaware District.

Q By a preacher? A Yes sir.

Q But not in accordance with the laws of the Cherokee Nation? A No sir.

Q You married her this second time to comply with the laws of the Cherokee Nation? A Yes sir.

Q Was she your first wife? A Yes sir.

Q Were you her first husband? A No sir; she was married to a man by the name of Marqum[sic] when she married me.

Q Was he dead or alive? A He was dead.

Q From the date of your marriage, did you and she live together continuously until the time of her death? A Yes sir.

Q Since her death have you remarried? A Married another woman but she was a Cherokee.

Q When did you marry the second time? A 18th day of December, 1885.

Q What is her name? A Lucy.

Q Is she living or dead? A Dead.

Q When did she die? A She died in 1887, last day of July.

Q Was she a recognized citizen of the Cherokee Nation? A Yes. Father and mother both Cherokees.

Q What is her father's name? A Williams.

Q William what? A Harrison Williams, - he is living yet.

Q What is her mother's name? A Katie, - she is dead.

Q What is the full name of your second wife before you married her? A Her name?

Q Your second wife? A Lucy Williams is all I know about it.

Q From the time of your marriage to your second wife, did you and she live together as husband and wife until her death[sic] A Yes sir.

Q Since her death have you married again? A No sir.

Q Has your residence been continuously in the Cherokee Nation from the time of your marriage to your first wife in 71 or 72 up to the present time? A Yes sir. Haven't been no where else.

ON BEHALF OF THE COMMISSIONER:

The applicant Charles Barney is identified on the Cherokee tribal authenticated roll of 1880, Coowees Coowee District, opposite No. 375. The original marriage records for Delaware District Book "S", in the possession of the Commissioner to the Five Civilized Tribes, shows that license was granted Charles Barney to marry Francis C. Marqum December 19, 1870, and that said license was returned for record December 19, 1870.

Q Who married you? A Man by the name of E. Lowry, full-blood.

Q Was he a minister of the gospel? A Yes, I have heard him preach many a time.

Q Did he give you a certificate at the time he married you? A Jeff McGee did.

Q Who was Jeff McGee? A He was clerk of the District court at that time.

Q Jeff McGee is the fellow who married you when you were married to your wife in accordance with the laws of the Cherokee Nation? A I guess he was; the Indian couldn't write at all.

Q Have you a certificate from him? A I had a certificate but Bob McDaniel came and called for it, and I gave it to him to take to Tahlequah. He was a councilor[sic] at that time.

Q That certificate is not in your possession? A No sir; because they called for it and I handed it over to them.

Q Is this man McGee who married you in accordance with the Cherokee law now living?

A I think he is, - I wont[sic] be certain. I know E. Lowry is dead.

Q If it was necessary then you could get another certificate from him? A Yes, any time I would send for it.

(Witness dismissed).

I, S. T. Wright, stenographer to the Commissioner to the Five Civilized Tribes, on oath, state that I recorded the testimony and proceedings had in the above entitled cause on January 5, 1907, and that the above and foregoing is a true and correct transcript of my stenographic notes thereof taken on said date.

ST Wright

Subscribed and sworn to before me this January 5th, 1907.

Edward Merrick
NOTARY PUBLIC.

◇◇◇◇◇

(The marriage license below typed as given.)

COPY

This is to certify by me that Charley Bosney[sic] a white man was license to marry F Ceithia Morton a female Cherokee on the 19th Dec 1870 the licens executed Dec 19 1870 being with according to the Act past by the National Council bareing date Oct the 15 1855 In regard to white man marring in this nation.

T J McShee Ck, D.C.D.D.C.N.

The undersigned being first duly sworn states that as stenographer to the Commissioner to the Five Civilized Tribes, she made the above copy and that the same is a true and copy of the marriage record now on file in this office.

Lola M Champlin

Subscribed and sworn to before me this 12 day of January 1907.

Chas E Webster
Notary Public.

◇◇◇◇◇

C.E.W.   Cherokee 5552.

DEPARTMENT OF THE INTERIOR,

COMMISSIONER TO THE FIVE CIVILIZED TRIBES.

In the matter of the application for the enrollment of CHARLES BARNEY as a citizen by intermarriage of the Cherokee Nation.

_D_E_C_I_S_I_O_N_

THE RECORDS OF THIS OFFICE SHOW: That at Chelsea, Indian Territory, November 17th, 1900, application was received by the Commission to the Five Civilized Tribes for the enrollment of Charles Barney as a citizen by intermarriage of the Cherokee Nation. Further proceedings in the matter of said application were had at Muskogee, Indian Territory, October 11th, 1902 and January 5th, 1907.

THE EVIDENCE IN THIS CASE SHOWS: That the applicant herein, Charles Barney, a white man, was married in accordance with Cherokee law December 19th, 1870 to his wife, Catherine Barney, nee Ward, since deceased, who was at the time of said marriage a recognized citizen by blood of the Cherokee Nation, and who is identified on the Cherokee authenticated tribal roll of 1880, Cooweescoowee District No. 376, as a native Cherokee; that from the time of said marriage until the death of said Catherine Barney, which occurred April 8th, 1883, the said Charles Barney and Catherine Barney resided together as husband and wife and continuously lived in the Cherokee nation; that subsequent to the death of said Catherine Barney the said Charles Barney on December 18th, 1885, was married to one Lucy Barney, nee William, since deceased, who was at the time of said marriage a recognized citizen by blood of the Cherokee Nation, and who is identified on the Cherokee authenticated tribal roll of 1880, Cooweescoowee District, Page 205, No. 3364 as a native Cherokee; that said Charles Barney and Lucy Barney resided together as husband and wife and continuously lived in the Cherokee Nation until the death of said Lucy Barney, which occurred in July, 1887; that since the death of said Lucy Barney the said Charles Barney has not married, and that his residence has been continuously in the Cherokee Nation since December 19th, 1870. Said applicant is identified on the Cherokee authenticated tribal roll of 1880 and the Cherokee census roll of 1896 as a native Cherokee.

IT IS, THEREFORE, ORDERED AND ADJUDGED: That in accordance with the decision of the Supreme Court of the United States, dated November 5, 1906, in the cases of Daniel Red Bird et al. vs. the United States Nos. 125, 126, 127 and 128, the said applicant, Charles Barney is entitled, under the provision of Section Twenty-one of the Act of Congress approved June 28th, 1898 (30 Stats. 495), to enrollment as a citizen by intermarriage of the Cherokee Nation, and his application for enrollment as such is accordingly granted.

Tams Bixby
Commissioner.

Dated at Muskogee, Indian Territory,
this   JAN 23 1907

◇◇◇◇◇

Cherokee
5552

Muskogee, Indian Territory, January 23, 1907.

W. W. Hastings,
   Attorney for the Cherokee Nation,
      Muskogee, Indian Territory.

Dear Sir:

There is enclosed herewith a copy of the decision of the Commissioner to the Five Civilized Tribes, dated January 23, 1907, granting the application for the enrollment of Charles Barney as a citizen by intermarriage of the Cherokee Nation.

Respectfully,

Encl. H-59   Commissioner.
JMH

◇◇◇◇◇

Cherokee 5552   W.W.HASTINGS.   OFFICE OF   H.M. VANCE.
                    ATTORNEY.   SECRETARY.

𝔄𝔱𝔱𝔬𝔯𝔫𝔢𝔶 𝔣𝔬𝔯 𝔱𝔥𝔢 ℭ𝔥𝔢𝔯𝔬𝔨𝔢𝔢 ℜ𝔞𝔱𝔦𝔬𝔫,

MUSKOGEE, I. T.   January 23, 1907.

The Commissioner to the Five Civilized Tribes,
             Muskogee, Indian Territory.

Sir:

    Receipt is acknowledged of the testimony and of your decision enrolling Charles Barney as a citizen by intermarriage of the Cherokee Nation. Time for protesting said decision is waived and I consent that said person may be placed upon the schedule immediately.

        Respectfully,
           W. W. Hastings
           Attorney for Cherokee Nation.

◇◇◇◇◇

Cherokee
  5552

        Muskogee, Indian Territory, January 23, 1907.

Charles Barney,
    Foyil, Indian Territory.

Dear Sir:

    There is enclosed herewith a copy of the decision of the Commissioner to the Five Civilized Tribes, dated January 23, 1907, granting your application for enrollment as a citizen by intermarriage of the Cherokee Nation.

    You will be advised when your name has been placed upon a schedule of citizens of the Cherokee Nation and approved by the Secretary of the Interior.

        Respectfully,

E.R.C.   Commissioner.
Enc. E.C. 84.

Cher IW 105

◇◇◇◇◇

E.C.M.

DEPARTMENT OF THE INTERIOR,

COMMISSIONER TO THE FIVE CIVILIZED TRIBES.

———————

In the matter of the application for the enrollment of

STEPHEN D. BROWN

as an intermarried citizen of the Cherokee Nation.

———————

CHEROKEE 5593

◇◇◇◇◇

R

Department of the Interior,
Commission to the Five Civilized Tribes,
Chelsea, I. T. November 19th 19oo[sic].

In the matter of the enrollment of Stephen D. Brown for enrollment as a Cherokee citizen. He being sworn before the Commission testified as follows=[sic]

Q What is your name? A. Stephen D. Brown.
Q How old are you? A. 60.
Q What is your post office? A. Grove.
Q Are you a Cherokee by blood? A. ¥No sir, by adoption.
Q Have you no wife or children? A. No sir.
Q How long have you resided in the Cherokee Nation? A. Sine[sic] July 10" 1868.
Q Have you been outside of the Cherokee Nation for any purpose during the last three years? A. No sir.
Q When were you married? A. July 1868.
Q Was that the first and last time that you were ever married? A. Yes sir.
Q Never married since? A. No sir.
Q When did your wife die? A. 18 months ago.
Q Does your name appear on the 1880 roll? A. Yes sir.
Q What district were you living in in 1880? A. Deleware[sic].
Q What district were you living in in 1896? A. Deleware[sic].
Q What was the name of your father? A. Alexander.
Q What was the name of your mother? Al[sic] Mary.
Q Are your parents both dead? A. Yes sir.
Q They were never recognized as citizens of the Cherokee Nation? A. No sir.

Cherokee Intermarried White 1906
Volume IV

Q Have you any evidence of your marriage? A. Yes sir.

The applicant presents marriage license authorizing his marriage to Lucy Ward a citizen of the Cherokee Nation, issued on the 9th of July, 1868 by T. J. McGee, clerk of the District court of Deleware[sic] District. Applicant also presents marriage certificate showing that he was married according to the laws of the Cherokee Nation and under the license just cited.
Document is returned to the applicant.

1880 roll, page 225, No 256, Steven A[sic]. Brown, Deleware[sic] Dist. Adpt. What.
1896   565,   47 Steven A[sic]. Brown, Deleware[sic] dist.

The applicant applies for enrollment as a citizen by intermarriage of the Cherokee Nation. He has lived in the Cherokee Nation ever since 1868, and he presents a marriage license and certificate showing that he was married in 1868. He has lived with his wife continuously until her death about 18 months ago. He is identified on the authenticated 1880 roll and on the census roll of 1896 as an adopted white. He will be listed now by this Commission as a citizen by inter-marriage of the Cherokee Nation.

* *

Chas. von Weise being duly sworn states that as stenographer to the Commission to the Five Civilized Tribes he reported in full all the proceedings in the above cause and that the foregoing is a full, true and correct transcript of his stenographic notes therein.

Chas von Weise

Subscribed and sworn to before me this 19th of November, 1900.

CR Breckinridge
Commissioner.

◇◇◇◇◇

Statement of Applicant Taken Under Oath.

CHEROKEE BY BLOOD AND ADOPTION.

(60)

		Date	NOV 19 1900	1900.
Name	Stephen D. Brown	Grove I T		
District	DELAWARE.	Year	1880	Page 225	No. 256

Citizen by blood   No   Mother's citizenship
Intermarried citizen   Yes
Married under what law   Date of marriage
License   Certificate
Wife's name
District   Year   Page   No.
Citizen by blood   Mother's citizenship
Intermarried citizen

25

Cherokee Intermarried White 1906
Volume IV

Married under what law..Date of marriage........................
License..Certificate..

Names of Children:

	Dist.	Year	Page	No.	Age
	Dist.	Year	Page	No.	Age
	Dist.	Year	Page	No.	Age
	Dist.	Year	Page	No.	Age
	Dist.	Year	Page	No.	Age

1 on 1880 roll as Steven A. Brown

◇◇◇◇◇

JOR.
Cher. 5593.

Department of the Interior.
Commission to the Five Civilized Tribes.
Tahlequah, I. T., October 20, 1902.

SUPPLEMENTAL TESTIMONY in the matter of the application for the enrollment of STEPHEN BROWN as a citizen by intermarriage of the Cherokee Nation.

STEPHEN BROWN, being first duly sworn, and being examined, testified as follows:

BY COMMISSION: What is your name? A Stephen D. Brown.
Q How old are you? A Sixty-two.
Q What is your post office address? A Grove, Indian Territory.
Q The index to the Cherokee enrollment cards shows that you were listed for enrollment under the name of Stephen Brown, but your full name is Stephen D. Brown? A Yes sir, that is my initial.
Q Where did you make application for enrollment? A Chelsea.
Q In 1900? A I guess so, it was last November was a year ago.
Q You made application for enrollment as a citizen by intermarriage of the Cherokee Nation? A Yes sir.
Q What is the name of the wife through whom you claim your citizenship? A Lucy A. Ward.
Q Is she living? A No sir.
Q Was she a Cherokee by blood? A Yes sir.
Q When were you and she married? A Sometime in July, 1868.
Q Were you married to her at that time according to Cherokee law? A Yes sir.
Q Does you name appear upon the roll of 1880? A Yes sir.

Q How long has your wife, Lucy A. Brown, been dead? A She has been dead about three years and six months, I guess.

Q Were you ever married before you married her? A No sir.

Q Was she ever married before she married you? A No sir.

Q You were her first husband and she was your first wife? A Yes sir

Q Did you and she live together continuously until the time of her death? A We did.

Q Were you living together when she died? A Yes sir.

Q Were you ever separated? A No sir.

Q Have you resided in the Cherokee Nation continuously since you and she married? A Yes sir.

Q Did she reside in the Cherokee Nation continuously until the time of her death? A Yes sir.

Q Have you continued to resided[sic] in the Cherokee Nation after she died? A Yes sir.

Q Have you married since her death? A No sir.

Q Have you any minor children for whom you made application? A No sir, no children at all.

> This testimony will be filed with and made a part of the record in the matter of the application for the enrollment of Stephen Brown as a citizen by intermarriage of the Cherokee Nation, Cherokee straight card field No. 5593.

Wm. Hutchinson, being first duly sworn, states that as stenographer to the Commission to the Five Civilized Tribes he correctly recorded the testimony and proceedings in this case, and that the foregoing is a true and complete transcript of the stenographic notes thereof.

Wm Hutchinson

Subscribed and sworn to before me this 30th day of October, 1902.

John O Rosson
Notary Public.

◇◇◇◇◇

C.F.B.   Cherokee 5593

DEPARTMENT OF THE INTERIOR,
COMMISSIONER TO THE FIVE CIVILIZED TRIBES.
MUSKOGEE, IND. TER., JANUARY 5, 1907.

In the matter of the application for the enrollment of STEPHEN D.
BROWN as a citizen by intermarriage of the Cherokee Nation.

Applicant appears in person:

APPEARANCES:

Cherokee Nation represented by H. M. Vance,
on behalf of W. W. Hastings, Attorney.

On Behalf of Commissioner:

Q. What is your name? A. Stephen Dawley Brown.
Q. How old are you? A. Sixty-six, will be the 22nd day of next month.
Q. What is your postoffice address? A. Grove.
Q. Are you a citizen by intermarriage of the Cherokee Nation?
A. Yes sir, I have always thought I was.
Q. You claim the right to enrollment as such? A. I do.
Q. You have no Cherokee blood? A. None whatever.
Q. Your only claim to the right to enrollment as a citizen of the Cherokee Nation is by
virtue of your marriage to a citizen by blood of that Nation? A. Yes sir.
Q. What is the name of the citizen through whom you claim the right to enrollment?
A. Her maiden name was Lucy Ward.
Q. Is she living or dead? A. She is dead.
Q. When did she die? A. The 19th day of February, 1899.
Q. Was she a recognized citizen of the Cherokee Nation at the time you married her?
A. Yes sir.
Q. When did you marry her? A. Well, now, I cannot say positively whether I and her
was married on the same day that I got my license, or the next day. I can not say that
positively, I have my license here. (Presents License)
Q. You married your wife in accordance with Cherokee law, did you?
Q[sic] Yes sir, in accordance with the laws of the Cherokees.
Q. She was residing in the Cherokee country at that time was she? A. No sir; I was not
at that time. I came the next fall. I was married the 9th day of July, or the 10th, 1868,
and moved to the Cherokee Nation the second day of October, 1868.
Q. Was your wife a resident of the Cherokee Nation at the time of your marriage to her?
A. Yes sir, she was.
Q. In what District did you secure your marriage license?
A. In Delaware District.

The applicant presents a certified copy of a marriage license and certificate, showing
that on the 9th day of July, 1868, license was issued in accordance with the law of the

Cherokee Nation, by T. J. McGhee, Clerk of the District Court, Delaware District, Cherokee Nation, authorizing the marriage of S. D. Brown and Lucy Ward, a citizen of the Cherokee Nation.

This instrument will be filed with and made a part of the record in this case.

Q. Are you the person mentioned in this marriage license as S. D. Brown? A. Yes sir, I am the identical man.

Q. When were you married? A. Well, now, as I said, I can not tell you whether I was married on the ninth day of July or on the next day. It was either the ninth or the next day.

Q. You were married immediately after this license was issued, were you? A. Yes sir.

Q. By whom were you married? A. By E. Lowery Butler.

Q. Was he a Minister of the Gospel?

A. Yes sir; he was a preacher

Q. Did he give you a certificate at the time he married you?

A. It is on the back of the license there, sir.

Q. This is the only evidence you have?

A. Yes sir, that is the only evidence I have got/[sic]

Q. This man who married you was a Cherokee was he? A. Yes sir; I presume he was a fullblood.

Q. From the time of your marriage to your wife on July 10, 1868 did you and she continuously reside together as husband and wife until the time of her death?

A. Yes sir.

Q. And continuously lived in the Cherokee Nation?

A. Yes sir; that is from the second day of October, 1868.

Q. Have you removed from the Cherokee Nation since her heath? A. No sir.

Q. You have lived in the Cherokee Nation continuously since her death? A. Yes sir.

The applicant, Stephen D. Brown, is identified on the Cherokee authenticated trial roll of 1880, Delaware District, No. 256.

Q. Were you ever married more than that one time? A. No sir.

Q. Were you your wife's first husband? A. Yes sir.

The undersigned being first duly sworn states that as stenographer to the Commissioner to the Five Civilized Tribes she correctly recorded the testimony taken in this case, and that the foregoing is a full, true and correct transcript of her stenographic notes thereof.

Lucy M Bowman

Subscribed and sworn to before me this 5th day of January, 1907.

John E. Tidwell
Notary Public.

Cherokee Intermarried White 1906
Volume IV

◇◇◇◇◇

(The Marriage License below typed as given.)

Deleweere District (July the 9th. 1868
Cheroke Nation   (

      S.D.Brown is here by Licins to Marry Lucy ward a Cherokee wom a legal citizen of the Cherokee and to Become a tru and a legal citizen of the Cherokee Nation the said S.D.Brown having complied with the Laws of the Cherokee Nation hern this day Before me By oath truly allennats him self from the protection of all other governments and from this day and will a Bide By a surport the Laws and constitution of the Cherokee Nation the said S.D.Brown will Be truly and lofly married By Sum administer of the Gospel)
)

                                            Given from under My Hand in office this is the 9th day of July 1868

T.J.McGhee clk.D.C.D.D.
Cherokee Nation.

      this is to certify By me that the within is a true Copy from the Record; & also the original Licens on file in this office on this the 10th Day Oct 1887

T.J.McGhee   Clk Del Dist   C.N.

      On the back of said license there appears what purports to be a marriage certificate written in the Cherokee language, which cannot be translated.

      The undersigned being duly sworn states that as stenographer to the Commissioner to the Five Civilized Tribes, she made the above copy, and that the same is a true and correct copy of the instrument now on file in this office.

Mary Tabor Mallory

Subscribed and sworn to before me this the 16th day of January 1907.

Chas E Webster
Notary Public.

◇◇◇◇◇

E. C. M.   Cherokee 5593.

DEPARTMENT OF THE INTERIOR,
COMMISSIONER TO THE FIVE CIVILIZED TRIBES.

———————

In the matter of the application for the enrollment of Stephen D. Brown as a citizen by intermarriage of the Cherokee Nation.

_D_E_C_I_S_I_O_N_.

THE RECORDS OF THIS OFFICE SHOW: That on November 19, 1900, application was received by the Commission to the Five Civilized Tribes for the enrollment of Stephen D. Brown as a citizen by intermarriage of the Cherokee Nation. Further proceedings in the matter of said application were had at Tahlequah, Indian Territory, October 20, 1902, and Muskogee, Indian Territory, January 5, 1907.

THE EVIDENCE IN THIS CASE SHOWS: That the applicant herein, Stephen D. Brown, a white man, was married in accordance with Cherokee law in July, 18, to his wife Lucy Brown, nee Ward, deceased, who was at the time of said marriage a recognized citizen by blood of the Cherokee Nation, who is identified on the Cherokee authenticated tribal roll of 1880, Delaware District, No. 257, as a native Cherokee, marked "Dead". It is further shown that from the time of said marriage in July, 1868, until the death of said Lucy Brown on February 19, 1899, the said Stephen D. Brown and Lucy Brown resided together as husband and wife and continuously lived in the Cherokee Nation;   that since the death of said Lucy Brown, said Stephen D. Brown remained unmarried and continuously lived in the Cherokee Nation up to and including September 1, 1902. Said applicant is identified on the Cherokee authenticated tribal roll of 1880 and the Cherokee census roll of 1896 as an intermarried citizen of the Cherokee Nation.

IT IS THEREFORE ORDERED AND ADJUDGED: That in accordance with the decision of the Supreme Court of the United States, dated November 5, 1906, in the case of Daniel Red Bird et al. vs. the United States, Nos. 125, 126, 127 and 128, the said applicant, Stephen D. Brown is entitled under the provisions of Section 21, of the Act of Congress approved June 28, 1898 (30 Stats. 495), to enrollment as a citizen by intermarriage of the Cherokee Nation, and his application for enrollment as such is accordingly granted.

Tams Bixby
Commissioner.

Dated at Muskogee, Indian Territory,
this   JAN 23 1907

◇◇◇◇◇

Cherokee
5593

Muskogee, Indian Territory, December 27, 1906.

Stephen D. Brown,
Grove, Indian Territory.

Dear Sir:

November 6, 1906, the United States Supreme Court held that white persons who intermarried with Cherokee citizens according to Cherokee law prior to November 1, 1875, are entitled to enrollment and allotments of land as citizens of the Cherokee Nation.

You are advised that to properly determine your right to enrollment as a citizen by intermarriage of the Cherokee Nation, it will be necessary for you to appear before the Commissioner for the purpose of giving testimony as to the date of your marriage and whether or not your wife, by reason of your marriage to whom you claim the right to enrollment as a citizen of the Cherokee Nation, was a recognized citizen of the Cherokee Nation at the time of your marriage to her, and whether or not you were married to her in accordance with Cherokee laws.

You are therefore directed to appear before the Commissioner at Muskogee, Indian Territory, at 9 o'clock A. M., on Saturday, January 5, 1907, and give testimony as above indicated.

Respectfully,

S.W.   Acting Commissioner.

◇◇◇◇◇

Cherokee 5593

Muskogee, Indian Territory, January 24, 1907.

W. W. Hastings,
Attorney for the Cherokee Nation,
Muskogee, Indian Territory.

Dear Sir:

There is enclosed herewith copy of the decision of the Commissioner to the Five Civilized Tribes, dated January 23, 1907, granting the application for the enrollment of Stephen D. Brown as a citizen by intermarriage of the Cherokee Nation.

Respectfully,

Enc I-73   Commissioner.

RPI

◇◇◇◇◇

Cherokee 5593   W.W.HASTINGS.   OFFICE OF   H.M. VANCE.
                   ATTORNEY.   SECRETARY.

Attorney for the Cherokee Nation,

MUSKOGEE, I. T.   January 23, 1907.

The Commissioner to the Five Civilized Tribes,
        Muskogee, Indian Territory.

Sir:

Receipt is acknowledged of the testimony and of your decision enrolling Stephen D. Brown as a citizen by intermarriage of the Cherokee Nation. Time for protesting said decision is waived and I consent that said person may be placed upon the schedule immediately.

Respectfully,

W. W. Hastings
Attorney for the Cherokee Nation.

◇◇◇◇◇

Cherokee 5593

Muskogee, Indian Territory, January 23, 1907.

Stephen D. Brown,
        Grove, Indian Territory.

Dear Sir:

There is enclosed herewith copy of the decision of the Commissioner to the Five Civilized Tribes, dated January 23, 1907, granting the application for your enrollment as a citizen by intermarriage of the Cherokee Nation.

You will be advised when your name has been placed upon a schedule of citizens of the Cherokee Nation and approved by the Secretary of the Interior.

Respectfully,

Enc I-90   Commissioner.
RPI

◇◇◇◇◇

Cherokee
I.W. 105

Muskogee, Indian Territory, April 16, 1907.

Stephen D. Brown,
    Grove, Indian Territory.

Dear Sir:

Your marriage license and certificate filed in connection your application for enrollment as a citizen by intermarriage of the Cherokee Nation is returned to you herewith, copies of the same being retained in the files of this office.

Respectfully,

Encl. W-10.   Commissioner.
S.W.

Cher IW 106

◇◇◇◇◇

CFB

DEPARTMENT OF THE INTERIOR,

COMMISSIONER TO THE FIVE CIVILIZED TRIBES.

In the matter of the application for the enrollment of

JOSEPH B. ANTOINE

as a citizen by intermarriage of the Cherokee Nation.

CHEROKEE 5706.

○ ○ ○ ○ ○

Cherokee Intermarried White 1906
Volume IV

DEPARTMENT OF THE INTERIOR,
COMMISSION TO THE FIVE CIVILIZED TRIBES,
TAHLEQUAH, I.T., NOVEMBER 27th, 1900.

In the matter of the application of Joseph B. Antoine for the enrollment of himself, wife and child as citizens of the Cherokee Nation; said Antoine being sworn and examined by Commissioner Needles, testified as follows:

Q What is your name? A Joseph B. Antoine.
Q What is your age? A 60 past.
Q What is your post office address? A Tahlequah.
Q What district do you live in? A I live in Tahlequah.
Q Are you a recognized citizen of the Cherokee Nation? A Yes, sir.
Q By blood or intermarriage? A Intermarriage.
Q Who do you want to enroll? A My wife and little baby.
Q Yourself? A Yes, sir.
Q What is the name of your wife? A Cherry E.
Q When were you married to her? A February 27th, 1868.
Q Is she a white woman? A She is a Cherokee by blood.
Q What is the name of your children? A Olive Antoine.
Q How old is Olive? A She is 15 past.
    1880 Roll; page 500, #30, Joseph Antwine, Illinois.
1880~~1896~~ Roll; page 500, #31, Sarah Antwine, Illinois.
    1896 Roll; page 1275, #4, Joseph B. Antoine, Tahlequah.
    1896 Roll; page 1131, #21, Sarah Antoine, Tahlequah.
    1896 Roll; page 1131, #22, Olive Antoine, Tahlequah.
Q Olive is alive and living with you at this time? A Yes, sir.
Q Have you lived continuously with your wife ever since you married her? A Yes, sir.

Com'r Needles:--The name of Joseph B. Antoine appears upon the authenticated roll of 1880 and the census roll of 1896 as Joseph Antoine, and the name of his wife, Sarah E., is found upon the authenticated roll of 1880 and the census roll of 1896 as Sarah Antoine. The name of their child, Olive is found upon the census roll of 1896. They being duly identified according to the page and number of the roll as indicated in the testimony and having made satisfactory proof as to their residence, consequently the said Joseph B. Antoine will be duly listed for enrollment as a Cherokee citizen by intermarriage, and his wife, Sarah E. and child, Olive, will be duly listed for enrollment as Cherokee citizens by blood.

---oooOOOooo---

J. O. Rosson, being first duly sworn, states as stenographer to the Commission to the Five Civilized Tribes, he correctly recorded the testimony and proceedings in this case, and that the foregoing is a true and complete transcript of his stenographic notes thereof.

J.O. Rosson

Subscribed and sworn to before me this 27th day of November, 1900.

MD Green   NP

~~Commissioner~~.

◇◇◇◇◇

R.
Cher. 5706.

Department of the Interior.
Commission to the Five Civilized Tribes.
Tahlequah, I. T., October 1, 1902.

SUPPLEMENTAL TESTIMONY AND PROCEEDINGS in the matter of the application for the enrollment of JOSEPH B. ANTOINE as a citizen by intermarriage of the Cherokee Nation.

JOSEPH B. ANTOINE, being first duly sworn, and being examined, testified as follows:

BY COMMISSION: What is your name? A Joseph B. Antoine.
Q How old are you? A Sixty-two.
Q What is your post office address? A Tahlequah.
Q You are a white man, are you? A Yes sir.
Q Are you an applicant before this Commission for enrollment as a citizen by intermarriage of the Cherokee Nation? A Yes sir.
Q What is the name of your wife? A Sarah E. Antoine.
Q Is she living? A Yes sir.
Q Is she a Cherokee by blood? W[sic] Yes sir.
Q Do you claim your right to enrollment by reason of your marriage to her? A Yes sir.
Q When were you married to her? A Married in February, 1868.
Q Have you lived together continuously since that time? A Yes sir
Q Are you living together now? A Yes sir.   No
Q Were you ever married before you married her? A ~~Yes~~ sir.
Q Was she ever married before she married you? A No sir.
Q You have lived in the Cherokee Nation continuously since you made application for enrollment, have you? A Yes sir.

> This testimony will be filed with and made a part of the record in the matter of the application for the enrollment of Joseph B. Antoine as a citizen by intermarriage of the Cherokee Nation, Cherokee straight card field No. 5706.

Wm. Hutchinson, being first duly sworn, states that as stenographer to the Commission to the Five Civilized Tribes he correctly recorded the testimony and proceedings in this case, and that the foregoing is a true and complete transcript of his stenographic notes thereof.

Wm Hutchinson

Subscribed and sworn to before me this 1st day of October, 1902.

John O Rosson
Notary Public.

◇◇◇◇◇

Cherokee 5706.

Department of the Interior,
Commission to the Five Civilized Tribes,
Tahlequah, I. T., May 5, 1903.

In the matter of the application of Joseph B. Antoine for the enrollment of himself as a citizen by intermarriage, and for the enrollment of his wife, Sarah E. Antoine, and his daughter, Olive Antoine, as citizens by blood of the Cherokee Nation.

James W. Antoine, being duly sworn, and examined by the Commission, testified as follows:

Q State your name, age and residence? A James W. Antoine.
Q What is your age? Ahe[sic] thirty-one; postoffice Tahlequah.
Q You are a citizen of the Cherokee Nation? A Yes sir.
Q What is your father's name? A Joseph B. Antoine.
Q How old is he? A He is sixty-three or four, I forget which.
Q Where is he living? A Tahlequah.
Q He is a white man, is he? A yes sir.
Q How long has he been living in the Cherokee Nation? A I couldn't tell you that exactly either.
Q Twenty-five years? A I am thirtyone[sic] and there are two children older than I am; he has been here thirty-three or four years.
Q Continuously? A Yes sir.
Q Has he had a home anywhere else? A It seems to me it was twenty-five years ago he went to Colorado and stayed a while and then come back.
Q He didn't go there to make a home, did he? A No sir.
Q Is your mother living? A Yes sir.
Q Sarah E.? A Yes sir.
Q She has been living with your father ever since they were married?
A Yes sir, they are living together.
Q Have you a sister, Olive? A Yes sir.
Q Still under age? A Yes sir.
Q Living at home? A Yes sir.
Q And always lived with her parents? A Yes sir.

Cherokee Intermarried White 1906
Volume IV

The undersigned, being duly sworn, states that as stenographer to the Commission to the Five Civilized Tribes he correctly recorded the testimony and proceedings in this case, and that the foregoing is a true and correct transcript of his stenographic notes thereof.

E.G. Rothenberger

Subscribed and sworn to before me this 11th day of May, 1903.

Samuel Foreman
Notary Public.

◇◇◇◇◇

Cherokee 5706.

DEPARTMENT OF THE INTERIOR,
COMMISSIONER TO THE FIVE CIVILIZED TRIBES.
Muskogee, I. T. January 4, 1907.

In the matter of the application for the enrollment of JOSEPH B. ANTOINE, as a citizen by intermarriage of the Cherokee Nation.

Joseph B. Antoine being first duly sworn by B. P. Rasmus, a Notary Public for the Western District, Indian Territory, testified as follows:

By the Commissioner:
Q What is your name? A Joseph B. Antoine.
Q How old are you? A Sixty-six.
Q What is your postoffice address? A Tahlequah?[sic] I. T.
Q You are an applicant for enrollment as a citizen by intermarriage of the Cherokee nation[sic]? A Yes sir.
Q You have no Cherokee blood? A No sir.
Q The only claim that you make to the right to enrollment as a citizen of the Cherokee nation is by virtue of your marriage to a citizen by blood of the Cherokee nation[sic]? A Yes.
Q What is the name of the citizen through whom you claim that right? A Sarah E. West, was her maiden name.
Q Was Sarah E. West a recognized citizen of the Cherokee nation[sic] at the time you married her? A Yes sir.
Q Living in the Cherokee country, was she? A Yes sir.
Q Were you married to her in accordance with the laws of the Cherokee nation[sic]? A Yes sir.
Q In what didtrict[sic] did you marry her? A In Illinois District.
Q Was the license issued to you from that district? A It was issued from Tahlequah District.

Q You obtained your license then, in Tahlequah District? A Yes sir.

Q In the year 1868? A Yes sir, February, 1868.

Q Since the marriage of yourself to your wife Sarah E. Antoine, have you and she lived together as husband and wife continuously? A Yes sir.

Q And lived in the Cherokee nation[sic], have you? A Yes sir.

Q Were you ever married prior to your marriage to her? A No sir.

Q Was she ever married prior to her marriage to you? A No.

Q Have you any evidence of a documentary character showing your marriage to your wife? A Yes, I have it here.

Q It is on file in this office, is it? A Yes sir.

Q Your original marriage license and certificate?

A The marriage license and the certificate is on record.

Q On record on[sic] Tahlequah District? A Yes sir.

> Applicant presents an affidavit signed by Robert B. Ross of Tahlequah, I. T., stating that as clerk of Tahlequah District, he issued a license dated February 17, 1868, authorizing the marriage of Joseph B. Antoine, a white citizen of the United States to wed Miss Sarah E. West, a Cherokee citizen, and that he recorded said license in March, 1868.
> This affidavit will be filed with and made a part of the records in this case.

> The applicant, Joseph B. Antoine, is identified on the 1880 authenticated tribal roll of the Cherokee Nation, Illinois District, opposite No. 30.

> The name of his wife, Sarah E. Antoine, is included in an improved partial roll of citizens by blood of the Cherokee Nation, opposite No. 174.

Frances R. Lane upon oath states that as stenographer to the Commissioner to the Five Civilized Tribes she reported the testimony in the above entitled cause and that the foregoing is an accurate transcript of her stenographic notes thereof.

Frances R. Lane

Subscribed and sworn to before me this January 5, 1907.

Edward Merrick
Notary Public.

◇◇◇◇◇

Cherokee Intermarried White 1906
Volume IV

AFFIDAVIT

UNITED STATES OF AMERICA,)
INDIAN TERRITORY,)
NORTHERN DISTRICT.)

Personally appeared this day before me, William F. Rasmus, a Notary Public within and for the judicial District and Territory aforenamed, duly commissioned and acting as such, Robert B. Ross, to me personally well known to be reputable and entitled to credit, and who being by me first duly sworn upon his oath according to law, deposes and says, that his age is 62 years; That his residence is Tahlequah Ind. Ty; That his post-office address is Tahlequah Ind. Ty; That he is a Post Master by occupation; And affiant further states that, he was the Clerk of Tahlequah District, in which Mr. Joseph B. Antoine (a white citizen of the United States) obtained License to wed Miss Sarah E. West, a Cherokee citizen of the Cherokee Nation, Indian Territory, Said Mr. Robert B. Ross further states that he issued said License, to Mr. Joseph B. Antoine, to wed Miss Sarah E. West, of Fort Gibson, Ind. Ty. Dated, Feb. 27-1868; Mr. Robert B. Ross further states that he recorded said License of Mr. Joseph B. Antoine Dated March-1868, all of which is to the best of my knowledge and recollection.

(Signed) Robert B. Ross.

The undersigned, being first duly sworn, states that as stenographer to the Commissioner to the Five Civilized Tribes, she made the above copy, and that the same is a full, true and correct copy of the original affidavit now on file in this office.

Mattie M Pace

Subscribed and sworn to before me this January 16, 1907.

Chas E Webster
Notary Public.

◇◇◇◇◇◇

ACKNOWLEDGMENT

The next above and the within and foregoing affidavit, subscribed and sworn to before me at Tahlequah, Ind. Terry. this the 4th day of January, A. D. 1907.

My commission expires, April 12th 1909, (4th Term)

(Signed) Wm. F. Rasmus

Notary Public

SEAL

(The Affidavit above given again.)

◇◇◇◇◇

C.F.B.   Cherokee 5706.

DEPARTMENT OF THE INTERIOR,

COMMISSIONER TO THE FIVE CIVILIZED TRIBES.

In the matter of the application for the enrollment of JOSEPH B. ANTOINE as a citizen by intermarriage of the Cherokee Nation.

D E C I S I O N

THE RECORDS OF THIS OFFICE SHOW: That at Tahlequah, Indian Territory, October 27, 1900, application was received by the Commission to the Five Civilized Tribes for the enrollment of Joseph B. Antoine as a citizen by intermarriage of the Cherokee Nation. Further proceedings in the matter of said application were had at Tahlequah, Indian Territory, October 1, 1902, and May 5, 1903, and at Muskogee, Indian Territory, January 4, 1907.

THE EVIDENCE IN THIS CASE SHOWS: That the applicant herein, Joseph B. Antoine, a white man, was married in the year 1868, in accordance with Cherokee law, to Sarah E. West, who was at the time of said marriage a recognized citizen by blood of the Cherokee Nation, who is identified on the Cherokee authenticated tribal roll of 1880, Illinois District, No. 31, as a native Cherokee, and whose name appears on the approved partial roll of citizens by blood of the Cherokee Nation, opposite No. 28174; that since the time of said marriage the said Joseph B. and Sarah E. Antoine have resided together as husband and wife, and have continuously lived in the Cherokee Nation. Said applicant

41

is identified on the Cherokee authenticated tribal roll of 1880, and the Cherokee census roll of 1896, as an adopted white citizen of the Cherokee Nation.

IT IS, THEREFORE, ORDERED AND ADJUDGED: That in accordance with the decision of the Supreme Court of the United States, dated November 5, 1906, in the cases of Daniel Red Bird et al. vs. the United States, Nos. 125, 126, 127 and 128, the said applicant, Joseph B. Antoine, is entitled, under the provision of Section 21, of the Act of Congress approved June 28, 1898 (30 Stats., 495), to enrollment as a citizen by intermarriage of the Cherokee Nation, and his application for enrollment as such is accordingly granted.

Tams Bixby
Commissioner.

Dated at Muskogee, Indian Territory,
this   JAN 22 1907

◇◇◇◇◇

Cherokee 5706

Muskogee, Indian Territory, January 23, 1907.

W. W. Hastings,
Attorney for the Cherokee Nation,
Muskogee, Indian Territory.

Dear Sir:

There is enclosed herewith a copy of the decision of the Commissioner to the Five Civilized Tribes, dated January 23, 1907, granting the application for the enrollment of Joseph B. Antoine as a citizen by intermarriage of the Cherokee Nation.

Respectfully,

Encl. H-71   Commissioner.
JMH

◇◇◇◇◇

Cherokee 5706

W.W.HASTINGS. ATTORNEY.

OFFICE OF

H.M. VANCE. SECRETARY.

Attorney for the Cherokee Nation,

MUSKOGEE, I. T.   January 23, 1907.

The Commissioner to the Five Civilized Tribes,
Muskogee, Indian Territory.

Sir:

Receipt is acknowledged of the testimony and of your decision enrolling Joseph B. Antoine as a citizen by intermarriage of the Cherokee Nation. Time for protesting said decision is waived and I consent that said person may be placed upon the schedule immediately.

Respectfully,

W. W. Hastings
Attorney for Cherokee Nation.

◇◇◇◇◇

Cherokee
5706

Muskogee, Indian Territory, January 23, 1907.

Joseph B. Antoine,
Tahlequah, Indian Territory.

Dear Sir:

There is enclosed herewith a copy of the decision of the Commissioner to the Five Civilized Tribes, dated January 23, 1907, granting your application for enrollment as a citizen by intermarriage of the Cherokee Nation.

You will be advised when your name has been placed upon a schedule of citizens of the Cherokee Nation and approved by the Secretary of the Interior.

Respectfully,

E.R.C.
Enc. E.C. 92.

Commissioner.

◇◇◇◇◇

OK CFB
Cherokee 5706
I.W.   Granted

Cher IW 107

◇◇◇◇◇

E.C.M.

DEPARTMENT OF THE INTERIOR,

COMMISSIONER TO THE FIVE CIVILIZED TRIBES.

In the matter of the application for the enrollment of

YELL HASTINGS

as a citizen by intermarriage of the Cherokee Nation.

CHEROKEE 5823

◇◇◇◇◇

Department of the Interior,
Commission to the Five Civilized Tribes,
Tahlequah, I. T., November 29, 1900.

In the mater[sic] of the application of Yell Hastings for the enrollment of himself and wife as Cherokee citizens being sworn and examined by Commissioner Needles he testified as follows:

Q What is your name? A Yell Hastings.
Q What is your age? A 58.
Q What is your post-office address? A Maysville, Arkansas.
Q What district do you lve[sic] in? A Delaware.
Q You are a recognized citizen of the Cherokee Nation? A Yes sir.
Q By blood or intermarriage? A By intermarriage.
Q Who do you want to enroll, yourself and family? A Myself and wife.
Q What is the name of your wife? A Louisa J.
APPLICANT'S WIFE, LOUISA J. HASTINGS, HAVING BEEN SWORN, TESTIFD[sic]

Q What is your age, Mrs. Hastings? A 60.
Q Are you a citizen by blood? A Yes sir.
1880 roll page 268 #1296 W.T. Hasting[sic] Delaware District
1880 roll page 268 #1297 Louisa J. Hasting Delaware Dist
1896 roll page 574 #242 Yell Hastings Delaware District
1896 roll page 483 #1526 Louisa J. Hasting[sic] Delaware Dist

APPLICANT RECALLED:

Q How long have you lived in the Cherokee Nation? A About 33 years.
Q Living here now? A Yes sir.
Q Mrs. Hastings also? A Yes sir.

Com'r Needles: The name of Yell Hastings appears upon the authenticated roll f[sic] 1880 as W.T. Hasting, and upon the census roll of 1896 as Yell Hastings; the name of his wife Louisa J., is found upon the authenticated roll of 1880 as well as the census roll of 1896, she being duly identified thereon, and having made satisfactory proof as to residence, said Yell Hastings will be duly listed for enrollment as a Cherokee citizen by intermarriage, and his wife, Louisa J., as a Cherokee citizen by blood.

M.D. Green, being first duly sworn, states that as stenographer to the Commission to the Five Civilized Tribes he correctly recorded the testimony and proceedings in this case and that the foregoing is a true and complete transcript of his stenographic notes thereof.

MD Green

Subscribed and sworn to before me this 30th day of November 1900.

TB Needles
Commissioner.

◇◇◇◇◇

Cherokee 5823.

Department of the Interior,
Commission to the Five Civilized Tribes,
Muskogee, I. T., September 20, 1902.

In the matter of the application of Yell Hastings for enrollment as a citizen of the Cherokee Nation by intermarriage.

W. W. Hastings, being sworn and examined by the Commission, testified as follows:
Q What is your name, age and postoffice address? A My name is W. W. Hastings, age 35, postoffice Tahlequah.
Q Are you the son of Yell Hastings? A Yes sir.
Q Is he living? A Yes sir.
Q What is the name of his wife? A Louisa J. Hastings.
Q Is she living? A Yes sir.
Q Have they always lived in the Cherokee Nation since their marriage? A Yes sir.
Q Are they living there at the present time? A Yes sir.
Q Your father is a white man? A Yes sir.
Q Has he and your mother lived together continuously since their marriage? A Yes sir.

Q Living together at the present time? A Yes sir.

The undersigned, being duly sworn, states that as stenographer to the Commission to the Five Civilized Tribes he correctly recorded the testimony and proceedings in this case and that the foregoing is a true and correct transcript of his stenographic notes thereof.

E.G. Rothenberger

Subscribed and sworn to before me this 23rd day of September, 1902.

BC Jones
Notary Public.

◇◇◇◇◇

Cher
5823

Department of the Interior,
Commission to the Five Civilized Tribes,
Vinita, I. T., January 8, 1903.

In the matter of the application of YELL HASTINGS, for the enrollment of himself, as a citizen by intermarriage, and his wife, LOUISA J. HASTINGS, as a citizen by blood, of the Cherokee Nation:

W. W. HASTINGS, being first duly sworn, and examined, testified as follows:

Examined by the Commission:

Q Sate your name, age and residence ?
A My name is W. W. Hastings; age 36; post office address, Tahlequah, I. T.
Q You are a citizen of the Cherokee Nation ? A Yes sir, by blood.
Q Do you know Yell Hastings who is an applicant to be enrolled as a citizen by intermarriage of the Cherokee Nation ?
A Yes sir, he is my father.
Q What is his wife's name ? A Louisa Jane Hastings.
Q Was she his wife in 1880 ? A Yes sir.
Q Has your father, Yell Hastings, and his wife Louisa Jane, been living together ever since 1880 ? A Yes sir.
Q Never been separated ? A No sir.
Q And were living together on the first day of last September, as husband and wife ?
A Yes sir.
Q Your father, Yell Hastings, has made his home in the Cherokee Nation ever since 1880 has he ? A Yes sir.

Cherokee Intermarried White 1906
Volume IV

I, E. C. Bagwell, a stenographer to the Commission to the Five Civilized Tribes, being first duly sworn, states that the foregoing is an accurate transcript of the notes of the testimony and proceedings had in the above entitled cause, as the same were reported by Jesse O. Carr, stenographer, and by him read to me.

E.C. Bagwell

Subscribed and sworn to before me this February 9, 1903.

Samuel Foreman
Notary Public.

◇◇◇◇◇

Cherokee 5823.

DEPARTMENT OF THE INTERIOR,
COMMISSIONER TO THE FIVE CIVILIZED TRIBES.
MUSKOGEE, I. T., DECEMBER 27, 1906.

In the matter of the application for the enrollment of YELL HASTINGS as a citizen by intermarriage of the Cherokee Nation.

APPEARANCES:
>Applicant present in person.
>For Cherokee Nation, W. W. Hastings.

YELL HASTINGS, being first duly sworn by B. P. Rasmus, a Notary Public, testified as follows:

ON BEHALF OF THE COMMISSIONER:

Q What is your name? A Yell Hastings.
Q Your age? A 64.
Q What is your postoffice? A Maysville, Arkansas.
Q You are a white man? A Yes sir, I suppose so.
Q You are an intermarried citizen of the Cherokee Nation? A Yes sir.
Q What is the name of the Cherokee wife that you claim your right to enrollment through? A L. J. Williams.
Q Is her full name Louisa J.? A Yes sir, that is it.
Q When were you and she married? A Married in December, 1867, about the first.
Q Was that acording[sic] to a Cherokee license? A I think so sir.
Q Have you any documentary evidence of your marriage?
A None only sir that what is here.

47

Cherokee Intermarried White 1906
Volume IV

There is offered in evidence a certified copy of the record of Marriages, Delaware District, Cherokee Nation, certifying that W. Y. Hasting[sic], a white man was licensed to marry L. J. Williams, a Cherokee, on the first day of December, 1867, and that the license was executed and returned January 13, 1869.

Since this certificate of record was prepared the Commissioner has secured possession of the original marriage records of the Cherokee Nation, and the record of this marriage license is found in Record "S" of marriage Records of Delaware District, Cherokee Nation, and in the index of the contents of the record it is shown that the license referred to was executed and returned on January 13, 1868, instead of January 13, 1869. These marriage records are in the lawful custody of this office.

Q Have you and your wife lived together continuously since your marriage?
A Yes sir.
Q Were you living in the Cherokee Nation when you married? A Yes sir.
Q Have you both lived in the Cherokee Nation continuously since then? A Yes sir.
Q Was she a recognized Cherokee at the time of your marriage to her? A Yes sir.

The applicant and his wife, Louisa J. Hastings, are listed for enrollment on Cherokee Field Card No. 5823. They are identified on the 1880 Authenticated Roll of citizens of the Cherokee Nation opposite Nos. 1296 and 1297 respectively, Delaware District, and the name of his wife is included in a partial roll of Cherokee citizens by blood approved by the Secretary of the Interior opposite No. 13938.

BY MR. HASTINGS:

Q You were married twice to your present wife, were you not? A Yes sir.
Q When were you first married? A in 1864 I think.
Q In Arkansas? A Yes sir.
Q And this last marriage about which you have been testifying was when you were married in accordance with Cherokee law? A Yes sir that is it.
Q Now your wife's name is given upon this card, her maiden name is given as Stover, had she previously been married? A Yes sir.
Q What was her first husband's name? A Williams.
Q Was Williams dead before you and she married? A Yes sir.
Q You had been previously married? A Yes sir.
Q Was your first wife dead when you and Louisa J. Williams married? A Yes sir.
Q You have lived together continuously since your marriage? A Yes sir.
Q And are living now together as husband and wife? A Yes sir.

ON BEHALF OF THE COMMISSIONER:

Q Is your present wife the identical person mentioned in this marriage record as L. J. Williams? A Yes sir.

(Witness excused).

-------------------------oOo-------------------------

Geo. H. Lessley, being first duly sworn, states that as stenographer to the Commissioner to the Five Civilized Tribes he reported the proceedings had in the above entitled cause, and that the above and foregoing is a true and correct transcript of his stenographic notes thereof.

Geo H Lessley

Subscribed and sworn to before me this 2nd day of January, 1907.

John E. Tidwell
Notary Public.

◇◇◇◇◇

C O P Y .

This is to certify by me that W. Y. Haisting[sic], a white man, was licensed to marry L. J. Williams, a female Cherokee, on the 1st day of December, 1867, and the license executed and returned Jan. 13, 1869, being with according to the Act past[sic] by the National Council bearing date October 15, 1855, in regard to white men marrying in this Nation.

(Signed)   T. J. McGhee,

Clk. D. C. D. D. C. N.

I, A. B. Cunningham, Executive Secretary of the Cherokee Nation do hereby certify that the above and foregoing is a true copy from the marriage record Deleware[sic] District in the Executive Department of the Interior the Cherokee Nation, and I further certify that a tabulated list found on the second page of same book giving a list of white people marrying in accordance with Cherokee Law gives this same license as issued on December 1st, 1867 but returned on Janyary[sic] 13, 1868 instead of 1869, and i[sic] do so certify on this 22d day of December, 1906.

(Signed) A. B. Cunningham

Executive Secretary, Cherokee

SEAL.   Nation.

This certifies that the undersigned, being duly sworn, states that, as stenographer for the Commissioner to the Five Civilized Tribes, she made the above and foregoing copy, and that the same is a full, true and correct copy of the original instrument now on file in this office.

Georgia Coberly

Subscribed and sworn to before me this 18th day of January, 1907.

Chas E Webster
Notary Public.

◇◇◇◇◇

E C M   Cherokee 5823

DEPARTMENT OF THE INTERIOR,
COMMISSIONER TO THE FIVE CIVILIZED TRIBES.

———————

In the matter of the application for the enrollment of Yell Hastings as a citizen by intermarriage of the Cherokee Nation.

D E C I S I O N .

———————

THE RECORDS OF THIS OFFICE SHOW: That at Tahlequah, Indian Territory, November 29, 1900, application was received by the Commission to the Five Civilized Tribes for the enrollment of Yell Hastings as a citizen by intermarriage of the Cherokee Nation. Further proceedings in the matter of said application were had at Muskogee, Indian Territory, September 20, 1902, Vinita, Indian Territory, January 8, 1903 and Muskogee, Indian Territory, December 27, 1906.

THE EVIDENCE IN THIS CASE SHOWS: That the applicant herein, Yell Hastings, a white man, was married in accordance with Cherokee law January 13, 1868 to his wife Louisa J. Hastings, nee Stover, who was at the time of said marriage a recognized citizen by blood of the Cherokee Nation, and who is identified on the Cherokee authenticated tribal roll of 1880, Delaware District, No. 1297, as a native Cherokee, and whose name is included on the approved partial roll of citizens by blood of the Cherokee Nation, opposite number 13998. It is further shown that from the time of said marriage the said Yell Hastings and Louisa J. Hastings resided together as husband and wife and continuously lived in the Cherokee Nation up to and including September 1, 1902. Said applicant is identified on the Cherokee authenticated tribal roll of 1880 as "W.T. Hastings" and the Cherokee census roll of 1896 as an intermarried citizen of the Cherokee Nation.

IT IS THEREFORE ORDERED AND ADJUDGED: That in accordance with the decision of the Supreme Court of the United States, dated November 5, 1906, in the case of Daniel Red Bird, et al. vs. the United States, numbers 125, 126, 127, 128, the said applicant, Yell Hastings is entitled, under the provision of Section 21, of the Act of Congress approved June 28, 1898 (30th. Stats. 495), to enrollment as a citizen by intermarriage of the Cherokee Nation, and his application for enrollment as such is accordingly granted.

Tams Bixby
Commissioner.

Dated at Muskogee, Indian Territory,
this   JAN 23 1907

◇◇◇◇◇

Cherokee 5823

Muskogee, Indian Territory, January 23, 1907.

W. W. Hastings,
      Attorney for the Cherokee Nation,
           Muskogee, Indian Territory.

Dear Sir:

There is enclosed herewith a copy of the decision of the Commissioner to the Five Civilized Tribes, dated January 23, 1907, granting the application for the enrollment of Yell Hastings as a citizen by intermarriage of the Cherokee Nation.

Respectfully,

Encl. H-70
Commissioner.
JMH

◇◇◇◇◇

Cherokee 5823   W.W.HASTINGS. ATTORNEY.   OFFICE OF   H.M. VANCE. SECRETARY.

Attorney for the Cherokee Nation,
MUSKOGEE, I. T.   January 23, 1907.

The Commissioner to the Five Civilized Tribes,
        Muskogee, Indian Territory.
Sir:

Receipt is acknowledged of the testimony and of your decision enrolling Yell Hastings as a citizen by intermarriage of the Cherokee Nation. Time for protesting said decision is waived and I consent that said person may be placed upon the schedule immediately.

Respectfully,

W. W. Hastings
Attorney for Cherokee Nation/[sic]

◇◇◇◇◇

Cherokee Intermarried White 1906
Volume IV

Cherokee
5823

Muskogee, Indian Territory, January 23, 1907.

Yell Hastings,
Maysville, Arkansas.

Dear Sir:

There is enclosed herewith a copy of the decision of the Commissioner to the Five Civilized Tribes, dated January 23, 1907, granting your application for enrollment as a citizen by intermarriage of the Cherokee Nation.

You will be advised when your name has been placed upon a schedule of citizens of the Cherokee Nation and approved by the Secretary of the Interior.

Respectfully,

E.R.C.   Commissioner.
Enc. E.C. 91

<><><><><>

```
OK CFB

Cherokee 5823
I.W.
Granted
```

Cher IW 108

<><><><><>

C.E.W.

DEPARTMENT OF THE INTERIOR,

COMMISSIONER TO THE FIVE CIVILIZED TRIBES.

In the matter of the application for the enrollment of

ELIJAH STEPHENS

as a citizen by intermarriage of the Cherokee Nation.

CHEROKEE 6135

◇◇◇◇◇

Department of the Interior,
Commission to the Five Civilized Tribes,
Tahlequah, I. T. December, 5th 1900.

In the matter of the application of Elijah Stephens for the enrollment of himself and child as Cherokee citizens. He being sworn before Commissioner Neeedles[sic], testified as follows-

Q What is your name? A. Elijah Stephens.
Q How old are you? A. 51.
Q What is your post office address? A. Parkhill.
Q What district do you live in? A. Tahlequah.
Q Are you a recognized citizen of the Cherokee Nation? A. Yes sir.
Q By blood? A. No sir by adoption.
Q Who do you desire to have enrolled? A. Myself and children.
Q When were you married? A. 26 years ago.
Q What is your wifes[sic] name? A. Mary
Q How old is she? A. 45.
Q Is she a Cherokee by blood? A. Yes sir.
Q What are the names of your children? A. A[sic] Thomas F.
Q How old? [sic]. 17.
Q Next? A. James E.
Q How old? A. 12.
Q Next? A. Taylor C.
Q How old? A. 10.
Q Next? A. Albert
Q How old? A. 7.
Q Is Mary your first wife? A. Yes sir.

Q Are you living with her now? A. No sir she is dead.
Q These children are all living are they? A. Yes sir.
Q Have you always lived in the Cherokee Nation? A. Yes sir, since my marriage.
Q Living here now? A. Yes sir.
Q Have you married since the death of your wife? A. No sir.
Q Is your name on the 1880 roll? A. Yes sir.

1880 roll, page 389	No 1123,	Eliza[sic] Stephens, Flint dist.	
1896	935	180	Elijah Stephens Illinois dist.
1896	899	1669	Thomas Stephens "
1896	899	1670	James E. Stephens "
1896	899	1671	Taylor C. Stephens "
1896	899	1672	Albert Stephens "

Q Are these children all living with you? A. Yes sir.

The name of Elijah Stephens appears on the authenticated roll of 1880, and his wife Mary appears on said roll also, she being dead. His name also appears on the census roll of 1896 and the names of his children, Thomas F., James E., Taylor C., and Albert also appear on the census roll of 1896. They all being identified according to the page and number of the roll and having made satisfactory proof as to residence, the said Elijah Stephens will be listed for enrollment as a Cherokee citizen by intermarriage and his children as enumerated herein as Cherokee citizens by blood.

Chas. von Weise being sworn states that as stenographer to the Commission to the Five Civilized Tribes he reported in full all the proceedings in the above cause and that the foregoing is a full true and correct transcript of his stenographic notes therein.

Chas von Weise

Subscribed and sworn to before me this the 5th of December, 1900.

CR Breckinridge
Commissioner.

◇◇◇◇◇

(Illegible Initials)

Cherokee 6135

DEPARTMENT OF THE INTERIOR,
COMMISSION TO THE FIVE CIVILIZED TRIBES,
MUSKOGEE, IND. TER., OCT. 4, 1902.

In the matter of the application for the enrollment of Elijah Stephens et al. as citizens of the Cherokee Nation:

SUPPLEMENTAL STATEMENT.

An examination of the 1880 authenticated tribal roll of the Cherokee Nation shows that Mary Stephens is identified on that roll, at page 389, #1124, Flint District.

It is ordered that copies of this statement be filed with and made a part of the record in this case.

TB Needles
Commissioner.

◇◇◇◇◇

JOR.
Cher. 6135.

Department of the Interior.
Commission to the Five Civilized Tribes.
Tahlequah, I. T., October 11, 1902.

SUPPLEMENTAL TESTIMONY AND PROCEEDINGS in the matter of the application for the enrollment of ELIJAH STEPHENS as a citizen by intermarriage of the Cherokee Nation.

ELIJAH Stephens, being first duly sworn, and being examined, testified as follows:

BY COMMISSION: What is your name? A Elijah Stephens.
Q How old are you? A About fifty, I reckon, I don't know my age exactly.
Q What is your post office address? A Parkhill.
Q You are a white man, are you? A Yes sir.
Q Have you heretofore made application to this Commission for enrollment as a citizen by intermarriage of the Cherokee Nation? A Yes sir.
Q What is the name of your wife? A Mary A. C.
Q Is she living? A No sir.
Q Was she a Cherokee by blood? A Yes sir.
Q Do you claim your right to enrollment by reason of your marriage to her?
A Yes sir.

Cherokee Intermarried White 1906
Volume IV

Q When were you and she married? A It has been about twenty-six years ago.

Q Were you married to her at that time according to Cherokee law? A Yes sir.

Q Did you make satisfactory proof to the Commission when you made your application to the Commission of your marriage to her according to Cherokee law? A Yes sir.

Q Were you ever married before you married her? A No sir.

Q Was she ever married before she married you? A No sir.

Q You are her first husband and she is your first wife? A Yes sir.

Q How long has she been dead? A It has been about two years.

Q Did you and she live together continuously until the time of her death? A Yes sir.

Q Never separated at all? A No sir.

Q Have you married since she died? A No sir.

Q You still remain single? A Yes sir.

Q Have you resided in the Cherokee Nation continuously since you and your wife were married? A Yes sir.

Q Did she reside in the Cherokee Nation continuously until the time of her death?
A Yes sir.

> This testimony will be filed with and made a part of the record in the matter of the application for the enrollment of Elijah Stephens as a citizen by intermarriage of the Cherokee Nation, Cherokee straight card field No. 6135.

Wm. Hutchinson, being first duly sworn, states that as stenographer to the Commission to the Five Civilized Tribes he correctly recorded the testimony and proceedings in this case, and that the foregoing is a true and complete transcript of the stenographic notes thereof.

Wm Hutchinson

Subscribed and sworn to before me this 18th day of October, 1902.

John O Rosson
Notary Public.

◇◇◇◇◇

Cherokee Intermarried White 1906
Volume IV

CHEROKEE-6135.

DEPARTMENT OF THE INTERIOR,
COMMISSIONER TO THE FIVE CIVILIZED TRIBES.
Muskogee, Indian Territory?[sic] January 5, 1907.

In the matter of making proof of the marriage of Elijah Stevens[sic] to his Cherokee wife, prior to November 1, 1875.

Elijah Stevens, being duly sworn by B. P. Rasmus, a Notary Public, testified as follows.

COMMISSIONER:

Q. What is your name? A. Elijah Stevens.
Q. What is your age? A. 58.
Q. What is your post office address? A. Park Hill.
Q. Do you claim to be an intermarried citizen of the Cherokee Nation? A. Yes sir.
Q. Through whom do you claim your right as such? A. Mary Martin
Q. When were you married to her? A. In '74.
Q. What time? A. I don't know the date.
Q. About what time was it? A. It was in the fall.
Q. Were you married under a license? A. Yes sir.
Q. Where is your license? A. I thought that was it.
Q. What District were you married in? A. Going Snake.
Q. Who married you? A. A. preacher by the name of Ferguson.
Q. What was the name of the man that issued the license? A. Ben Goss.
Q. Were you ever married before you married Mary Martin? A. No sir.
Q. Was she ever married before she married you? A. No sir.
Q. How long have you lived together as husband and wife? A. Up till about 7 years ago.
Q. You lived with her as her husband up to the time of her death? A. Yes sir.
Q. She died seven years ago? A. Yes sir I think so.
Q. In 1889? A. Yes sir.
Q. Have you married again since her death? A. No sir.
Q. Did you live continuously in the Cherokee Nation since your marriage to Mary Martin in 1874 up to the present time? A. Yes sir.

(Commissioner -- The applicant is identified upon the 1880 Cherokee Roll, opposite No. 1123, Flint District.)

Cherokee Intermarried White 1906
Volume IV

(Commissioner -- It will be necessary for you to furnish this office with proof of the fact that you were married under a Cherokee license, in compliance with the Cherokee law prior to November 1, 1875.)

(Commissioner-- The applicant offers in evidence the marriage license issued to him on November 20, 1874 by B. P. Goss to marry Rebecca Martin.)

Witness excused.

Eula Jeanes Branson, being sworn, states that she correctly reported the proceedings had in the above entitled matter on the 5th. day of January, 1907.

Eula Jeanes Branson

Subscribed and sworn to before me this the 8th. day of January, 1907.

Walter W. Chappell
Notary Public.

◇◇◇◇◇

COPY

Cherokee Nation

G. S. Dist

By the authority in me vested by the law of the Cherokee Nation I do hereby grant license of marriage unto Elijah Stevens a citizen of the United States of good moral character and of industrious habits (as per petition) to marry Miss Mary Martin a Cherokee by birth and a daughter of Ham Martin and Rebeca[sic] Martin having complied with the requirements of the law regulating intermarriage with white men

Given from under my hand in office this the 20 of Nov 1874.

(Signed) B. F. Goss Clerk
G. S. Dist C. N.

I hereby certify that I have joined together by marriage the persons whose names appear in the within licens[sic] according to the laws of the Cherokee Nation on the 20 day of Nov 1874.

(Signed) T. R. Ferguson
Ordaned[sic] minister of the Baptist Church.

The undersigned being first duly sworn states that as stenographer to the Commissioner to the Five Civilized Tribes, she made the above copy and that the same is a true and correct copy of the original marriage license and certificate now on file in this office.

Lola M. Champlin

Subscribed and sworn to before me this 14 day of January 1970.

Chas E Webster
Notary Public.

◇◇◇◇◇

C.E.W.   Cherokee 6135.

DEPARTMENT OF THE INTERIOR.

COMMISSIONER TO THE FIVE CIVILIZED TRIBES.

. . . .

In the matter of the application for the enrollment of Elijah Stephens as a citizen by intermarriage of the Cherokee Nation.

D E C I S I O N .

THE RECORDS OF THIS OFFICE SHOW: That at Tahlequah, Indian Territory, December 5, 1900, application was received by the Commission to the Five Civilized Tribes for the enrollment of Elijah Stephens, as a citizen by intermarriage of the Cherokee Nation. Further proceedings in the matter of said application were had at Muskogee, Indian Territory, October 4, 1902, and at Tahlequah, Indian Territory, January 5, 1907.

THE EVIDENCE IN THIS CASE SHOWS: That the applicant herein, Elijah Stephens, a white man, was married in accordance with Cherokee law November 20, 1874, to one Mary Stephens, nee Martin, since deceased, who was at the time of said marriage a recognized citizen by blood of the Cherokee Nation, and who is identified on the Cherokee authenticated roll of 1880, Flint District, page 389, number 1124, as a citizen by blood of the Cherokee Nation; and that after said marriage the said Elijah Stephens and Mary Stephens lived together as husband and wife until her death which occurred about the year 1899; that since the death of the said Mary Stephens the said Elijah Stephens has not married; and that he has continuously lived in the Cherokee Nation since November 20, 1874. Said Elijah Stephens is identified o the Cherokee authenticated roll of 1880, and the Cherokee census roll of 1896 as an intermarried citizen of the Cherokee Nation.

IT IS, THEREFORE, ORDERED AND ADJUDGED: That in accordance with the decision of the Supreme Court of the United States, dated November 5, 1906, in the case of Daniel Red Bird, et al., vs. the United States, Nos. 125, 126, 127 and 128, the said applicant Elijah Stephens is entitled, under the provision of Section 21 of the Act of Congress approved June 28, 1898 (30 Stats. 495), to enrollment, as a citizen by intermarriage of the Cherokee Nation, and his application for enrollment as such is accordingly granted.

Tams Bixby
Commissioner.

Dated at Muskogee, Indian Territory,
this   JAN 23 1907

◇◇◇◇◇

Cherokee
I.W. 108

Muskogee, Indian Territory, April 16, 1907.

Elijah Stephens,
      Park Hill, Indian Territory.

Dear Sir:

Your marriage license and certificate filed in connection with your application for enrollment as a citizen by intermarriage of the Cherokee Nation, is returned to you herewith, copies of the same being retained in the files of this office.

Respectfully,

Encl. W-11.   Commissioner.
S.W.

◇◇◇◇◇

Cherokee I.W.
 # 108

Muskogee, Indian Territory, July 13, 1907.

Elijah Stephens,
      Muskogee, Indian Territory.

Dear Sir:

In compliance with your verbal request you are advised the records of this office show that your name is included in the schedule of citizens by intermarriage of the Cherokee Nation, approved by the Secretary of the Interior, February 25, 1907.

Respectfully

Commissioner.

MTM

◇◇◇◇◇◇

Cherokee 6138

Muskogee, Indian Territory, January 23, 1907.

W. W. Hastings,
      Attorney for the Cherokee Nation,
           Muskogee, Indian Territory.

Dear Sir:

      There is enclosed herewith of the decision of the Commissioner to the Five Civilized Tribes, dated January 23, 1908, granting the application for the enrollment of Elijah Stephens as a citizen by intermarriage of the Cherokee Nation.

Respectfully,

Enc I-70

RPI

◇◇◇◇◇◇

Cherokee 6135.   W.W.HASTINGS.   OFFICE OF   H.M. VANCE.
                   ATTORNEY.   SECRETARY.

Attorney for the Cherokee Nation,
MUSKOGEE, I. T.   January 23, 1907.

The Commissioner to the Five Civilized Tribes,
      Muskogee, Indian Territory.

Sir:

      Receipt is acknowledged of the testimony and of your decision enrolling Elijah Stephens as a citizen by intermarriage of the Cherokee Nation. Time for protesting said decision is waived and I consent that said person may be placed upon the schedule immediately.

Respectfully,

W. W. Hastings
Attorney for the Cherokee Nation.

◇◇◇◇◇◇

Cherokee 6138

Muskogee, Indian Territory, January 23, 1907.

Elijah Stephens,
        Park Hill, Indian Territory.

Dear Si:

        There is enclosed herewith a copy of the decision of the Commissioner to the Five Civilized Tribes, dated January 23, 1907, granting the application for your enrollment of as a citizen by intermarriage of the Cherokee Nation.

        You will be advised when your name has been placed upon a schedule of citizens of the Cherokee Nation and approved by the Secretary of the Interior.

Respectfully,

Encl. H-103   Commissioner.
    JMH

Cher IW 109

◇◇◇◇◇

F.R.

DEPARTMENT OF THE INTERIOR,
COMMISSIONER TO THE FIVE CIVILIZED TRIBES.

In the matter of the application for the enrollment of

Savelon S. Boyles

as a citizen by intermarriage of the Cherokee Nation.

CHEROKEE 6285.

◇◇◇◇◇

Cherokee Intermarried White 1906
Volume IV

Department of the Interior.
Commission to the Five Civilized Tribes.
Tahlequah, I. T., December 8, 1900.

In the matter of the application of Savelon S. Boyles for the enrollment of himself, wife and children as Cherokee citizens; he being sworn and examined by Commissioner T. B. Needles, testified as follows:

Q What is your name? A Savelon S. Boyles.
Q How old are you? A 56.
Q What is your postoffice? A Tahlequah.
Q What district do you line in? A Tahleqah[sic] district.
Q Are you a recognized citizen of the Cherokee Nation? A I am.
Q By blood? A No sir, by adoption.
Q Who do you desire to enroll? A My wife and children.
Q Have you any certificate of marriage? A Yes sir.
Q You and your wife on the 1880 roll? A Yes sir.
Q What is the name of your wife? A Martha.
Q What is her age? A 46.
Q Whar[sic] are the names of your children? A Oliver O.
Q How old is Oliver O.? A 18 past.
Q Next child? William H. H[sic].
Q How old is he? A He's seven years past.
Q You always lived in the Cherokee Nation? A I have snce[sic] '63 mostly.
Q Lived with your wife continuously since that time? A Yes sir.
Q Never been separated? A No sir.
Q These children living with you? A Yes sir.
1880 roll; page 734, #81, S. S. Boyles, Tahlequah district
1880 roll; page 734, #82, Martha Boyles, Tahlequah district
1896 roll; page 1275, #14, Savelon S. Boyles, Tahlequah district.
1896 roll; page 1135, #104, Martha Boyles, Tahlequah district.
1896 roll; page 1135, #106, Oliver O. Boyles, Tahlequah district
1896 roll; page 1135, #108, William H. Boyles., Tahlequah district

Commissioner Needles-
The name of Savelon S. Boyles is found upon the authenticated roll of 1880 as S. S. Boyles. His wife, Martha, is found upon said roll. They are also found upon the Census roll of 1896. The name of the two children, Oliver O. and William H. H., are found upon the Census roll of 1896. They are all duly identified, and makes satisfactory proof as to residence; consequently, the said Savelon S. Boyles will be duly listed for enrollment as a Cherokee citizen by intermarriage, his wife, Martha, and two children as enumerated herein, as Cherokee citizens by blood.

E.G. Rothenberger, being duly sworn, states that as stenographer to the Commission to the Five Civilized Tribes, he reported in full the testimony and proceedings in the above case, and that the foregoing is a full, true and correct transcript of his stenographic notes in the said case.

E.G. Rothenberger

Subscribed and sworn to before me this 10th day of December, 1900.

C R Breckinridge
Commissioner.

◇◇◇◇◇

R.
Cher. 6285.

Department of the Interior.
Commission to the Five Civilized Tribes.
Tahlequah, I. T., September 29 1902.

SUPPLEMENTAL TESTIMONY AND PROCEEDINGS in the matter of the application for the enrollment of SAVELON S. BOYLES as a citizen by intermarriage of the Cherokee Nation.

SAVELON S. BOYLES, being first duly sworn, and being examined, testified as follows:

BY COMMISSION: What is your name? A Savelon S. Boyles.
Q How old are you? A Fifty-nine in January.
Q What is your post office address? A Tahlequah.
Q You are a white man, are you? A Yes sir.
Q You have heretofore made application to this Commission for enrollment as a citizen by marriage of the Cherokee Nation? A Yes sir.
Q What is the name of your wife? A Martha Boyles.
Q Is she living? A Yes sir.
Q Were you married to her according to Cherokee law[sic] A Yes sir.
Q She is a Cherokee by blood? A Yes sir.
Q Have you and she lived together continuously since the date of your marriage?
A Never been apart. Lived together all the time.
Q Have you resided in the Cherokee Nation continuously since the date of your application? A Yes sir, never been out.
Q You claim your right to enrollment by reason of your marriage to your Cherokee wife?
A Yes sir.

This testimony will be filed with and made and made a part of the record in the matter of the application for the enrollment of Savelon S. Boyles, Cherokee straight card field No. 6285.

Wm. Hutchinson, being first duly sworn, states that as stenographer to the Commission to the Five Civilized Tribes he correctly recorded the testimony and proceedings in this case and that the foregoing is a true and complete transcript of his stenographic notes thereof.

Wm Hutchinson

Subscribed and sworn to before me this 29th day of September, 1902.

John O Rosson
Notary Public.

◇◇◇◇◇

C.F.B.

Cherokee 6285.

DEPARTMENT OF THE INTERIOR,
COMMISSIONER TO THE FIVE CIVILIZED TRIBES.
MUSKOGEE, I. T., JANUARY 7, 1907.

In the matter of the application for the enrollment of SAVELON S. BOYLES as a citizen by intermarriage of the Cherokee Nation.

APPEARANCES: Applicant appears in person.
                 W. W. Hastings, Attorney for Cherokee Nation.

SAVELON S. BOYLES, being first duly sworn by John E. Tidwell, Notary Public, testified as follows:

ON BEHALF OF THE COMMISSIONER:

Q What is your name? A Savelon S. Boyles.
Q What is your age? A I will be 63 Friday.
Q What is your post office address? A Tahlequah, I. T.
Q You are an applicant for enrollment as a citizen by intermarriage of the Cherokee Nation, are you? A Yes sir.
Q Your only claim to the right to enrollment as a citizen of the Cherokee Nation is by virtue of your marriage to a citizen by blood of the Cherokee Nation, is it? A Yes sir.
Q What is the name of the citizen? A Martha Boyles.
Q Is she living? A Yes sir.
Q When did you marry her? A I married her on the 30th of March, '75.
Q Was she a recognized citizen of the Cherokee Nation? A Yes sir.
Q Living in the Cherokee Country, was she? A Yes sir.

Q Was she your first wife? A No sir.

Q Was your first wife dead? A Yes sir, she died in September, 1872.

Q Was she a white woman or a Cherokee? A Cherokee.

Q Was your second wife married prior to her marriage to you? A No sir.

Q Since your marriage to your second wife, have you and she continuously lived
together as husband and wife? A Yes sir.

Q And have lived all those years in the Cherokee Nation, have you? A Yes sir.

Q You claim the right to enrollment through your second wife, do you not? A Yes sir.

Q Did you marry her in accordance with Cherokee law? A Yes sir.

"The applicant presents an original license, showing that on March 29, 1875, license was issued, in accordance with Cherokee law, authorizing the marriage of S. S. Boyles, a white man, and a citizen of the United States, and Miss Martha Wofford, a Cherokee. A certificate on the back of said license shows that said parties were united in marriage, in accordance with the terms of said license, March 30, 1875, by J. R. Hendrick, Judge, District Court, Tahlequah District.

The applicant, Savelon S. Boyles, is identified on the Cherokee authenticated roll of 1880, Tahlequah District, No. 81. His wife, Martha Boyles, is identified on said roll at No. 82, and her name appears in the approved partial roll of citizens of the Cherokee Nation, opposite No. 14993.

The undersigned, being first duly sworn, states that as stenographer to the Commissioner to the Five Civilized Tribes, she correctly recorded the above and foregoing testimony, and that the same is a full, true and correct transcript of her stenographic notes thereof.

Sarah Waters

Subscribed and sworn to before me this 9th day of January, 1907.

John E. Tidwell
Notary Public.

◇◇◇◇◇

CERTIFIED COPY.

Cherokee Nation)
Tahlequah District.)

Know all men by these presents, that I, O. P. Daniel Clerk of said District by virtue of the authority in me vested by law do hereby grant License to Mr. S. S. Boyles, a white man and citizen of the United States, to marry Miss Martha Wofford, a Cherokee, he the said S. S. Boyles having complied with the law regulating intermarriage with white men.

Cherokee Intermarried White 1906
Volume IV

Therefore, any ordained minister of the Gospel, or any Judge of the Courts of the Cherokee nation[sic] are hereby authorized and empowered to solemnize the Rite of Matrimony between the above named parties and return this instrument with certificate of marriage to the office for record.

Given from under my hand on this the 29th day of March, A. D., 1875.

(Signed) O. P. Daniel, Clk.
Tahlequah Districe[sic], C. N.

I hereby certify that I have this day solemnized the Rites of Matrimony Between the above named parties, according to the ceremonies, and of the Authority of the Law done at this offices[sic] this the 30th day of March, A. D., 1875
(Signed) J. R. Hendricks, Judge
of the District Court in and for
Tahlequah Dist., Cherokee Nation.

I do certify that the within license has been recorded in the Clerk's office of Tahlequah District.

(Signed) Allen Ross, Clerk,
Tahlequah District,
Tahlequah District,
February 4th, 1878
Cherokee Nation.
(SEAL).
Endorsed:
Marriage License of
S. S. Boyles
To
Martha Wofford.

I, Frances R. Lane, a stenographer to the Commissioner to the Five Civilized Tribes, do hereby certify that the above and foregoing is a true and complete copy of a marriage license and certificate issued to S. S. Boyles and Miss Mary Wofford, now on file with the records of this office in the matter of the application for the enrollment of S. S. Boyles as a citizen by intermarriage of the Cherokee Nation, Cherokee 6285.

Frances R Lane

Subscribed and sworn to before me this January 15, 1907.

Edward Merrick
Notary Public.

◇◇◇◇◇

F.R.   Cherokee 6285.

DEPARTMENT OF THE INTERIOR,

COMMISSIONER TO THE FIVE CIVILIZED TRIBES.

In the matter of the application for the enrollment of Savelon S. Boyles as a citizen by intermarriage of the Cherokee Nation.

D E C I S I O N .

THE RECORDS OF THIS OFFICE SHOW: That December 8, 1900, application was received by the Commission to the Five Civilized Tribes for the enrollment of Savelon S. Boyles as a citizen by intermarriage of the Cherokee Nation. Further proceedings in the matter of said application were had at Tahlequah, Indian Territory, September 29, 1902, and at Muskogee, Indian Territory, January 7, 1907.

THE EVIDENCE IN THIS CASE SHOWS: That the applicant herein, Savelon S. Boyles, a white man, was married in accordance with the Cherokee law, March 30, 1875, to his wife, Martha Boyles (nee Wofford), who was at the time of said marriage, a recognized citizen by blood of the Cherokee Nation, who is identified on the Cherokee authenticated tribal roll of 1880, Tahlequah District, No. 82, as a native Cherokee, and whose name is included in the approved partial roll of citizens by blood of the Cherokee Nation opposite No. 14993. It is further shown that, from the time of said marriage, the said Savelon S. Boyles and Martha Boyles resided together as husband and wife and continuously lived in the Cherokee Nation up to and including September 1, 1902. The said applicant is identified on the Cherokee authenticated tribal roll of 1880, and the Cherokee Census Roll of 1896, as an intermarried citizen of the Cherokee Nation.

IT IS, THEREFORE, ORDERED AND ADJUDGED: That in accordance with the decision of the Supreme Court of the United States, dated November 5, 1906, in the cases of Daniel Red Bird et al., vs. the United States, Nos. 125, 126, 127 and 128, the said applicant, Savelon S. Boyles, is entitled, under the provision of Section twenty-one of the Act of Congress approved June 28, 1898 (30 Stats., 495), to enrollment as a citizen by intermarriage of the Cherokee Nation, and his application for enrollment as such is accordingly granted.

Tams Bixby
Commissioner.

Dated at Muskogee, Indian Territory,
this   JAN 21 1907

◇◇◇◇◇

Cherokee Intermarried White 1906
Volume IV

Cherokee 6285

Muskogee, Indian Territory, January 21, 1907.

W. W. Hastings,
    Attorney for the Cherokee Nation,
        Muskogee, Indian Territory.

Dear Sir:

      There is enclosed herewith copy of the decision of the Commissioner to the Five Civilized Tribes, dated January 21, 1907, granting the application for the enrollment of Savelon S. Boyles as a citizen by intermarriage of the Cherokee Nation.

            Respectfully,

Enc I-43   Commissioner.

RPI

◇◇◇◇◇

Cherokee 6285   W.W.HASTINGS. ATTORNEY.   OFFICE OF   H.M. VANCE. SECRETARY.

Attorney for the Cherokee Nation,
MUSKOGEE, I. T. January 21, 1907.

The Commissioner to the Five Civilized Tribes,
    Muskogee, Indian Territory.

Sir:

      Receipt is acknowledged of the testimony and of your decision enrolling Savelon S. Boyles as a citizen by intermarriage of the Cherokee Nation. Time for protesting said decision is waived and I consent that said person may be placed upon the schedule immediately.

            Respectfully,
              W. W. Hastings
              Attorney for the Cherokee Nation.

◇◇◇◇◇

Cherokee 6285

Muskogee, Indian Territory, January 24, 1907.

Savelon S. Boyles,
    Tahlequah, Indian Territory.

Dear Sir:

    There is enclosed herewith copy of the decision of the Commissioner to the Five Civilized Tribes, dated January 21, 1907, granting the application for your enrollment as a citizen by intermarriage of the Cherokee Nation.

    You will be advised when your name has been placed upon a schedule of citizens of the Cherokee Nation and approved by the Secretary of the Interior.

Respectfully,

Enc I-95   Commissioner.

RPI

Cher IW 110

◇◇◇◇◇

F.R.

DEPARTMENT OF THE INTERIOR,

COMMISSIONER TO THE FIVE CIVILIZED TRIBES.

In the matter of the application for the enrollment of

REBECCA C. ROBBINS

as a citizen by intermarriage of the Cherokee Nation.

CHEROKEE 6297.

◇◇◇◇◇

Cherokee Intermarried White 1906
Volume IV

Department of the Interior.
Commission to the Five Civilized Tribes
Tahlequah, I. T. December 8th 1900.

In the matter of the application of Rebecca Caroline Robbins for the enrollment of herself, son and nephew as Cherokee citizens. She being sworn before Commissioner Needles, testified as follows-

Q What is your name? A. Rebecca Caroline Robbins.
Q What is your age? A. 55.
Q What is your post office address? A. Tahlequah
Q What district do you live in? A. Tahlequah.
Q Are you a recognized Cherokee citizen? A. Yes sir.
Q By blood or inter-marriage? A. Inter-marriage.
Q Who do you want to have enrolled? A. Myself, son and nephew.
Q What is your husband's name? A. Benjamin Robbins.
Q Is he living? A. No sir.
Q When were you married to him? A. Somewhere in the '70s
Q Was he a Cherokee by blood? A. Yes sir
Q Have you married since his death? A. No sir I am a widow.
Q When did he die? A. 18 years ago
Q Did you live with him continuouslt[sic] from the time you married him until he died? A. Yes sir.
Q What is the name of your child? A. Doc Robbins.
Q How old is he? A⸱ 19.
Q What is the name of your nephew? A. Joshua Robbins.
Q What is his age? A. *(Illegible)*
Q What is his fathers[sic] name? A. Joshua Robbins.
Q What is his mothers[sic] name? A. Algerean Robbins.
Q Are they living? A. Both are dead.
Q Was his father Joshua a Cherokee by blood? A. Yes sir.
Q Was his mother Algerean a Cherokee by blood? A. No sir she was a white woman.

1880 roll, page 42, No 1153, R. C. Robbins, Canadian dist.

1880	42	1152	B. F. Robbins "
1896	1247	219	Caroline Robbins Tahlequah "
1896	1231	2708	Dock Robbins
1896	1045	109	Josh Robbins, Orphan roll, Saline dist.
1880	798	1823	Joshua Robbins, Tahlequah
1880	798	1824	Aljarine[sic] Robbins "

Q Is Joshua and Algerean Robbins, the father and mother of Joshua Robbins for whom you now apply for enrollment? A. Yes sir.
Q Do these children both live with you? A. Yes sir.

The name of Rebecca C. Robbins appears on the authenticated roll of 1880 as R. C. Robbins, an inter-married white, and on the census roll of 1896 as Caroline Robbins. The name of her son Doc Robbins is found on the census roll of 1896, and the name of Joshua Robbins for whom the applicant also applies for enrollment, appears on the census roll of 1896 and he is duly identified as the child of Joshua and Algerean Robbins, whose names appear on the authenticated roll of 1880. They are all duly identified and have made satisfactory proof as to residence therefore the said Rebecca Caroline Robbins and her son Doc Robbins and her nephew Joshua Robbins will be duly listed for enrollment as Cherokee citizens by blood.

Chas. von Weise, being sworn states that as stenographer to the Commission to the Five Civilized Tribes he reported in full all the proceedings in the above cause and that the foregoing is a full, true and correct transcript of his stenographic notes therein.

Chas von Weise

Subscribed and sworn to before me
this 10th of December, 1900.

CR Breckinridge

Commissioner.

◇◇◇◇◇

H.
Cher. 6297.

Department of the Interior.
Commission to the Five Civilized Tribes.
Tahlequah, I. T., October 6, 1902.

SUPPLEMENTAL TESTIMONY AND PROCEEDINGS in the matter of the application for the enrollment of REBECCA C. ROBBINS as a citizen by intermarriage of the Cherokee Nation.

REBECCA C. ROBBINS, being first duly sworn, and being examined, testified as follows:

BY COMMISSION: What is your name? A Rebeca C. Robbins.
Q How old are you? A Fifty-six.
Q What is your post office address? A Tahlequah.
Q You are a white woman, are you? A Yes sir.
Q Have you heretofore made application to this Commission for enrollment as a citizen by intermarriage of the Cherokee Nation? A Yes sir.
Q What is the name of your husband? A Benjamin Robbins.
Q Is he living? A No sir
Q Was he a Cherokee by blood? A Yes sir.
Q Did you and he live together continuously until the time of his death? A Yes sir.

Q Do you claim your right to enrollment by reason of your marriage to him? A Yes sir.
Q You have not married since his death? A No sir.
Q Were you ever married before you married him? A No sir.
Q Was he ever married before he married you? A No sir.
Q Have you resided in the Cherokee Nation continuously since the date of your application for enrollment? A Yes sir.

> This testimony will be filed with and made a part of the record in the matter of the application for the enrollment of Rebecca C. Robbins as a citizen by intermarriage of the Cherokee Nation, Cherokee straitht[sic] card field No. 6297.

Wm. Hutchinson, being first duly sworn, states that as stenographer to the Commission to the Five Civilized Tribes he correctly recorded the testimony and proceedings in this case, and that the foregoing is a true and complete transcript of his stenographic notes thereof. in this case, and that the foregoing is a true and complete transcript of the stenographic notes thereof.

Wm Hutchinson

Subscribed and sworn to before me this 8th day of October, 1902.

John O Rosson
Notary Public.

◇◇◇◇◇

Cherokee
No. 6297

DEPARTMENT OF THE INTERIOR
COMMISSIONER TO THE FIVE CIVILIZED TRIBES

Muskogee, Indian Territory
January 4, 1907

In the matter of the application of Rebecca C. Robbins for enrollment as a citizen by intermarriage of the Cherokee Nation.

The applicant being first duly sworn testified as follows:

Q What is your name? A Rebecca Caroline Robbins is my name
Q How old are you? A I am 61
Q What is your postoffice address? A Matory[sic]
Q Do you claim to be a citizen by intermarriage of the Cherokee Nation? A Yes sir
Q Through whom do you claim your intermarried rights? A Benjamin Robbins my husband.
Q When were you married to Benjamin Robbins? A In '66

Cherokee Intermarried White 1906
Volume IV

Q What time? A In 1866

Q What time of the year? A September 20, 1866

Q Where were you married? A In the Choctaw Nation near Armstrong's Academy.

Q Who married you? A Old man---Isaac Sanders, he was a Cherokee

Q Was he a minister of the gospel[sic]

A Yes sir.

Q Did he give you a certificate? A No sir there wasn't nothing like that called for them days.

Q How long did you live in the Choctaw Nation A 1 year

Q Where did you go then? A We came to the Cherokee Nation

Q Have you lived in the Cherokee Nation ever since? A I have, I haven't been out of it since

Q Were you ever married before you married Benjamin Robbins?

A No sir. He was my only husband

Q Was he ever married before he married you? A No sir He wasn't

Q Is he living now? A No sir he's been dead for 23 years

Q Was your husband recognized as a citizen by blood of the Cherokee Nation at the time he married in 1866? A Yes sir

Q Where was he born? A He was born in the Cherokee Nation.

Q Were you always recognized as a citizen by adoption of the Cherokee Nation after your marriage to your husband? A Yes sir I have been recognized ever since.

Q Your rights were never questioned after you came up here from the Choctaw Nation?

A No sir.

The applicant is identified on the 1880 Cherokee Roll, Canadian District opposite No. 1153

Q Did you have any children by Benjamin Robbins? A I have three

Q What are their names?

A The oldest is Milo Tehee Robbins

Q What is the next one? A Richard Butler and Doc Robbins

Q Is Doc living with you at this time? A Yes sir.

Q How old is he A 25 years old

It appears from the Census card records of this office that Doc Robbins is enrolled opposite No. 29940 on the final roll of citizens by blood and that he is listed as the son of the applicant and Benjamin Robbins

Witness excused

James A. King being called as witness in behalf of the applicant being duly sworn, testified as follows:

Q What is your name? A King--James A.

Q How old are you? A 53

Q What is your postoffice address? A Tahlequah

74

Q Are you acquainted with Rebecca C. Robbins? A I have not been personally acquainted with her. I was at Sulphur Springs Choctaw Nation and Mr. Josh Robbins, he married about that time and his son Benjamin Robbins married--I think they married sisters

Q Who did Benjamin Robbins marry? A I didn't know these people, but I think he married a woman by the name of Post

Q You know then that Benjamin Robbins married a woman by the name of Post?
A Yes sir.

Q Do you know what her given name was? A No sir, I don't know her given name-- they lived quite a bit south of us.

Witness excused

Rebecca C. Robbins the applicant, recalled:

Q Mrs. Robbins was your maiden name Post? A Yes sir

Q What was your father's name? A William Post

Q What was your mother's name? A Rebeca Post

Q The records of this office show that her name was Elizabeth Post. What do you say your mother's name was Betty or Rebecca?

Q[sic] They always called her Becky--that's what my father always called her-- Pecky[sic] Post

----

J. M. Smith being called as a witness on behalf of the applicant and being first duly sworn, testified as follows:

Q What is your name? A J. M. Smith

Q How old are you? A 73

Q What is your postoffice address? A Tahlequah

Q Are you a citizen of the Cherokee Nation? A Yes sir I live in the Cherokee Nation

Q Are you acquainted with Rebecca C. Robbins? A Yes sir

Q This one? [sic] Yes I know her

Q Did you know Benjamin Robbins? A I knew Benjamin Robbins

Q What relation was Benjamin Robbins to Rebecca C. Robbins? A Husband as I understood it.

Q Did they live together as husband and wife? A Did when I first saw them

Q When did you first see them? A 38 or 40 years ago

Q Where was that? A I saw them at Tahlequah when they come up there after the war

Q Where was that? A I saw them at Tahlequah when they come up there after the war

Q Have you know them ever since they came to Tahlequah after the war. A I haven't seen them for four or five years, but then I knew them before that.

Q They always held themselves out in the community as husband and wife?
A Yes sir

Q Was Benjamin Robbins recognized as a citizen by blood of the Cherokee Nation in his life-time? A He drew mony[sic] as an old settler.

Q Was his wife Rebecca C. Robbins recognized as a citizen by adoption of the Cherokee Nation? A Yes sir

Witness excused

Gertrude Hanna being duly sworn, states that as stenographer to the Commissioner to the Five Civilized Tribes Five Civilized Tribes she reported the proceedings had in the above entitled case on January 4, 1907 and that the above and foregoing is a true and correct transcript of her stenographic notes thereof stenographic notes taken therein.

Gertrude Hanna

Subscribed and sworn to before me this 5 day of January, 1907

Walter W. Chappell
Notary Public

◇◇◇◇◇

F.R.   Cherokee 6297.

DEPARTMENT OF THE INTERIOR,
COMMISSIONER TO THE FIVE CIVILIZED TRIBES.

In the matter of the application for the enrollment of Rebecca C. Robbins as a citizen by intermarriage of the Cherokee Nation.

D E C I S I O N .

THE RECORDS OF THIS OFFICE SHOW: That on December 8, 1900, application was received by the Commission to the Five Civilized Tribes for the enrollment of Rebecca C. Robbins as a citizen by intermarriage of the Cherokee Nation. Further proceedings in the matter of said application were had at Tahlequah, Indian Territory, October 6, 1902, and at Muskogee, Indian Territory, January 4, 1907/

THE EVIDENCE IN THIS CASE SHOWS: That the applicant herein, Rebecca C. Robbins, a white woman, was lawfully married September 20, 1866, to Benjamin Robbins, who was at the time of said marriage a recognized citizen by blood of the Cherokee Nation, who is identified on the Cherokee authenticated tribal roll of 1880, Canadian District, No. 1152, as a native Cherokee. It is further shown that from the time of said marriage the said Benjamin Robbins and Rebecca C. Robbins resided together as husband and wife until the death of said Benjamin Robbins in 1884. That the applicant has not remarried, and has resided continuously in the Cherokee Nation from 1867 up to

76

and including September 1, 1902. Said applicant is identified of[sic] the Cherokee authenticated tribal roll of 1880, and the Cherokee census roll of 1896 as an intermarried citizen of the Cherokee Nation.

IT IS, THEREFORE, ORDERED AND ADJUDGED: That in accordance with the decision of the Supreme Court of the United States, dated November 5, 1906, in the cases of Daniel Red Bird et al., vs. the United States, Nos. 125, 126, 127 and 128, the said applicant, Rebecca C. Robbins is entitled, under the provisions of Section 21 of the Act of Congress approved June 28, 1898 (30 Stats., 495), to enrollment as a citizen by intermarriage of the Cherokee Nation, and her application for enrollment as such is accordingly granted.

Tams Bixby
Commissioner.

Dated at Muskogee, Indian Territory,
this   JAN 23 1907

◇◇◇◇◇

Cherokee 6297

Muskogee, Indian Territory, January 23, 1907.

W. W. Hastings,
   Attorney for the Cherokee Nation,
      Muskogee, Indian Territory.

Dear Sir:

There is enclosed herewith copy of the decision of the Commissioner to the Five Civilized Tribes, dated January 18, 1907, granting the application for the enrollment of Rebecca C. Robbins as a citizen by intermarriage of the Cherokee Nation.

Respectfully,

Enc I-77   Commissioner.

RPI

◇◇◇◇◇

Cherokee 6297

W.W.HASTINGS.
ATTORNEY.

OFFICE OF

H.M. VANCE.
SECRETARY.

Attorney for the Cherokee Nation,

MUSKOGEE, I. T.   January 23, 1907.

The Commissioner to the Five Civilized Tribes,
Muskogee, Indian Territory.

Sir:

Receipt is acknowledged of the testimony and of your decision enrolling Rebecca C. Robbins as a citizen by intermarriage of the Cherokee Nation. Time for protesting said decision is waived and I consent that said person may be placed upon the schedule immediately.

Respectfully,

W. W. Hastings
Attorney for the Cherokee Nation.

◇◇◇◇◇

Cherokee 6297

Muskogee, Indian Territory, January 23, 1907.

Rebecca C. Robbins,
Tahlequah, Indian Territory.

Dear Madam:

There is enclosed herewith a copy of the decision of the Commissioner to the Five Civilized Tribes, dated January 23, 1907, granting the application for your enrollment as a citizen by intermarriage of the Cherokee Nation.

You will be advised when your name has been placed upon a schedule of citizens of the Cherokee Nation and approved by the Secretary of the Interior.

Respectfully,

Enc I-95

Commissioner.

RPI

Cher IW 111

◇◇◇◇◇

DEPARTMENT OF THE INTERIOR,

COMMISSIONER TO THE FIVE CIVILIZED TRIBES.

In the matter of the application for the enrollment of

Jacob M. Hiser

as a citizen by intermarriage of the Cherokee Nation.

CHEROKEE 6492.

◇◇◇◇◇

Department of the,
Commission to the Five Civilized Tribes,
Tahlequah, I. T. December, 10th 1900.

In the matter of the application of Jacob M. Hiser for the enrollment of himself and six children as Cherokee citizens. He being sworn before Commissioner Breckinridge, testified as follows-

Q What is your name? A. Jacob M. Hiser.
Q How old are you? A. 53.
Q What is your post office? A. Mayesville[sic], Arkansas.
Q What district do you live in? A. Deleware[sic].
Q Who do you desire to have enrolled, yourself and family? A. Yes sir
Q Have you a wife? A. Yes sir.
Q How many children have you? A. Six.
Q Are they all at home and living with you and under twenty-one years old. A. Yes sir all but Mavry J. a daughter who is 24 years old.
Q She will have to apply for herself. A. I wish that I could make the application for her as she is living with me and it is so far from here we went to Fairland and could not get in as the croud[sic] was so large and you left before our time came.
Q Is your daughter un-married? A. Yes sir.
Q How far do you live from here? A. Fifty miles or more.
Q Did you come here for the purpose of enrolling? A. Yes sir.
Q Well under the circumstances we will let you apply for her.
Q Are you a Cherokee by blood? A. No sir a white man.
Q Is your wife a Cherokee by blood? A. Yes sir.
Q Are you on the 1880 roll? A. Yes sir.

79

Q How long have you lived here? A. Ever since 1872.
Q Give me the name of your wife? A. Martha E.
Q How old is your wife? A. 46.
Q When did you marry her? A. In 1872.
Q Have you and she been living together continuously ever since? A. Yes sir.
Q What was her fathers[sic] name? A. Daniel Tittle.
Q Is he living? A. No sir.
Q Give me her mothers[sic] name? A. Rosanna.
Q Is she living? A. No sir.
Q Give me the names of your children? A. Mavry J.
Q How old? A. 24.
Q Next child? A. Daniel A. J.
Q How old? A. 20.
Q Next child? Okey M.
Q How old? A. 18.
Q Next child? A. James D.
Q How old? A. 16.
Q Next child? A. Hugh F.
Q How old? A. o5[sic].
Q Next child? A. Olive.
Q How old? A. 9.
Q Are these children all living now? A. Yes sir.
Q Has your wife always lived in the Cherokee Nation? A. Yes sir.

1880 roll, page 269 No 1313, F. M. Hizer[sic], Deleware[sic].

1880	269	1314, Martha E. Hizer	"
1880	269	1316 Marah F. Hizer	"
1896	+574	246 Jacob M. Hiser,	"
1896	484	1539 Martha E. Hiser	"
1896	484	1541 Mavery J. Hiser	"
1896	484	1543 Daniel J. Hiser	"
1896	484	1544 O.K. Myrtle Hiser	"
1896	484	1545 James D. Hiser	"
1896	484	1546 Hugh F. Hiser	"
1896	484	1547 Olive Hiser	"

The applicant applies for the enrollment of himself, wife and six children. He is identified on the rolls of 1880 and 1896 as an adopted Cherokee. He is a white man, and has lived with his Cherokee wife ever since their marriage prior to 1880, and he will be listed now for enrollment as a Cherokee by adoption. His wife is identified with her husband on the rolls of 1880 and 1896, she has lived in the Cherokee Nation all her life, is a native Cherokee, and will be listed for enrollment as a Cherokee by blood. The applicant is permitted to apply for his oldest child mentioned in the testimony, Mavry J. Hiser, who is now 24 years of age, a daughter, and whom he states is at home some fifty miles away and that it would work a hardship and be difficult and very inconvenient for her to come here and apply for herself. As she is still unmarried and in his family, and as he came here from his home for the express purpose of making this application, he will be permitted to apply for her. She is duly identified on the rolls of 1880 and 1896, is living and will be listed now for enrollment as a Cherokee by blood. The remaining children, Daniel A. J., Okey M., James D., Hugh F., and Olive Hiser, are all duly identified on the roll of 1896 they are minors, and all living. They will now be listed for enrollment as Cherokees by blood.

Chas. von Weise, being sworn states that as stenographer to the Commission to the Five Civilized Tribes he reported in full, all the proceedings in the above cause and the above is a full, true and correct transcript of his stenographic notes therein.

Chas von Weise

Subscribed and sworn to before me this the 15th of December, 1900.

CR Breckinridge

Commissioner.

◇◇◇◇◇

JOR.
Cher. 6492.

Department of the Interior.
Commission to the Five Civilized Tribes.
Tahlequah, I. T., October 20, 1902.

SUPPLEMENTAL TESTIMONY in the matter of the application for the enrollment of JACOB M. HISER as a citizen by intermarriage, and for the enrollment of MAVERY J. HISER as a citizen by blood of the Cherokee Nation.

JACOB M. HISER, being first duly sworn, and being examined, testified as follows:

BY COMMISSION: What is your name? A Jacob M. Hiser.
Q How old are you? A Fifty-five.
Q What is your post office address? A Mayesville[sic], Arkansas.
Q You are a white man, are you? A Yes sir.
Q Have you heretofore made application to this Commission for enrollment as a citizen by intermarriage of the Cherokee Nation? A Yes sir.
Q What is the name of your wife? A Martha E. Hiser.
Q Is she living? A Yes sir.
Q Is she a Cherokee by blood? A Yes sir.
Q Do you claim your right to enrollment by reason of your marriage to her? A Yes sir.
Q When were you and she married? A In 1872.
Q Were you married to her at that time according to Cherokee law? A Yes sir.
Q Does your name appear upon the roll of 1880? A Yes sir.
Q Were you ever married before you married her? A No sir.

Cherokee Intermarried White 1906
Volume IV

Q Was she ever married before she married you? A No sir.

Q You are her first husband and she is your first wife? A Yes sir.

Q Have you and she lived together continuously since your married? A Yes sir.

Q Were you living together on the 1st day of Septenber[sic], 1902? A Yes sir.

Q You have never been separatee[sic] at all? A No sir.

Q Have you resided in the Cherokee Nation continuously since you and she married?
A Yes sir.

Q Has she also? A Yes sir.

Q You have how many children that you made application for?
A Six, I believe I made application for.

Q Are all of these children living at this time? A Yes sir.

Q You state that one of your children is married? A Yes sir.

Q Which one? A The oldest one, Mavery J.

Q She is your daughter, is she, by your present wife? A Yes sir.

Q What is her present name? Dubois.

Q What is the full name of her husband? A Jacob Dubois.

Q Is he a Cherokee? A No sir.

Q White man? A Yes sir.

Q When were they married? A I don't know as I remember exactly.

Q About a year ago? A Yes sir.

Q Have they any children? A No sir.

This testimony will be filed with and made a part of the record in the matter of the application for the enrollment of Jacob M. Hiser as a citizen by intermarriage, and for the enrollment of Mavery J. Hiser as a citizen by blood, of the Cherokee Nation, Cherokee straight card field No. 6492.

Wm. Hutchinson, being first duly sworn, states that as stenographer to the Commission to the Five Civilized Tribes he correctly recorded the testimony and proceedings in this case, and that the foregoing is a true and complete transcript of his stenographic notes thereof.

Wm Hutchinson

Subscribed and sworn to before me this 30th day of October, 1902.

John O Rosson
Notary Public.

◇◇◇◇◇

Cherokee Intermarried White 1906
Volume IV

Cherokee 6492.

DEPARTMENT OF THE INTERIOR,
COMMISSIONER TO THE FIVE CIVILIZED TRIBES.
MUSKOGEE, I. T., DECEMBER 27, 1906.

In the matter of the application for the enrollment of JACOB M. HISER, as a citizen by intermarriage of the Cherokee Nation.

APPEARANCES:
    For Applicant, Present in person.
    For Cherokee Nation, W. W. Hastings.

JACOB M. HISER, being first duly sworn by B. P. Rasmus, a Notary Public, testified as follows:

ON BEHALF OF THE COMMISSIONER:

Q What is your name? A Jacob M. Hiser
Q How old are you? A 60.
Q What is your postoffice? A Maysville, Arkansas.
Q You are a white man? A Yes sir
Q Claim citizenship by intermarriage in the Cherokee Nation? A Yes sir.
Q What is the name of your wife? A Martha E. Tittle before I married her.
Q Is she living? A No sir.
Q When did she die? A She died December 9, 1904.

An affidavit showing the death of the witness's wife on the date he gives is on file with this office

Q When were you and your wife married? A 1872.
Q What day? A September 11th, I believe.
Q Who married you? A A fellow named J. O. Wood, a Pracher.
Q Have you any documentary evedecne[sic] of your marriage? A Nothing more than that.

The witness offers a certified copy of the record of his marriage according to Cherokee law, said certificate being signed by J. R. Hastings, Clerk of Delaware District, Cherokee Nation, under the Seal of the Nation. The original marriage record from which this certificate is made is in the lawful custody of this office, and the record is found in Book "S" of the Recrod[sic] of Marriage, Delaware District, Cherokee Nation.

Q Have you and your wife lived together continuously since your marriage?
A Yes sir, until her death.

The Marriage Record shows that the license was issued on September 5, 1872, and was executed and returned on October 14, 1872.

Q Did the man who married you give you a certificate? A He signed the license I recorded; he just certified on the back of it.

Q He made his certificate on the back, did he? A Yes sir

Q Were you married under authority of the license issued you that has been mentioned in the testimony? A Yes sir

Q Have you and your wife lived together continuously since your marriage? A Yes sir, up until her death.

Q Was she a recognized Cherokee by blood when you married? A Yes sir.

Q Was she living in the Cherokee Nation? A Yes sir.

Q Had you ever been married before you married her? A No sir

Q Had she ever been married before she married you? A No sir.

-----------------------oOo-----------------------

Geo. H. Lessley, being first duly sworn, states that as stenographer to the Commissioner to the Five Civilized Tribes, he reported the proceedings had in the above entitled cause, and that the above and foregoing is a true and correct trascript[sic] of his stenographic notes thereof.

Geo H Lessley

Subscribed and sworn to before me this 10th day of January, 1907.

John E. Tidwell
Notary Public.

◇◇◇◇◇

(COPY)

OFFICE OF
J. R. HASTINGS,
CLERK OF DELAWARE DISTRICT, C.N.

Maysville, Ark., July 26, 1897.

This is to certify by me that Jacob Hiser, a white man, was licensed to marry M. E. Tittle, a female Cherokee on the 5th Sept. 1872, and the license executed and returned on the 15th Oct. 1872, being in accordance with an Act of the National Council bearing date Oct. 15th, 1855, regulating intermarriage of white men with citizens of this Nation.

J. T. Cunningham,

Clerk, D.D.C.N.

I hereby certify that the above is
a true and correct copy of marriage
license on file in this office.

J.R. Hastings, C.D.D., C.N.

I, Alma Miriam Kline, a stenographer to
the Commissioner to the Five Civilized
Tribes hereby certify that the above
is a full, true and correct copy of a
certified copy of the marriage record of
Jacob Hiser and M. T[sic]. Tittle as shown by
the records now in the possession of this
office in the matter of the application
of Jacob Hiser for enrollment as a citizen
by intermarriage of the Cherokee Nation.

Alma Miriam Kline

Dated this 17th day of Jany 1907.

Walter W. Chappell

◇◇◇◇◇

F.R.   Cherokee 6492.

DEPARTMENT OF THE INTERIOR,

COMMISSIONER TO THE FIVE CIVILIZED TRIBES.

In the matter of the application for the enrollment of Jacob M. Hiser as a citizen by intermarriage of the Cherokee Nation.

D E C I S I O N

THE RECORDS OF THIS OFFICE SHOW: That December 10, 1900, application was received by the Commission to the Five Civilized Tribes for the enrollment of Jacob M. Hiser as a citizen by intermarriage of the Cherokee Nation. Further proceedings in the matter of said application were had at Tahlequah, Indian Territory, October 20, 1902, and at Muskogee, Indian Territory, December 27, 1906.

THE EVIDENCE IN THIS CASE SHOWS: That the applicant herein, Jacob M. Hiser, a white man, was married in accordance with the Cherokee law September 11, 1872, to his wife, Martha E. Hiser (nee Tittle) who was at the time of said marriage a recognized citizen by blood of the Cherokee Nation, who is identified on the Cherokee authenticated tribal roll of 1880, Delaware District No. 1314, as a native Cherokee, and whose name is included in the approved partial roll of citizens by blood of the Cherokee Nation opposite No. 15544. It is further shown that, from the time of said marriage, the said Jacob M. Hiser and Martha E. Hiser resided together as husband and wife and continuously lived in the Cherokee Nation up to and including September 1, 1902. The said applicant is identified on the Cherokee authenticated tribal roll of 1880, and the Cherokee Census Roll of 1896, as an intermarried citizen of the Cherokee Nation.

It is, THEREFORE, ORDERED AND ADJUDGED: That in accordance with the decision of the Supreme Court of the United States, dated November 5, 1906, in the cases of Daniel Red Bird et al., vs. the United States, Nos. 125, 126, 127 and 128, the said applicant, Jacob M. Hiser, is entitled, under the provisions of Section 21 of the Act of Congress approved June 28, 1898 (30 Stats., 495), to enrollment as a citizen by intermarriage of the Cherokee Nation, and his application for enrollment as such is accordingly granted.

Tams Bixby   Commissioner.

Dated at Muskogee, Indian Territory,
this   JAN 23 1907

◇◇◇◇◇

Cherokee 6492

Muskogee, Indian Territory, January 23, 1907.

W. W. Hastings,
      Attorney for the Cherokee Nation,
           Muskogee, Indian Territory.

Dear Sir:

      There is enclosed herewith a copy of the decision of the Commissioner to the Five Civilized Tribes, dated January 22, 1907, granting the application for the enrollment of Jacob M. Hiser as a citizen by intermarriage of the Cherokee Nation.

Respectfully,

Encl. H-26

Commissioner.

JMH

◇◇◇◇◇

Cherokee 6492   W.W.HASTINGS.   OFFICE OF   H.M. VANCE.
                 ATTORNEY.   SECRETARY.

Attorney for the Cherokee Nation,
MUSKOGEE, I. T.   January 23, 1907.

The Commissioner to the Five Civilized Tribes,
           Muskogee, Indian Territory.

Sir:

      Receipt is acknowledged of the testimony and of your decision enrolling Jacob M. Hiser as a citizen by intermarriage of the Cherokee Nation. Time for protesting said decision is waived and I consent that said person may be placed upon the schedule immediately.

Respectfully,
W. W. Hastings
Attorney for Cherokee Nation.

◇◇◇◇◇

Cherokee 6492

Muskogee, Indian Territory, January 23, 1907.

Jacob M. Hiser,
      Maysville, Arkansas.

Dear Sir:

      There is enclosed herewith a copy of the decision of the Commissioner to the Five Civilized Tribes, dated January 23, 1907, granting the application for your enrollment as a citizen by intermarriage of the Cherokee Nation.

Respectfully,

Encl. H-100   Commissioner.
JMH

Cher IW 112

◇◇◇◇◇

CFB

DEPARTMENT OF THE INTERIOR,

COMMISSIONER TO THE FIVE CIVILIZED TRIBES.

In the matter of the application for the enrollment of

CHARLES PATTERSON

as a citizen by intermarriage of the Cherokee Nation.

CHEROKEE 6531.

〜〜〜〜〜

Cherokee Intermarried White 1906
Volume IV

Department of the Interior,
Commission to the Five Civilized Tribes,
Tahlequah, I. T. December 12th 1900.

In the matter of the application of Charles Patterson for the enrollment of himself and one child as Cherokee citizens. He being sworn before Commissioner Needles, testified as follows-

Q What is your name? A. Charles Patterson.
Q What is your age? A. 53.
Q What is your post office address? A. Stillwell[sic].
Q What district do you live in? A. Flint.
Q Are you a recognized citizen of the Cherokee Nation? A. Yes sir.
Q By blood or inter-marraige[sic]? A. Inter-marriage.
Q Who do you desire to have enrolled? A. Myself and youngest boy, Joseph A. Patterson.
Q Have you a certificate of marriage? A. (No response)
Q Is your wife living? A. No sir.
Q What is her name? A. Caroline.
Q How old is Joseph A.   A. 18 years old.

1880 roll, page 385 No 1018, Chas. Patterson, Flint dist.

1880	385	1019	Caroline Patterson	"
1896	715	60	Charlie Patterson	"
1896	688	1332	Joseph A. Patterson	"

Q Is he living? A. Yes sir.
Q Have you ever been married since the death of your wife? A. No sir.
Q Have you always lived in the Cherokee Nation since your marriage? A Yes sir.
Q Did you live with your wife continuously since your marriage? A. Yes sir until she died.

The name of Charles Patterson appears on the authenticated roll of 1880 as welll[sic] as the census roll of 1896 as in[sic] inter-married white, and the name of his wife Caroline appears on the authenticated 1880 roll and the name of his son Joseph A. Patterson appears on the census roll of 1896, and is duly identified as the child of the applicant and his deceased wife Caroline, whose name appears on the authenticated roll of 1880. They both being duly identified according to the page and number of the roll, and having made satisfactory proof as to residence the said Charles Patterson will be listed for enrollment as a Cherokee a Cherokee[sic] citizen by inter-marriage and his son Joseph A. Patterson as a Cherokee citizen by blood.

Chas. von Weise, being sworn states that as stenographer to the Commission to the Five Civilized Tribes he reported in full all the proceedings in the above entitled cause and that the foregoing is a full, true and correct transcript of his stenographic notes therein.

Chas von Weise

Subscribed and sworn to before me this the 13th of December, 1900.

TB Needles
Commissioner.

◇◇◇◇◇

JOR.
Cher. 6531.

Department of the Interior.
Commission to the Five Civilized Tribes.
Tahlequah, IT., October 22, 1902.

SUPPLEMENTAL TESTIMONY in the matter of the application for the enrollment of CHARLES PATTERSON as a citizen by intermarriage of the Cherokee Nation.

CHARLES PATTERSON, being first duly sworn, and being examined, testified as follows:

BY COMMISSION: What is your name? A Charles Patterson.
Q How old are you? A Fifty-five.
Q What is your post office address? A Stilwell.
Q You are a white man, are you? A Yes sir.
Q Have you heretofore made application to this Commission for enrollment as a citizen by intermarriage of the Cherokee Nation? A Yes sir.
Q What is the name of your wife through whom you claim your citizenship? A Caroline Damron.
Q Is she living? A No sir, she is dead.
Q When did she die? A In 1890, eleven years ago.
Q When were you and she married? A In 1872, I believe.
Q Were you married at that time according to Cherokee law? A Yes sir.
Q Does your name appear upon the roll of 1880? A Yes sir.
Q Were you ever married before you married her? A No sir.
Q Was she ever married before she married you? A No sir.
Q You are her first husband and she is your first wife? A Yes sir.
Q Did you and she live together continuously until the time of her death? A Yes sir.
Q Were you living together when she died? A Yes sir.
Q Were you ever separated from her? A No sir.
Q Have you married since she died? A No sir.
Q You have continued to live single? A Yes sir.
Q How long have you continued to reside in the Cherokee Nation? A Thirty two years, about.
Q Continuously? A Yes sir.
Q How long had your wife resided in the Cherokee Nation? A All her life.

Q Born and raised in the Cherokee Nation? A Yes sir.
Q Lived here continuously all her life? A Yes sir, except during the Civil War, she was a minor then.
Q You have how many minor children that you made application for? A Just one.
Q Is that child living at this time? A Yes sir.
Q You have had no children die sibce[sic] you were enrolled? A No sir.

This testimony will be filed with and made a part of the record in the matter of the application for the enrollment of Charles Patterson as a citizen by intermarriage of the Cherokee Nation, straight card field No. 6531.

Wm. Hutchinson, being first duly sworn, states that as stenographer to the Commission to the Five Civilized Tribes he correctly recorded the testimony and proceedings in this case, and that the foregoing is a true and complete transcript of his stenographic notes thereof.

Wm Hutchinson

Subscribed and sworn to before me this 11th day of November, 1902.

BC Jones
N.P.

◇◇◇◇◇

CHEROKEE-6531.

DEPARTMENT OF THE INTERIOR,
COMMISSIONER TO THE FIVE CIVILIZED TRIBES.
Muskogee, Indian Territory, January 5, 1907.

In the matter of making proof of the marriage of Charles Patterson to his Cherokee wife, prior to November 1, 1875.

Charles Patterson , being duly sworn by John E. Tidwell, Notary Public, testified as follows:

COMMISSIONER:

Q. What is your name? A. Charles Patterson.
Q. What is your age? A. 59.
Q. What is your post office address? A. Stilwell.
Q. You claim to be a citizen by intermarriage of the Cherokee Nation? A. Yes sir.
Q. Through whom do you claim your intermarried rights? A. Caroline Dameron.

Q. When were you married to her? A. June 2, 1871.

Q. Where? A. In Flint District.

Q. Were you ever married prior to the time you married Caroline Dameron? A. No sir.

Q. Was she ever married before she married you? A. No sir.

Q. Is Caroline Dameron living at this time? A. No sir.

Q. When did she die? A. The 20th of June, 1891.

Q. Have you ever married again? A. No sir.

Q. Have you lived in the Cherokee Nation continuously since your marriage in 1871 up to the present time? A. Yes sir.

Q. Were you married under a Cherokee license? A. Yes sir.

Q. Have you got that license with you? A. No, it is on record in Flint District.

(Commissioner -- Applicant is identified upon the 1880 Roll, Flint District, opposite No. 1018.) (on page 117 of Book "B" of marriage records of Flint District it is shown that a license was issued to the applicant by James W. Adair, Clerk of the Court, to marry Caroline Dameron, a cherokee[sic] citizen, on June 2, 1871, and that the applicant was married under said license by Rev. W. A. Duncan on June 2, 1871.)

Witness excused.

Eula Jeanes Branson, being sworn, states that she correctly reported the proceedings had in the above and foregoing, on the 5th. day of January, 1907.

Eula Jeanes Branson

Subscribed and sworn to before me this 7th. day of January, 1907.

Walter W. Chappell

◇◇◇◇◇

C. F. B.   Cherokee 6531.

DEPARTMENT OF THE INTERIOR,

COMMISSIONER TO THE FIVE CIVILIZED TRIBES.

In the matter of the application for the enrollment of CHARLES PATTERSON as a citizen by intermarriage of the Cherokee Nation.

D E C I S I O N

THE RECORDS OF THIS OFFICE SHOW: That at Tahlequah, Indian Territory, December 12, 1900, application was received by the Commission to the Five Civilized Tribes for the enrollment of Charles Patterson as a citizen by intermarriage of the Cherokee Nation. Further proceedings in the matter of said application were had at Tahlequah, Indian Territory, October 22, 1902, and at Muskogee, Indian Territory, January 5, 1907.

THE EVIDENCE IN THIS CASE SHOWS: That the applicant herein, Charles Patterson, a white man, was married in accordance with Cherokee law June 2, 1981, to one Caroline Dameron, who was at the time of said marriage a recognized citizen by blood of the Cherokee Nation, and who is identified on the Cherokee authenticated tribal roll of 1880, Flint District, page 385, No. 1019, as a native Cherokee; that the said Charles and Caroline Patterson resided together as husband and wife until the time of the death of said Caroline Patterson, which occurred June 20, 1891; that since the death of said Caroline Patterson said Charles Patterson has not married; and that he has continuously lived in the Cherokee Nation since June 2, 1871. Said applicant is identified on the Cherokee authenticated tribal roll of 1880, and the Cherokee census roll of 1896, as an intermarried citizen of the Cherokee Nation.

IT IS, THEREFORE, ORDERED AND ADJUDGED: That in accordance with the decision of the Supreme Court of the United States, dated November 5, 1906, in the cases of Daniel Red Bird et al. vs. the United States, Nos. 125, 126, 127 and 128, the said applicant, Charles Patterson, is entitled, under the provisions of Section 21, of the Act of Congress approved June 28, 1898 (30 Stats., 495), to enrollment as a citizen by intermarriage of the Cherokee Nation, and his application for enrollment as such is accordingly granted.

Tams Bixby
Commissioner.

Dated at Muskogee, Indian Territory,
this   JAN 21 1907

◇◇◇◇◇

Cherokee
6531

Muskogee, Indian Territory, January 21, 1907.

W. W. Hastings,
      Attorney for the Cherokee Nation,
          Muskogee, Indian Territory.

Dear Sir:

      These is enclosed herewith copy of the decision of the Commissioner to the Five Civilized Tribes, dated January 21, 1907, granting the application for your enrollment of Charles Patterson as a citizen by intermarriage of the Cherokee Nation.

                Respectfully,

Enc I-24   Commissioner.

RPI

Cherokee 6531   ◇◇◇◇◇

W.W.HASTINGS.   OFFICE OF   H.M. VANCE.
ATTORNEY.   SECRETARY.
Attorney for the Cherokee Nation,
MUSKOGEE, I. T. January 21, 1907.

The Commissioner to the Five Civilized Tribes,
      Muskogee, Indian Territory.

Sir:

      Receipt is acknowledged of the testimony and of your decision enrolling Charles Patterson as a citizen by intermarriage of the Cherokee Nation. Time for protesting said decision is waived and I consent that said person may be placed upon the schedule immediately.

                Respectfully,
                    W. W. Hastings
                    Attorney for the Cherokee Nation.

◇◇◇◇◇

94

Cherokee 6531

Muskogee, Indian Territory January 24, 1907.

Charles Patterson,
    Stilwell, Indian Territory.

Dear Sir:

There is enclosed herewith copy of the decision of the Commissioner to the Five Civilized Tribes, dated January 21, 1907, granting the application for your enrollment as a citizen by intermarriage of the Cherokee Nation.

You will be advised when your name has been placed upon a schedule of citizens of the Cherokee Nation and approved by the Secretary of the Interior.

Respectfully,

Enc I-102   Commissioner.

RPI

Cher IW 113

◇◇◇◇◇

C.E.W.

DEPARTMENT OF THE INTERIOR,

COMMISSIONER TO THE FIVE CIVILIZED TRIBES.

In the matter of the application for the enrollment of

WILLIAM F. RASMUS

as a citizen by intermarriage of the Cherokee Nation.

CHEROKEE 6648

◇◇◇◇◇

95

Cherokee Intermarried White 1906
Volume IV

Department of the Interior,
Commission to the Five Civilized Tribes,
Tahlequah, I. T. December 14th 1900.

In the mater[sic] of the application of William F. Rasmus for the enrollment of himself and wife as Cherokee citizens. He being sworn before Commissioner Needles, testified as follows:

Q What is your name? A. William F. Rasmus.
Q What is your age? A. 62.
Q What is your post office? A. Tahlequah
Q What district do you live in? A. Tahlequah.
Q Are you a recognized citizen of the Cherokee Nation? A. Yes sir.
Q By blood? A. No sir by adoption.
Q Who do you want to have enrolled? A. Myself and wife.
Q What is her name? A. Josephine C.
Q Is she a Cherokee by blood? A. Yes sir.
Q How old is she? A. 60./
Q Have you lived in the Territory ever since 1880? A. Yes sir.
Q Have you lived continuously with your wife since your marriage to her? A. Yes sir.

1880 roll, page   798 No 1837, Wm. F. Rasmus, Tahlequah district.
1880   798   1838 Josephine Rasmus   "
1896   1287   218 William F. Rasmus   "
1896   1230   2681 Josephine C. Rasmus   "

The name of William F. Rasmus and his wife Josephine C. Rasmus appear on the authenticated roll of 1880 and the census roll of 1896, he as an inter-married white and she as a Cherokee citizen by blood. They are both duly identified and having made satisfactory proof as to residence, consequently the said William F. Rasmus will be duly listed for enrollment as a Cherokee citizen by inter-marriage and his wife Josephine C. as a Cherokee citizen by blood.

Chas. von Weise, being sworn states that as stenographer to the Commission to the Five Civilized Tribes he reported in full all the proceedings in the above cause and that the foregoing is a full, true and correct transcript of his stenographic notes therein.

                                          Chas von Weise

Subscribed and sworn to before me this the 10th of January, 1901.

                              CR Breckinridge
                              Commissioner.

◇◇◇◇◇

R.
Cher. 6648.

Department of the Interior.
Commission to the Five Civilized Tribes.
Tahlequah, I. T., September 29, 1902.

SUPPLEMENTAL TESTIMONY AND PROCEEDINGS in the matter of the application for the enrollment of WILLIAM F. RASMUS as a citizen by intermarriage of the Cherokee Nation.

WILLIAM F. RASMUS, being first duly sworn, and being examined, testified as follows:

BY COMMISSION: What is your name? A William F. Rasmus.
Q How old are you? A I am sixty-four years of age the 5th day of September.
Q What is your post office address? A Tahlequah.
Q You are a white man? A Yes sir.
Q Have you heretofore made application to this Commission for enrollment as a citizen by intermarriage of the Cherokee Nation? A Yes sir.
Q What is the name of your wife? A Josephine C. Rasmus.
Q Is she a Cherokee by blood? A Yes sir.
Q Do you claim your right to enrollment by reason of your marriage to her? A Yes sir.
Q Have you and she lived together continuously since the date of your marriage?
A Yes sir.
Q She is living at present? A Yes sir, at Tahlequah.
Q Were you ever married before you married her? A No sir.
Q Was she ever married before she married you? A No sir.
Q You have resided in the Cherokee Nation continuously since you made application, have you? A Yes sir.

> The testimony will be filed with and made a part of the record in the matter of the application for the enrollment of William F. Rasmus as a citizen by intermarriage of the Cherokee Nation, Cherokee straight card filed No. 6648.

Wm. Hutchinson, being first duly sworn, states that as stenographer to the Commission to the Five Civilized Tribes he correctly recorded the testimony and proceedings in this case, and that the foregoing is a true and complete transcript of the stenographic notes thereof.

Wm Hutchinson

Cherokee Intermarried White 1906
Volume IV

Subscribed and sworn to before me this 29th day of September, 1902.

John O Rosson
Notary Public.

◇◇◇◇◇

(The above Supplemental Testimony and Proceedings given again.)

◇◇◇◇◇

C. F. B.   Cherokee 6648.

DEPARTMENT OF THE INTERIOR,
COMMISSION TO THE FIVE CIVILIZED TRIBES.
Muskogee, Indian Territory, January 8, 1907.

In the Matter of the Application for the Enrollment of William F. Rasmus as a citizen by intermarriage of the Cherokee Nation.

Applicant appears in person.

APPEARANCES:

Cherokee Nation represented by
W. W. Hastings, Attorney.

William F. Rasmus being first duly sworn by John E. Tidwell, Notary Public, testified as follows:

ON BEHALF OF COMMISSIONER.

Q What is your name?   A William F. Rasmus.
Q What is your age: A 68 last September.
Q What is your post office address?
A Tahlequah, Cherokee Nation, Indian Territory.
Q You are an applicant for enrollment as a citizen by intermarriage of the Cherokee Nation?
A I am.
Q You have no Cherokee blood?   A None.
Q Your only claim to the right to enrollment as a citizen of the Cherokee Nation is by virtue of your marriage to a citizen by blood?
A Yes sir.
Q What is the name of the citizen through whom you claim that right?
A Josephine C. Rasmus. Her maiden name was Josephine C. Dannenberg.
Q When did you marry her?
A September 4, 1866.
Q Is she living now?
A She is.

Q In what district did you marry her?

A Flint District.

Q Was she a recognized citizen of the Cherokee Nation at the time you married her?

A She was.

Q Living in the Cherokee country?

A Yes sir.

Q You married her in accordance with the laws of the Cherokee Nation?

A I did.

Q Your license was issued in Flint District?

A No sir, issued by the Cherokee National council. At that time they didn't consider that the clerks had full authority.

The applicant presents original marriage license and certificate issued by H. D. Reese, Clerk National Council Cherokee Nation, in 1886, authorizing the marriage of William F. Rasmus, a citizen of the United States, and Josephine Dannenberg, a citizen of the Cherokee Nation. The certificate attached shows that said parties were united in marriage in accordance with the terms of said license, September 4, 1866, by Reverend Young Ewing. This instrument will be copies and a copy filed with and made a part of the record in this case.

The applicant, William F. Rasmus is identified on the Cherokee authenticated tribal roll of 1880, Tahlequah district, No. 1837. His wife, Josephine C. Rasmus, appears on said roll at No. 1838 and her name is included in the approved partial roll of citizens of the Cherokee Nation, opposite No. 1589.

The undersigned being first duly sworn states that as stenographer to the Commission to the Five Civilized Tribes, she recorded the testimony taken in this case and that the foregoing is a full, true and correct transcript of her stenographic notes thereof.

Myrtle Hill

Subscribed and sworn to before me this the 12th day of January, 1907.

Chas E. Webster
Notary Public.

<><><><><>

Cherokee 6648.

License.

Is hereby granted to Wm. F. Rasmus, a citizen of the United States, to be joined in the bonds of Matrimony, unto Miss Josephine Dannenberg of the Cherokee Nation. He, the said W. F. Rasmus having fully complied with the law, rules and regulations, of the National Council, in such cases made and provided.

Given from under my hand the ____ of _____ 1866.

H. D. Reese,

Clerk National Committee.

I hereby certify that I have this day placed the above license on record in this office this 23rd day of November A. D. 1877.

D. R. Hicks, Clerk,

(SEAL)   Tahlequah District, C. N.

This is to certify that on this day and dait[sic] September the 4th, 1866, I did beeing[sic] a Minister of the M. E. Church South, solemnized the Rights of Matrimony between the parties hos[sic] names appear within.

Given under my hand this day and dait fire said.

Rev. Young Ewing.

⟡⟡⟡⟡⟡

C.E.W.   Cherokee 6648.

DEPARTMENT OF THE INTERIOR,

COMMISSIONER TO THE FIVE CIVILIZED TRIBES.

_____

In the matter of the application for the enrollment of William F. Rasmus, as a citizen by intermarriage of the Cherokee Nation.

D E C I S I O N

THE RECORDS OF THIS OFFICE SHOW: That at Tahlequah, Indian Territory, December 14, 1900, application was received by the Commission to the Five Civilized Tribes for the enrollment of William F. Rasmus, as a citizen by intermarriage of the Cherokee Nation. Further proceedings in the matter of said application were had at

Tahlequah, Indian Territory, September 29, 1902, and at Muskogee, Indian Territory, January 8, 1907.

THE EVIDENCE IN THIS CASE SHOWS: That the applicant herein, William F. Rasmus, a white man, was married in accordance with Cherokee law September 4, 1866 to his wife, Josephine C. Rasmus, nee Dannenberg, who was at the time of said marriage a recognized citizen by blood of the Cherokee Nation, who is identified on the Cherokee authenticated tribal roll of 1880, Tahlequah District, page 798 number 1838, as a native Cherokee, and whose name is included in the approved partial roll of citizens by blood of the Cherokee Nation, oposite[sic] number 15891. It is further shown that from the time of said marriage the said William F. Rasmus and Josephine C. Rasmus resided together as husband and wife and have continuously lived in the Cherokee Nation. Said applicant is identified on the Cherokee authenticated tribal roll of 1880, and the Cherokee census roll of 1896 as an intermarried citizen of the Cherokee Nation.

IT IS, THEREFORE ORDERED AND ADJUDGED: That in accordance with the decision of the Supreme Court of the United States, dated November 5, 1906, in the cases of Daniel Red Bird, et al., vs. the United States, Nos. 125, 126, 127 and 128, the said applicant William F. Rasmus is entitled, under the provision of Section 21 of the Act of Congress approved June 28, 1898 (30 Stats., 495), to enrollment, as a citizen by intermarriage of the Cherokee Nation, and his application for enrollment as such is accordingly granted.

Tams Bixby
Commissioner.

Dated at Muskogee, Indian Territory,
this   JAN 23 1907

◇◇◇◇◇

Muskogee, Indian Territory, January 7, 1907.

William F. Rasmus,
    Tahlequah, Indian Territory.

Sir:

Replying to your letter of January 2, 1907, in connection with your aplication[sic] for enrollment as a citizen by intermarriage of the Cherokee Nation, and in which you state you will appear before the Commissioner during the week commencing January 6, 1907, you are advised that you will be permitted to appear on any day of that week.

Respectfully,

S.W.   Commissioner.

◇◇◇◇◇

COPY

Tahlequah, Cherokee Nation, Ind. Terry,

January 10th., 1907.

Hon. Tams Bixby,

U. S. Commissioner to the Five Civilized Tribes,

Muskogee, Ind. Terry.

Sir:

I desire to give notice that in my personal examination before your office on the 8th. inst. as an intermarried white citizen of the Cherokee Nation, it occurs to me that I may have stated that my marriage on September, 4th. 1866, should have taken place in Flint District Cherokee Nation, Ind. Terry., and if so, is an error, and desire the same corrected to read, "in Going-Snake District, Cherokee Nation, Ind. Terry.[sic]

Very respectfully,

Wm. F. Rasmus.

◇◇◇◇◇

Cherokee 6648

Muskogee, Indian Territory, January 23, 1907.

W. W. Hastings,

Attorney for the Cherokee Nation,

Muskogee, Indian Territory.

Dear Sir:

There is enclosed herewith copy of the decision of the Commissioner to the Five Civilized Tribes, dated January 23, 1907, granting the application for the enrollment of William F. Rasmus as a citizen by intermarriage of the Cherokee Nation.

Respectfully,

Enc I-71   Commissioner.

RPI

◇◇◇◇◇

Cherokee 6648   W.W.HASTINGS. ATTORNEY.   OFFICE OF   H.M. VANCE. SECRETARY.

Attorney for the Cherokee Nation,

MUSKOGEE, I. T.   January 23, 1907.

The Commissioner to the Five Civilized Tribes,
    Muskogee, Indian Territory.

Sir:

    Receipt is acknowledged of the testimony and of your decision enrolling William F. Rasmus as a citizen by intermarriage of the Cherokee Nation. Time for protesting said decision is waived and I consent that said person may be placed upon the schedule immediately.

      Respectfully,
       W. W. Hastings
       Attorney for the Cherokee Nation.

◇◇◇◇◇

Cherokee 6648

    Muskogee, Indian Territory, January 24, 1907.

William F. Rasmus,
    Tahlequah, Indian Territory.

Dear Sir:

    There is enclosed herewith a copy of the decision of the Commissioner to the Five Civilized Tribes, dated January 23, 1907, granting your application for the enrollment as a citizen by intermarriage of the Cherokee Nation.

    You will be advised when your name has been placed upon a schedule of citizens of the Cherokee Nation and approved by the Secretary of the Interior.

      Respectfully,

Encl. H-20   Commissioner.
JMH

◇◇◇◇◇

Cherokee
I.W. 113

Muskogee, Indian Territory, April 16, 1907.

William F. Rasmus,
    Tahlequah, Indian Territory.

Dear Sir:

Your marriage license and certificate filed in connection with your application for enrollment as a citizen by intermarriage of the Cherokee Nation is returned to you herewith, copies of the same being retained in the files of this office.

Respectfully,

Encl. W-21
S.W.

Commissioner.

Cher IW 114

◇◇◇◇◇

F.R.

DEPARTMENT OF THE INTERIOR,

COMMISSIONER TO THE FIVE CIVILIZED TRIBES.

In the matter of the application for the enrollment of

Mary R. Harnage

as a citizen by intermarriage of the Cherokee Nation.

Cherokee 6756.

◇◇◇◇◇

Cherokee Intermarried White 1906
Volume IV

Department of the Interior,
Commission to the Five Civilized Tribes,
Tahlequah, I.T., December 15, 1900.

In the matter of the application of William Thomas Harnage for the enrollment of himself, wife and children as Cherokee citizens; being sworn and examined by Commissioner Breckinridge he testified as follows:

Q Give me your full name? A William Thomas Harnage
Q How old are you? A 53
Q What is your post-office? A Tahlequah.
Q In what district do you live? A Tahlequah.
Q Do you want to enroll yourself and family? A Yes sir.
Q Have you a wife? A Yes sir.
Q How many children have you? A I have four that's not enrolled/[sic]
Q Are you a Cherokee by blood? A Yes sir.
Q Is your wife a Cherokee by blood? A Mo[sic] sir.
Q White woman is she? A Yes sir.
Q Have you lived in the Cherokee Nation all your live? A No sir, I have been here since 1872 I believe.
Q You are on the roll of 1880 are you? A Yes sir.
Q Give me the name of your father? A John G. Harnage.
Q Is he dead? A Yes sir.
Q Give me the name of your mother? A Emily W. Harnage.
Q Is she dead? A Yes sir.
Q Give me the name of your wife? A Mary R.
Q How old is she? A She is 50 years old.
Q When were you and she married? A Married in 1870.
Q Have you lived together ever since? A Yes sir.
Q Is she with you on the roll of 1880? A Yes sir.
Q Give me the names of your children? A Rosanna.
Q How old is that child? A 18.
Q Next child? A William Custus.
Q How old is that child? A 16
Q Now the next child? A Lena,
Q No middle name? A No sir.
Q How old is that child? A 14
Q The next child? A Ruth B.
Q How old is that child? A 11
Q That's all is it? A Yes sir.
1880 roll page 701 #635 Wm. Harnage Sequoyah native
1880 roll page 701 #636 Mary Harnage Sequoyah native
1896 roll page 1183 #1453 William T. Harnage   "
1896 roll page 1281 #110 Mary Harnage   "
1896 roll page 1183 #1457 Rose A. Harnage   "
1896 roll page 1184 #1458 William C. Harnage   "

Cherokee Intermarried White 1906
Volume IV

1896 roll page 1184 #1459 Lena Harnage   "
1896 roll page 1184 #1460 Ruth B. Harnage   "

    Com'r Breckinridge: The applicant applies for the enrollment of himself, his wife and four children; he is identified on the rolls of 1880 and 1896 as a native Cherokee; he has lived in the Cherokee Nation since 1872, and he will now be listed for enrollment as a Cherokee by blood.

    His wife is a white woman; she is identified with him on the rolls of 1880 and 1896; they have lived together ever since their marriage in 1870 and she will now be listed for enrollment as a Cherokee by adoption; the four children named in the testimony are duly identified on the roll of 1896; they are living and will be listed for enrollment as Cherokees by blood.

    M.D. Green, being first duly sworn, states that as stenographer to the Commission to the Five Civilized Tribes he correctly recorded the testimony and proceedings in this case and that the foregoing is a true and complete transcript of his stenographic notes thereof.

MD Green

Subscribed and sworn to before me this December 17, 1900.

TB Needles
Commissioner.

◇◇◇◇◇

R.
Cher. 6756.

Department of the Interior.
Commission to the Five Civilized Tribes.
Tahlequah, I. T., October 3, 1902.

    SUPPLEMENTAL TESTIMONY AND PROCEEDINGS in the matter of the application for the enrollment of MARY R. HARNAGE as a citizen by intermarriage of the Cherokee Nation.

    MARY R. HARNAGE, being first duly sworn, and being examined, testified as follows:

BY COMMISSION: What is your name? A Mary R. Harnage.
Q How old are you? A Fifty-two.
Q What is your post office address? A Tahlequah.
Q Are you a white woman? A Yes sir.
Q Have you heretofore made application to this Commission for enrollment as a citizen by intermarriage of the Cherokee Nation? A My husband did for me.
Q What is the name of your husband? A William T. Harnage.

Q Is he living? A Yes sir.
Q Is he a Cherokee by blood? A Yes sir.
Q Do you claim your right to enrollment by reason of your marriage to him? A Yes sir.
Q When were you married? A In 1870, December 25th.
Q Have you and he lived together continuously since that time? A Yes sir.
Q Have you resided in the Cherokee Nation continuously since the time you were married? A No sir, we came here in December, 1871.
Q Have you resided in the Cherokee Nation continuously since that time? A Yes sir, was here ever since.
Q Were you ever married before you married him? A No sir.
Q Was he ever married before he married you? A No sir.

This testimony will be filed with and made a part of the record in the matter of the application for the enrollment of Mary R. Harnage as a citizen by intermarriage of the Cherokee Nation, Cherokee straight card field No. 6756.

Wm. Hutchinson, being first duly sworn, states that as stenographer to the Commission to the Five Civilized Tribes he correctly recorded the testimony and proceedings in this case, and that the foregoing is a true and complete transcript of the stenographic notes thereof.

Wm Hutchinson

Subscribed and zsworn[sic] to before me this 3rd day of Octber[sic], 1902.

John O Rosson
Notary Public.

◇◇◇◇◇

DEPARTMENT OF THE INTERIOR
COMMISSIONER TO THE FIVE CIVILIZED TRIBES
Muskogee, Indian Territory
January 4, 1907   Cherokee
No. 6756

In the matter of the application for the enrollment of Mary R. Harnage as a citizen by intermarriage of the Cherokee Nation

The applicant being duly sworn testified as follows:

Q What is your name? A Mary R. Harnage
Q How old are you? A I am 56 last October.
Q What is your postoffice address? A Tahlequah
Q Do you claim to be a citizen by intermarriage of the Cherokee Nation? A Yes sir.
Q Through whom do you claim your intermarried rights? A William T. Harnage

Cherokee Intermarried White 1906
Volume IV

Q When were you married to William T. Harnage? A Married on December 25, 1870
Q Where? A Texas
Q Was William Harnage a recognized citizen of the Cherokee Nation at that time?
A He was an Indian by blood---Yes he was a citizen of the Nation
Q Where was he born? A Born here in the Nation--Flint District
Q How long did you live in Texas after your marriage? A 1 year We came here in November, 1872
Q Was William T. Harnage readmitted to citizenship after he came back here in 1872?
A Well, I can't tell you exactly what time.
Q Have you any documentary evidence of your marriage to William T. Harnage? A No sir, none at all. In Texas the license was turned over to the minister and he turned it to the county clerk
Q What was the name of the minister that married you? A Rev. Bellamy.
Q Were you ever married before you married William T. Harnage? A No sir.
Q Was he ever married before he married you? A No sir
Q Is he living at this time? A Yes sir.
Q Have you lived together as husband and wife ever since 1870 up to the present time?
A Yes sir
Q Is he here today? A No sir, he's not here today--his two sisters re here

The applicant is identified on the 1880 Cherokee Roll Shequoyah[sic] District opposite No. 636. Her husband through whom she claims her right to enrollment is identified on said roll, said district, opposite No. 635. He is also identified on the final roll of citizens by blood of the Cherokee Nation, opposite No. 16170.

Q Has your husband held property in the Cherokee Nation ever since you came here in 1872? A Yes sir
Q Always vted[sic] in the Cherokee elections? A Yes sir
Q Are you sure he was re-admitted to citizenship in the Cherokee Nation prior to 1875?
A Why I can't swear to it--his sisters can.

Witness excused.

Ida H. Ewers being called as a witness for the applicant and being first duly sworn, testified as follows:

Q What is your name? A Ida H. Ewers
Q How old are you? A 53
Q What is your postoffice address? A Centralia, I.T.
Q Are you acquainted with Mary R. Harnage? A Yes sir
Q Do you know her husband, William T. Harnage? A Yes sir, he's my brother.
Q Do you know when they were married? A I was at the wedding.
Q When were they married? A December 25, 1870.
Q Was your brother William T. Harnage a recognized citizen of the Cherokee Nation at the time he married in 1870? A Yes we always were--he was born in the Cherokee Nation

Q How long had he been living in Texas when he married Mary R. Harnage? A I don't remember, but he had been in this country since the war and came back there, I reckon three or four years he stayed away and came back soon after they were married, I think it was in a year

Q Do you know that he was readmitted when he returned to the Cherokee Nation in 1872? A I was not there, but it was the rule, we were all readmitted when we came back home, we have always kept on the roll.

Witness excused

Belle H. Scott being called as a witness for the applicant and being first duly sworn testified as follows:

Q What is your name? A Belle H. Scott
Q What is your postoffice address? A Fort Gibson.
Q How old are you? A 51
Q Are you a recognized citizen by blood of the Cherokee Nation? A Yes sir.
Q Do you know Mary R. Harnage? A I do
Q Is she any relation to you? A She's my sister-in-law--my brother's wife. Her husband is William T. Harnage
Q Do you know when they were married? A They were married in 1870
Q Were you present at the marriage? A Yes sir
Q Where were they married? A In Texas
Q Were you living in Texas at that time? A Yes sir
Q When did you return to the Nation?
A He, my brother came back in '66 but I didn't come back until '76
Q Your brother came back in 1866? A Yes sir
Q Do you know when your brother was readmitted to citizenship in the Cherokee Nation? A I can't exactly say, but our father never allowed our citizenship to expire during his lifetime. Of course after my brother came back he attended to that himself
Q Was your brother William T. Harnage always recognized as a citizen by blood of the Cherokee Nation? A Yes sir

Witness excused

Gertrude Hanna, being duly sworn, states that she reported the proceedings had in the above numbered case on January 4, 1907 and that the above and foregoing is a true and correct transcript of her stenographic notes taken therein.

Gertrude Hanna

Subscribed and sworn to before me this 5 day of January, 1907

Walter W. Chappell
Notary Public.

◇◇◇◇◇

F.R.   Cherokee 6756.

DEPARTMENT OF THE INTERIOR,

COMMISSIONER TO THE FIVE CIVILIZED TRIBES.

In the matter of the application for the enrollment of Mary R. Harnage as a citizen by intermarriage of the Cherokee Nation.

D E C I S I O N.

THE RECORDS OF THIS OFFICE SHOW: That December 15, 1900, application was received by the Commission to the Five Civilized Tribes for the enrollment of Mary R. Harnage as a citizen by intermarriage of the Cherokee Nation. Further proceedings in the matter of said application were had at Tahlequah, Indian Territory, October 3, 1902, and at Muskogee, Indian Territory, January 4, 1907.

THE EVIDENCE IN THIS CASE SHOWS: That the applicant herein, Mary R. Harnage, a white woman, was lawfully married December 25, 1870, to her husband William T. Harnage, who was at the time of said marriage, a recognized citizen by blood of the Cherokee Nation, who is identified on the Cherokee authenticated tribal roll of 1880, Sequoyah District No. 635, as a native Cherokee, and whose name is included on the approved partial roll of citizens by blood of the Cherokee Nation opposite No. 16170. It is further shown that, from November 1872, the said William T. Harnage and Mary R. Harnage resided together as husband and wife and continuously lived in the Cherokee Nation up to and including September 1, 1902. The said applicant is identified on the Cherokee authenticated tribal roll of 1880, and the Cherokee Census Roll of 1896, as an intermarried citizen of the Cherokee Nation.

It Is, THEREFORE, ORDERED AND ADJUDGED: That in accordance with the decision of the Supreme Court of the United States, dated November 5, 1906, in the cases of Daniel Red Bird et al., vs. the United States, Nos. 125, 126, 127 and 128, the said applicant, Mary R. Harnage, is entitled under the provisions of Section twenty-one of the Act of Congress approved June 28, 1898 (30 Stats., 495), to enrollment as a citizen by intermarriage of the Cherokee Nation, and her application for enrollment as such is accordingly granted.

Cherokee Intermarried White 1906
Volume IV

Tams Bixby
Commissioner.

Dated at Muskogee, Indian Territory,
this   JAN 23 1907

◇◇◇◇◇

Cherokee 6756

Muskogee, Indian Territory, January 23, 1907.

W. W. Hastings,
     Attorney for the Cherokee Nation,
         Muskogee, Indian Territory.

Dear Sir:

     There is enclosed herewith a copy of the decision of the Commissioner to the Five Civilized Tribes, dated January 23, 1907, granting the application for the enrollment of Mary R. Harnage as a citizen by intermarriage of the Cherokee Nation.

Respectfully,

Encl. H-65   Commissioner.
JMH

◇◇◇◇◇

Cherokee 6756

W.W.HASTINGS.   OFFICE OF   H.M. VANCE.
ATTORNEY.   SECRETARY.

Attorney for the Cherokee Nation,
MUSKOGEE, I. T.   January 23, 1907.

The Commissioner to the Five Civilized Tribes,
         Muskogee, Indian Territory.

Sir:

     Receipt is acknowledged of the testimony and of your decision enrolling Mary R. Harnage as a citizen by intermarriage of the Cherokee Nation. Time for protesting said decision is waived and I consent that said person may be placed upon the schedule immediately.

Respectfully,
W. W. Hastings
Attorney for Cherokee Nation.

◇◇◇◇◇

**Cherokee Intermarried White 1906
Volume IV**

Cherokee 6756

Muskogee, Indian Territory, January 23, 1907.

Mary R. Harnage,
Tahlequah, Indian Territory.

Dear Madam:

There is enclosed herewith a copy of the decision of the Commissioner to the Five Civilized Tribes, dated January 23, 1907, granting the application for your enrollment as a citizen by intermarriage of the Cherokee Nation.

You will be advised when your name has been placed upon a schedule of citizens of the Cherokee Nation and approved by the Secretary of the Interior.

Respectfully,

Encl. H-87   Commissioner.

Cher IW 115

◇◇◇◇◇

F.R.

DEPARTMENT OF THE INTERIOR,
COMMISSIONER TO THE FIVE CIVILIZED TRIBES.

In the matter of the application for the enrollment of

Maggie J. Wolfe

as a citizen by intermarriage of the Cherokee Nation.

Cherokee 6898.

◇◇◇◇◇

DEPARTMENT OF THE INTERIOR,
COMMISSION TO THE FIVE CIVILIZED TRIBES.
TAHLEQUAH, I.T., DECEMBER 18th, 1900.

IN THE MATTER OF THE APPLICATION OF Thomas P. Wolfe for the enrollment of himself and wife as citizens of the Cherokee Nation, and he being sworn and edamined[sic] by Commissioner, T. B. Needles, testified as follows:

Q What is your name? A Thomas P. Wolfe.
Q What is your age? A Fifty one.
Q What is your Postoffice address? A Tahlequah.
Q What district do you live in? A Tahlequah.
Q Are you a recognized citizen of the Cherokee Nation? A Yes sir.
Q By blood? A Yes sir; I was born and raised right here in this town.
Q Whom do you want to enroll? A Myself and wife.
Q What is the name of your wife? A Maggie J.
Q What is her age? A Forty five.
Q Is she a citizen by blood? A No sir.
Q When did you marry her? A In '74.

(1880 Roll, Page 821, #2553, Thomas P. Wolf[sic], Tahlequah D'st)
(1880 Roll, Page 821, #2554, Maggie Wolf, Tahlequah D'st)
(1896 Roll, Page 1268, #3716, Thomas Wolfe, Tahlequah D'st)
(1896 Roll, Page 1292, #295, Magie J. Wolfe, Tahlequah D'st)

Q Have you always lived in the Cherokee nation; you and your wife?
A Yes sir; we went south during the war.

Com'r. T. B. Needles: The name of Thomas P. Wolfe appears upon the authenticated roll of 1880, as well as the census roll of 1896, as a Cherokee by blood. The name of his wife, Maggie J. appears upon the authenticated roll of 1880 and upon the census roll of 1896, as Maggie J. Wolfe, as a citizen by adoption.

They both being dully[sic] identified, and making satisfactory proof of residence, the said Thomas P. Wolfe will be duly listed for enrollment as a Cherokee citizen by blood, and his wife, Maggie J. Wolfe as a Cherokee citizen by intermarriage.

The undersigned, being sworn, states that as stenographer to the Commission to the Five Civilized Tribes, he correctly recorded the testimony and proceedings in this case, and that the foregoing is a true and complete transcript of his stenographic notes thereof.

R R Cravens

Cherokee Intermarried White 1906
Volume IV

Subscribed and sworn to before me this 11th day of January, 1901.

CR Breckinridge
COMMISSIONER.

◇◇◇◇◇

JOR.
Cher. 6898.

Department of the Interior.
Commission to the Five Civilized Tribes.
Tahlequah, I. T., October 9, 1902.

SUPPLEMENTAL TESTIMONY AND PROCEEDINGS in the matter of the application for the enrollment of MAGGIE J. WOLFE as a citizen by intermarriage of the Cherokee Nation.

MAGGIE J. WOLFE, being first duly sworn, and being examined, testified as follows:

BY COMMISSION: What is your name? A Maggie J. Wolfe.
Q How old are you? A Forty-eight.
Q What is your post office address? A Tahlequah.
Q You are a white woman, are you? A Yes sir.
Q Have you heretofore madd[sic] application to this Commission for enrollment as a citizen by intermarriage of the Cherokee Nation? A ~~Yes sir~~. No sir.
Q Has your husband made application for you? A I don't recollect, I registered, that is all.
Q You have been enrolled? A I have not been enrolled, no sir.
Q You have never been before the Commission? A Yes sir, I enrolled last winter with the Dawes Commission.
Q What is the name of your husband? A Thomas P. Wolfe.
Q Is he living? A Yes sir.
Q Is he a Cherokee by blood? A Yes sir.
Q Do you claim your right to enrollment by reason of your marriage to him? A Yes sir.
Q When were you and he married? A In 1874, twenty-eight years ago.
Q At the time application was made for your enrollment, was satisfactory proof made to the Commission of your marriage to him? A Yes sir.
Q Have you and he lived together continuously ever since that time[sic] A Yes sir.
Q Were you and he living together on the 1st day of September, 1902[sic]
A Yes sir, we have lived together all the time.
Q You have never been separated at all? A No sir, we have lived together cince[sic] 1874.
Q Were you ever married before you married him? A No sir.
Q Was he ever married before he married you? A No sir.
Q You are his first wife and he is your first husband? A Yes sir.

114

Q Have you resided in the Cherokee Nation continuously ever since you and he were married in 1874? A Yes sir, we have never lived anywhere else.
Q Has he also? A Yes sir.
Q You have no children? A No sir.
Q Your husband has never made application for the enrollment of any children? A No sir.

This testimony will be filed with and made a part of the record in the matter of the application for the enrollment of Maggie J. Wolfe as a citizen by intermarriage of the Cherokee Nation, Cherokee straight card field No. 6898.

Wm. Hutchinson, being first duly sworn, states that as stenographer to the Commission to the Five Civilized Tribes he correctly recorded the testimony and proceedings in this case, and that the foregoing is a true and complete transcript of the stenographic notes thereof.

Wm Hutchinson

Subscribed and sworn to before me this 16th day of October, 1902.

John O Rosson
Notary Public.

◇◇◇◇◇

Cherokee
No. 6898

DEPARTMENT OF THE INTERIOR
COMMISSIONER TO THE FIVE CIVILIZED TRIBES

Muskogee, Indian Territory

January 4, 1907

In the matter of the application of Maggie J. Wolfe for enrollment as a citizen by intermarriage of the Cherokee Nation.

The applicant being duly sworn, testified as follows:

Q What is your name? A Maggie J. Wolfe
Q How old are you.[sic] A 53
Q What is your postoffice address? A Tahlequah, Cherokee Nation.
Q Do you claim to be a citizen by intermarriage of the Cherokee Nation? A Yes sir.
Q Through whom do you claim your rights? A T. P. Wolfe
Q Thomas P. Wolfe? A Yes sir
Q When were you married to Thomas P. Wolfe? A In '74

Cherokee Intermarried White 1906
Volume IV

Q What time? A July 8th, 1874.

Q Was Thomas P. Wolfe a recognized citizen by blood of the Cherokee Nation at the time you married him in 1874? A Yes sir

Q Where were you married? A Park Hill, Tahlequah District.

Q Who married you? A Rev. McSpadden.

Q Did he give you a certificate? A Yes sir and it got lost

Q Were you ever married before you married Thomas P. Wolfe? A No sir

Q Was he ever married before he married you? A Not as I know of, no he never was married before.

Q Did you live together as husband and wife from the time of your marriage in 1874 up to the present time? A Yes sir

Q Have you always been recognized as a citizen by adoption since your marriage in 1874? A Yes sir

The applicant is identified on the 1880 Cherokee roll, Tahlequah District opposite No. 2554. Her husband through whom she claims her right to enrollment is identified on said roll opposite No. 2553. He is also identified on the final roll of citizens by blood of the Cherokee Nation opposite No. 16472

Witness excused.

Thomas P. Wolfe being called as a witness for the applicant, and being duly sworn, testified as follows:

Q What is your name? A Thomas P. Wolfe

Q How old are you? A. 57

Q What is your postoffice address? A Tahlequah.

Q Do you know Maggie J. Wolfe? A Yes sir

Q What relation is she to you? [sic] She's my wife.

Q When was you married to Maggie J. Wolfe.[sic] A Married July 8, 1874.

Q Were you ever married before you married Maggie J. Wolfe? A No sir

Q Have you lived together continuously since your marriage in '74 up to the present time in the Cherokee Nation? A Yes sir

Q Were you a recognized citizen by blood of the Cherokee Nation at the time you married your wife in '74? A Yes sir

Witness excused.

Cul Thorne being called as a witness for the applicant, and being duly sworn, testified as follows:

Q What is your name? A. Cul Thorn[sic]

Q Your age? A 54 years of age

Q What is your postoffice address? A Tahlequah

Q Are you acquainted with Thomas P. Wolfe and Maggie J. Wolfe? A Yes sir.

Q How long have you known them? A Since he was a little boy.

Q Do you know when they were married? A Yes sir

Q Were you present at their marriage? A Yes sir

Q Was Thomas P. Wolfe a recognized citizen of he[sic] Cherokee Nation, by blood, at the time they were married? A Yes sir, always was.

Q Have they always lived together as husband and wife ever since they were married?
A Yes sir

Witness excused.

Gertrude Hanna, being duly sworn, states that as stenographer to the Commissioner to the Five Civilized Tribes she reported the proceedings had in the above numbered case on January 4, 1907, and that the above and foregoing is a true and correct transcript of her stenographic notes taken therein.

Gertrude Hanna

Subscribed and sworn to before me this 5 day of January, 1907.

Walter W Chappell
Notary Public

◇◇◇◇◇

F.R.   Cherokee 6898.

DEPARTMENT OF THE INTERIOR,

COMMISSIONER TO THE FIVE CIVILIZED TRIBES.

In the matter of the application for the enrollment of Maggie J. Wolfe as a citizen by intermarriage of the Cherokee Nation.

D E C I S I O N.

THE RECORDS OF THIS OFFICE SHOW: That December 18, 1900, application was received by the Commission to the Five Civilized Tribes for the enrollment of Maggie J. Wolfe as a citizen by intermarriage of the Cherokee Nation. Further proceedings in the matter of said application were had at Tahlequah, Indian Territory, October 9, 1902, and at Muskogee, Indian Territory, January 4, 1907.

THE EVIDENCE IN THIS CASE SHOWS: That the applicant herein, Maggie J. Wolfe, a white woman, was lawfully married July 8, 1874, to her husband, Thomas P. Wolfe, who was at the time of said marriage, a recognized citizen by blood of the Cherokee Nation, who is identified on the Cherokee authenticated tribal roll of 1880, Tahlequah District No. 2553, as a native Cherokee, and whose name is included in the approved partial roll of citizens by blood of the Cherokee Nation opposite No. 16472. It is further shown that, from the time of said marriage, the said Thomas P. Wolfe and Maggie J. Wolfe resided together as husband and wife and continuously lived in the Cherokee Nation up to and including September 1, 1902. The said applicant is identified on the Cherokee authenticated tribal roll of 1880, and the Cherokee Census Roll of 1896, as an intermarried citizen of the Cherokee Nation.

IT IS, THEREFORE, ORDERED AND ADJUDGED: That in accordance with the decision of the Supreme Court of the United States, dated November 5, 1906, in the cases of Daniel Red Bird et al., vs. the United States, Nos. 125, 126, 127 and 128, the said applicant, Maggie J. Wolfe, is entitled, under the provisions of Section twenty-one of the Act of Congress approved June 28, 1898 (30 Stats., 495), to enrollment as a citizen by intermarriage of the Cherokee Nation, and her application for enrollment as such is accordingly granted.

Tams Bixby
Commissioner.

Dated at Muskogee, Indian Territory,
this   JAN 23 1907

◇◇◇◇◇

Cherokee
6898

Muskogee, Indian Territory, January 28, 1907.

W. W. Hastings,
    Attorney for the Cherokee Nation,
        Muskogee, Indian Territory.

Dear Sir:

There is enclosed herewith a copy of the decision of the Commissioner to the Five Civilized Tribes, dated January 22, 1907, granting the application for the enrollment of Maggie J. Wolfe as a citizen by intermarriage of the Cherokee Nation.

Respectfully,

Encl. H-25   Commissioner.
JMH

◇◇◇◇◇

Cherokee 6898

W.W.HASTINGS.
ATTORNEY.

OFFICE OF

H.M. VANCE.
SECRETARY.

Attorney for the Cherokee Nation,

Muskogee, I. T.   January 23, 1907.

The Commissioner to the Five Civilized Tribes,
Muskogee, Indian Territory.

Sir:

Receipt is acknowledged of the testimony and of your decision enrolling Maggie J. Wolfe as a citizen by intermarriage of the Cherokee Nation. Time for protesting said decision is waived and I consent that said person may be placed upon the schedule immediately.

Yours very truly,
W. W. Hastings
Attorney for Cherokee Nation.

◇◇◇◇◇

Cherokee 6898

Muskogee, Indian Territory, January 23, 1907.

Maggie J. Wolfe,
Tahlequah, Indian Territory.

Dear Madam:

There is enclosed herewith copy of the decision of the Commissioner to the Five Civilized Tribes, dated January 23, 1907, granting the application for your enrollment as a citizen by intermarriage of the Cherokee Nation.

You will be advised when your name has been placed upon a schedule of citizens of the Cherokee Nation and approved by the Secretary of the Interior.

Respectfully,

Enc I-87

Commissioner.

RPI

Cher IW 116

◇◇◇◇◇

Cherokee Intermarried White 1906
Volume IV

F.R.

DEPARTMENT OF THE INTERIOR,
COMMISSIONER TO THE FIVE CIVILIZED TRIBES.

In the matter of the application for the enrollment of

NANCY J. RIDER
as a citizen by intermarriage of the Cherokee Nation.

Cherokee 6963.

◇◇◇◇◇

Department of the Interior.
Commission to the Five Civilized Tribes.
Tahlequah, I. T., December 19, 1900.

In the matter of the application of Wilson Rider for the enrollment of himself, wife and children as Cherokee citizens; he being sworn and examined by Commissioner T. B. Needles, testified as follows:

Q What is your name? A Wilson Rider.
Q How old are you? A About 61.
Q What is your postoffice? A Tahlequah
Q What district do you lve[sic] in? A Illinois district.
Q Are you a recognized citizen of the Cherokee Nation? A I guess so.
Q By blood? A I guess so; I have been raised here.
Q Who do you want to enroll; yourself? A Myself and two little girls.
Q Your wife? A Yes sir.
Q What is the name of your wife? A Nancy J. Stevens was her name.
Q Is she a citizen by blood? A No sir, she's a white woman.
Q How old is she? A I expect I don't know exactly how old she is. I expect she is about 48.
Q When did you marry her? A I guess its[sic] been about 29 years ago.
Q What is the girl's name? A Mahala.
Q How old is she? A 14.
Q The other girl's name? A Julia.
Q How old is she? A 12.
Q Got any more children? A No sir.
1880 roll; page 796, #1759, Wilson Rider, Tahlequah district
1880 roll; page 796, #1760, Nancy Rider, Tahlequah district.
1896 roll; page 893, #1516, Wilson Rider, Illinois district.

1896 roll; page 934, #165, Jane Rider, Illinois district.
        893, #1518, Mahala Rider, "   "
        893, #1519, Julia Rider,   "   "

Q These two girls are home, and living with you? A Yes sir.
Q You always lived in the Cherokee Nation? A Yes sir.
Q Your wife? A Yes sir.

Commissioner Needles-
    The name of Wilson Rider appears upon the authenticated roll of 1880 as well as the Census roll of 1896 as a Cherokee by blood. The name of his wife, Nancy J., appears upon the authenticated roll of 1880 as Nancy Rider, and upon the Census roll of 1896 as Jane Rider, as a citizen by intermarriage. The names of his two children, Mahala and Julia, appear upon the Census roll of 1896. They are all duly identified, and make satisfactory proof as to residence, consequently Wilson Rider and his two children as enumerated herein, will be duly listed for enrollment as Cherokee citizens by blood, and his wife, Nancy J., as a Cherokee citizen by intermarriage.

E. G. Rothenberger, being duly sworn, states that as stenographer to the Commission to the Five Civilized Tribes, he reported in full the testimony and proceedings in the above case, and that the foregoing is a full, true and correct transcript of his stenographic notes in said case.

E.G. Rothenberger

Subscribed and sworn to before me this 10th day of January, 1901.

T.B. Needles
Commissioner.

◇◇◇◇◇

JOR.
Cher. 6963.

Department of the Interior.
Commission to the Five Civilized Tribes.
Tahlequah, I. T., October 8, 1902.

    SUPPLEMENTAL TESTIMONY AND PROCEEDINGS in the matter of the application for the enrollment of NANCY J. RIDER as a citizen by intermarriage of the Cherokee Nation.

    NANCY J. RIDER, being first duly sworn, and being examined, testified as follows:

BY COMMISSION: What is your name? A Nancy J. Rider.
Q How old are you? A About forty, as near as I can get at it. I am not certain.
Q What is your post office address? A Tahlequah.

121

Q You are a white woman? A Yes sir.

Q Has application heretofore been made to this Commission for your enrollment as a citizen by intermarriage of the Cherokee Nation? A Yes sir.

Q What is the name of your husband? A Wilson Rider.

Q Is he living? A Yes sir.

Q Is he a Cherokee by blood? A Yes sir.

Q Do you claim your right to enrollment by reason of your marriage to him? A Yes sir.

Q When were you and he married? A It has been something over thirty years ago. I have no record of it, it is thirty-one or -two years back.

Q When application was made for your enrollment to the Commission, was satisfactory proof of your marriage made? A Yes sir.

Q Have you and your husband lived together continuously ever since you were married? A Yes sir.

Q Are you living together now? A Yes sir.

Q Were you living together on the 1st day of September, 1902? A Yes sir.

Q Never been separated at all? A No sir.

Q Were you ever married before you married him? A No sir.

Q Was he ever married before he married you? A No sir, not that I know of.

Q Have you ever heard that he was? A No sir.

Q Have you any reason to believe that he was ever married before he married you? A No sir.

Q He is your first husband and you are his first wife? A Yes sir.

Q Have you resided in the Cherokee Nation continuously since you and he were married? A Yes sir, been right here.

Q Has he? A Yes sir.

Q You have how many children that application was made for with your family? A Two.

Q Are both those children living? A Yes sir.

This testimony will be filed with and made a part of the record in the matter of the application for the enrollment of Nancy J. Rider as a citizen by intermarriage of the Cherokee Nation, Cherokee straight card field No. 6963.

Wm. Hutchinson, being first duly sworn, states that as stenographer to the Commission to the Five Civilized Tribes he correctly recorded the testimony and proceedings in this case, and that the foregoing is a true and complete transcript of the stenographic notes thereof.

Wm Hutchinson

Subscribed and sworn to before me this 14th day of October, 1902.

John O Rosson
NP

◇◇◇◇◇

Cherokee Intermarried White 1906
Volume IV

Cherokee #6963.
DEPARTMENT OF THE INTERIOR,
COMMISSION TO THE FIVE CIVILIZED TRIBES.
CHEROKEE LAND OFFICE.
Tahlequah, I. T., January 17, 1905.

In the matter of the application of Wilson Rider for the enrollment of himself, his wife, Nancy J., and children, Mahala and Julia Rider as citizens by blood of the Cherokee Nation.

SUPPLEMENTAL TESTIMONY.

Mahala Crossland, being sworn and examined by the Commission, testified as follows:

Q What is your name? A Mahala Crossland.
Q How old are you? A Going on 21.
Q What is your postoffice? A Manard.
Q Are you a Cherokee by blood? A Yes ma'am.
Q Are you a daughter of Wilson Rider? A Yes'm.
Q Have you married since you enrolled? A Yes'm.
Q What is the name of your husband? A Pink Crossland.
Q Is he a citizen of the Cherokee Nation? A No, white man.
Q When were you married? A November 14, 1901.
Q Are you and he living together now? A Yes'm.

- - - - - - - - - - - - -

I, May Hudson, state upon oath that as stenographer to the Commission to the Five Civilized Tribes I correctly recorded the supplemental testimony in this case and that the foregoing is a true and complete transcript of my stenographic notes thereof.

May Hudson

Subscribed and sworn to before me this 18th day of January, 1905.

Samuel Foreman
Notary Public.

◇◇◇◇◇

CHEROKEE-6963.

DEPARTMENT OF THE INTERIOR,
COMMISSIONER TO THE FIVE CIVILIZED TRIBES.
Muskogee, Indian Territory, January 5, 1907.

In the matter of making proof of the marriage of Nancy J. Rider to her Cherokee husband, prior to November 1, 1875.

Nancy J. Rider, after having first been duly sworn by B. P Rasmus, a Notary Public, testified as follows:

COMMISSIONER:

Q. What is your name? A. Nancy J. Rider.
Q. What is your age? A. 50.
Q. What is your post office address? A. Tahlequah.
Q. Do you claim rights as an intermarried citizen of the Cherokee Nation? A. Yes sir.
Q. Through whom do you claim your intermarried rights? A. Wilson Rider.
Q. When were you married to Wilson Rider? A. In '71, as well as I remember.
Q. Where were you married? A. In Flint District.
Q. Did the Judge give you a certificate? A. No sir.
Q. Were you ever married before you married Wilson Rider? A. No sir.
Q. Was he ever married before he married you? A. No sir.
Q. You have lived together continuously since your marriage in '71 up to the present time? A. Yes sir.

(Commissioner -- The applicant is identified upon the 1880 Roll, Tahlequah District, opposite No. 1766. Her husband, through whom she claims her right to enrollment, is identified upon said roll in said district, opposite No. 1759. He is also identified upon the final roll of citizens by blood of the Cherokee Nation, opposite No. 16619.)

Q. Was your husband a recognized citizen of the Cherokee Nation at the time you were married in '71? A. Yes sir.
Q. Was he born in the Cherokee Nation? A. Yes sir.
Q. Always lived in the Cherokee Nation? A. Yes sir.
Q. Have you any witnesses here today who know of your marriage to Wilson Rider? A. No sir, there were just Mr. Cristy, the Judge who married us, and his wife and two boys present at the marriage.

Witness excused.

Cherokee Intermarried White 1906
Volume IV

Martin Wallace, after having first been duly sworn by B. P. Rasmus, a Notary Public, testified as follows:

COMMISSIONER:

Q. What is your name? A. Martin Wallace.
Q. How old are you? A. 60.
Q. What is your post office address? A. Tahlequah.
Q. Are you acquainted with Wilson Rider and Nancy J. Rider? A. Yes sir.
Q. How long have you known them? A. Since '71 or '72.
Q. Do you know whether or not they were married? A. I wasn't present when they were married.
Q. Have they always held themselves out as husband and wife in the community in which they live? A. Yes sir. It has always been the understanding in the community in which they live that they have been married since 1871.

Witness excused.

Elijah Stevens, after having first been duly sworn, by B. P. Rasmus, a Notary Public, testified as follows:

COMMISSIONER:

Q. What is your name? A. Elijah Stevens.
Q. What is your age? A. 58.
Q. Your post office? A. Park Hill.
Q. Are you acquainted with Wilson Rider and Nancy J. Rider? A. Yes sir.
Q. How long have you known them? A. I have known them always. She is my sister.
Q. Nancy Rider is? A. Yes sir.
Q. Do you know when they were married? A. No, I don't know the year.
Q. They have always been recognized as man and wife since they were married?
A. Yes sir.

Witness excused.

Eula Jeanes Branson, being sworn, states that she correctly reported the proceedings had in the above and foregoing, on the 5th. day of January, 1907.

Eula Jeanes Branson

Subscribed and sworn to before me, this 8th. day of January, 1907.

Walter W Chappell
Notary Public.

◇◇◇◇◇

F. R.   Cherokee 6963.

DEPARTMENT OF THE INTERIOR,
COMMISSIONER TO THE FIVE CIVILIZED TRIBES.

———————————

In the matter of the application for the enrollment of Nancy J. Rider as a citizen by intermarriage of the Cherokee Nation.

D E C I S I O N

THE RECORDS OF THIS OFFICE SHOW: That at Tahlequah, Indian Territory, December 19, 1900, Wilson Rider appeared before the Commission to the Five Civilized Tribes and made application for the enrollment of himself and his two minor children, Mahala and Julia Rider, as citizens by blood of the Cherokee Nation, and for the enrollment of his wife, Nancy J. Rider (nee Stevens), as a citizen by intermarriage of the Cherokee Nation. The application for the enrollment of said Wilson Rider and his two minor children, Mahala and Julia Rider, has been heretofore disposed of, and their rights to enrollment will not be considered in this decision. In the matter of the application for the enrollment of said Nancy J. Rider, further proceedings were had   before the Commission to the Five Civilized Tribes at Tahlequah, Indian Territory, October 8, 1902, and January 17, 1905, and also, before the Commissioner to the Five Civilized Tribes, at Muskogee, Indian Territory, January 5, 1907.

THE EVIDENCE IN THIS CASE SHOWS: That the applicant herein, Nancy J. Rider, a white woman, was married in accordance with the Cherokee law in 1871, to her husband, Wilson Rider, who as at the time of said marriage, a recognized citizen by blood of the Cherokee Nation, who is identified on the Cherokee authenticated tribal roll of 1880, Tahlequah District, Number 1759, as a native Cherokee, and whose name appears opposite No. 16619 on the approved partial roll of citizens of the Cherokee Nation, and that since said marriage the said Wilson Rider and his wife, Nancy J. Rider, have lived together as husband and wife, and have continuously lived in the Cherokee Nation. The said Nancy J. Rider is identified on the Cherokee authenticated tribal roll of 1880 as an intermarried citizen of the Cherokee Nation.

IT IS, THEREFORE, ORDERED AND ADJUDGED: That in accordance with the decision of the Supreme Court of the United States, dated November 5, 1906, in the cases of Daniel Red Bird et al., vs. the United States, Nos. 125, 126, 127 and 128, the said applicant, Nancy J. Rider, is entitled, under the provisions of Section 21 of the Act of Congress approved June 28, 1898 (30 Stats., 495), to enrollment as a citizen by intermarriage of the Cherokee Nation, and her application for enrollment as such is accordingly granted.

Tams Bixby   Commissioner.

Dated at Muskogee, Indian Territory,
this   JAN 21 1907

◇◇◇◇◇

Cherokee 6963

Muskogee, Indian Territory, January 21, 1907.

W. W. Hastings,
    Attorney for the Cherokee Nation,
        Muskogee, Indian Territory.

Dear Sir:

There is enclosed herewith copy of the decision of the Commissioner to the Five Civilized Tribes, dated January 21, 1907, granting the application for the enrollment of Nancy J. Rider as a citizen by intermarriage of the Cherokee Nation.

Respectfully,

Enc I-23   Commissioner.

RPI

◇◇◇◇◇

Cherokee 6963   W.W.HASTINGS.   OFFICE OF   H.M. VANCE.
                 ATTORNEY.   SECRETARY.
Attorney for the Cherokee Nation,
MUSKOGEE, I. T.   January 21, 1907.

Commissioner to the Five Civilized Tribes,
    Muskogee, Indian Territory.

Sir:

Receipt is acknowledged of the testimony and of your decision enrolling Nancy J. Rider as a citizen by intermarriage of the Cherokee Nation. Time for protesting said decision is waived and I consent that said person may be placed upon the schedule immediately.

Respectfully,
                        W. W. Hastings
                        Attorney for the Cherokee Nation.

◇◇◇◇◇

Cherokee 6963

Muskogee, Indian Territory, January 24, 1907.

Nancy J. Rider,
Tahlequah, Indian Territory.

Dear Madam:

There is enclosed herewith copy of the decision of the Commissioner to the Five Civilized Tribes, dated January 21, 1907, granting the application for your enrollment as a citizen by intermarriage of the Cherokee Nation.

You will be advised when your name has been placed upon a schedule of citizens of the Cherokee Nation and approved by the Secretary of the Interior.

Respectfully,

Enc I-108.   Commissioner.

RPI

Cher IW 117

◇◇◇◇◇

DEPARTMENT OF THE INTERIOR,

COMMISSIONER TO THE FIVE CIVILIZED TRIBES.

In the matter of the application for the enrollment of

WILLIAM B. BECK

as a citizen by intermarriage of the Cherokee Nation.

Cherokee 7279.

◇◇◇◇◇

Cherokee Intermarried White 1906
Volume IV

DEPARTMENT OF THE INTERIOR.

COMMISSION TO THE FIVE CIVILIZED TRIBES.

MUSKOGEE, I.T., FEBUARY[sic] 15th, 1901.

IN THE MATTER OF THE APPLICATION OF WILLIAM BL[sic] BECK FOR THE ENROLLMENT OF HIMSELF AND WIFE AS CITIZENS OF THE CHEROKEE NATION, AND SAID BECK BEING SWORN AND EXAMINED BY COMMISSIONER, C. R. BRECKINRIDGE TESTIFIED AS FOLLOWS:

Q Give me your full name? A William B. Beck.
Q How old are you? A My age is fifty three.
Q What is your Postoffice? A Fawn.
Q In what district do you live? A Canadian District, Cherokee Nation.
Q Who is it you want to have enrolled; yourself and family?
A Myself, wife and a little orphan girl we have.
Q That is all? A Yes, sir.
Q Are you a Cherokee by blood? A No, sir.
Q White man? A Yes, sir.
Q Is your wife a Cherokee by blood? A Yes, sir.
Q Let me see your marriage license and certificate?
A I haven't got it.
Q When were you married? A In '70.
Q To your present wife? A Yes sir.
Q Have you lived in the Cherokee Nation with her ever since you married her in 1870?
A Yes, sir.
Q Give me the name of your wife, please? A Malinda J.
Q How old is she? A She's about fifty years old.
Q Has she lived in the Cherokee Nation all her life? A No, sir.
Q But she's lived here since 1870? A Yes, sir; '69.
Q Give me the name of her father? A Moses Crittenden.
Q Is he dead? A Yes, sir.
Q Give me the name of her mother? A Edie.
Q Is she dead? A Yes, sir.
Q Is this orphan child related to you? A It is an orphan child some relation to my wife.
A Is it of your name? A No, sir, it's[sic] name is Quinton.

Tribal Rolls of citizens of the Cherokee Nation examined and the names of applicants appear thereon as follows:
    1880 Authenticated Roll, Page 39, #1081, W. B. Peck, Canadian District.
        Note on 1896 Census Roll reads as follows: "This family appears on the roll of 1880 as Peck."
    1880 Roll, Page 39, #1082, M. J. Peck, Indian Territory Canadian District.
    1896 Roll, Page 85, #17, William B. Beck, Canadian District.

1896 Roll, Page 5, #114, Malinda J. Beck, Canadian District.

Com'r. C. R. Breckinridge: The applicant applies for the enrollment of himself and wife: The application of the orphan child will be taken up on a separate card. He and his wife are both identified on the rolls of 1880 and 1896, he as an adopted Cherokee, he being a white man, and his wife as a Cherokee by blood. They have lived in the Cherokee Nation ever since their marriage in 1870 and they will now be listed for enrollment, he as a Cherokee by intermarriage and his wife as a Cherokee by blood.

The undersigned, being sworn, states that as stenographer to the Commission to the Five Civilized Tribes, he correctly recorded the testimony and proceedings in this case, and that the foregoing is a true and complete transcript of his stenographic notes thereof.

R R Cravens

Subscribed and sworn to before me
this 15th day of Febuary[sic], 1901.

TB Needles
COMMISSIONER.

◇◇◇◇◇

Cherokee 7279.

Department of the Interior,
Commission to the Five Civilized Tribes,
Muskogee, I. T., September 29, 1902.

In the matter of the application of William B. Beck for the enrollment of himself as a citizen by intermarriage, and for the enrollment of his wife, Malinda J. Beck, as a citizen by blood of the Cherokee Nation; he being sworn and examined by the Commission, testified as follows:

Q What is your name? A William B. Beck.
Q What is your age? A 54.
Q What is your postoffice? A Fawn.
Q Are you the same William B. Beck who made application to the Commission for enrollment on February 15, 1901? A Yes sir.
Q What is your wife's name? A Malinda J.
Q Is she a citizen by blood? A Yes sir.
Q When were you and Malinda J. married? A We were first married in '66 and intermarried in '70 or '71, I am not positive now.
Q Were you ever married before you married this wife? A No sir.
Q Was she ever married? A No sir.
Q She is your first wife and you are her first husband? A Yes sir.
Q Have you and she lived together continuously from the time of your marriage as husband and wife? A We have.
Q Have you ever been separated? A Never.

Q And you have never married any other woman since your marriage to this woman? A No sir.

Q You and she are living together a husband and wife on the first day of September, 1902? A Yes sir.

Q How long have you lived in the Cherokee Nation, Mr. Beck? A I have lived here since '68, been living in the Cherokee Nation ever since continuously, excepting short times.

Q Those you go out for visits? A Yes, not over a month or six weeks at a time.

Q Has your wife been living with you in the nation all that time? A All the time, yes sir.

The undersigned, being duly sworn, states that as stenographer to the Commission to the Five Civilized Tribes he correctly recorded the testimony and proceedings in this case, and that the foregoing is a true and correct transcript of the stenographic notes thereof.

E.G. Rothenberger

Subscribed and sworn to before me this 16th day of October, 1902.

BC Jones
Notary Public.

◇◇◇◇◇

CHEROKEE-7279.

DEPARTMENT OF THE INTERIOR,
COMMISSIONER TO THE FIVE CIVILIZED TRIBES.
Muskogee, Indian Territory, January 5, 1907.

In the matter of making proof of the marriage of William B. Beck to his Cherokee wife, prior to November 1, 1875.

William B. Beck, being first duly sworn by B. P. Rasmus, a Notary Public, testified as follows:

COMMISSIONER:

Q. What is your name? A. William B. Beck.
Q. What is your age? A. 59.
Q. Do you claim to be a citizen by intermarriage of the Cherokee Nation? A. Yes sir.
Q. Through whom do you claim that right? A. Malinda J. Crittenden.

Cherokee Intermarried White 1906
Volume IV

Q. When were you married to her? A. First in 1866, and then intermarried with her in 1871.
Q. Where were you married the first time? A. In the State of Arkansas.
Q. Where the second time? A. In Going Snake District.
Q. Were you married under the Cherokee law either time? A. Yes sir, the last time.
Q. Have you got the license? A. No, I lost it.
Q. Were you ever married before you married Malinda J. Crittenden? A. No sir.
Q. Was she ever married before she married you? A. No sir.
Q. Where were you living at the time you were married the second time?
   A. In Going Snake District.
Q. Have you lived together continuously in the Cherokee Nation as man and wife since your second marriage? A. Yes sir.

(Commissioner -- Applicant is identified upon the 1880 Roll, Canadian District, opposite No. 1081. His wife, through whom he claims, is identified upon the 1880 Roll, in said District, opposite No. 1082; and also on the final roll of citizens by blood of the Cherokee Nation, opposite No. 17315.)

Q. What has become of your marriage license? A. I don't know. I got my license but they are worn out or misplaced in some way.
Q. You are sure that you got them in Going Snake District? A. Yes sir.
Q. Who issued them to you? A. John Thornton.
Q. Who married you the second time? A. Jusge[sic] Glover Thornton.
Q. When was the last time you saw your license? A. I couldn't remember.
Q. You know they are gone? A. Yes sir.
Q. Have you any witnesses here today who know of your second marriage? A. Not that I know of positively but my wife -- she is here. There are others here who know about it, but they were not present when we were married.

Witness excused.

Malinda J. Beck, being first duly sworn by B. P. Rasmus, a Notary Public, testified as follows:

COMMISSIONER:

Q. What is your name? A. Malinda J. Beck.
Q. How old are you? A. 56.
Q. What is your post office? A. Fawn.
Q. Do you know William B. Beck? A. Yes sir.
Q. What relation are you to him? A. I am his wife.
Q. When were you married to him? A. The first time was in '66.
Q. Where were you married in '66? A. In Arkansas.
Q. Where were you married the second time? A. In Going Snake District.
Q. Were you a citizen of the Cherokee Nation at the time of your marriage to William B. Beck? A. No sir, not in '66.

Q. When were you admitted to citizenship? A. Either in '69 or '70, and I don't remember which.

Q. Did you get a decree of the Court admitting you? A. My father had his whole family admitted. I was grown and married, but he had me admitted with the rest.

Q. You were remarried after you were admitted, under the Cherokee law? A. Yes sir.

Q. Were you ever married before you married William B. Beck? A. No sir.

Q. Have you lived in the Cherokee Nation continuously, as husband and wife, since your marriage in '66? A. Yes sir.

Q. Has William B. Beck been recognized as a citizen ever since he married you?
A. Yes sir.

Q. Voted in the Cherokee Nation? A. Yes sir.

Q. Held property in the Cherokee Nation? A. Yes sir.

Witness excused.

J. Frank Phillips, being first duly sworn by B. P. Rasmus, a Notary Public, testified as follows:

COMMISSIONER:

Q. What is your name? A. J. Frank Phillips.

Q. What is your age? A. 54.

Q. What is you post office address? A. Texana[sic].

Q. Are you acquainted with William B. Beck and Malinda J. Beck? A. Yes sir.

Q. How long have you known them? A. I have known her ever since I have known anybody. I lived right by her, and we are first cousins. I have always known her.

Q. Are you a citizen of the Cherokee Nation? A. Yes sir.

Q. By blood? A. Yes sir.

Q. Do you know when William B. Beck and Malinda J. Beck were married? I mean the second time? A. I know when it was, but I wasn't present.

Q. Do you know that they were married under the Cherokee law? A. That was the talk.

Q. Do you know when Malinda J. Beck was admitted to citizenship in the Cherokee Nation? A. No, I don't know exactly the date. I know that she was somewhere about '68 or '69. She was admitted to citizenship with Mose Crittenden and is family in '68 or '69

Q. Has William B. Beck been recognized as a citizen of the Cherokee Nation ever since his marriage to Malinda J. Beck? A. Yes sir.

Q. You have never heard his rights disputed in any manner? I never have. I have known of him being on juries and everything just the same as a Cherokee

Witness excused.

William B. Beck recalled.

I was once elected from Canadian District to the Cherokee National Council.

Q. When was that? A. It has been 10 or 12 years ago.

Witness excused.

Edward Still, being first duly sworn, before B. P. Rasmus, a Notary Public, testified as follows:

<u>COMMISSIONER:</u>

Q. What is your name? A. Edward Still.
Q. How old are you? A. 59.
Q. What is your post office address? A. Tahlequah.
Q. Do you know William B. Beck? A. Yes sir.
Q. And Malinda J. Beck? A. Yes sir.
Q. Do you know anything about their second marriage in Going Snake District? A. All I know was that they moved from Polk County Arkansas to the Cherokee Nation.
Q. Was Malinda J. Beck recognized as a citizen when she returned to the Nation? A. Yes sir.
Q. When was she admitted to citizenship after she returned? A. She was admitted when old man Mose Crittenden was admitted.
Q. When was that? A. Either in '68 or '69.
Q. Do you know anything of their second marriage? A. Only by hearsay. They claimed they had to be married the second time.
Q. Do you remember the circumstance of a petition being circulated for them? A. Yes sir.
Q. Did you sign his petition? A. I don't think I did.
Q. Do you know who did sign it? A. I think Black Still did. I heard him talking about it. He said that was the first white man's petition he ever signed.
Q. You heard him talking about it? A. Yes, we were all neighbors together.
Q. Has William Beck been recognized as a citizen by adoption of the Cherokee Nation ever since his marriage to Malinda J. Beck? A. Yes sir. I have seen him vote.
Q. When is the first time you remember to have seen him vote? A. I think he voted the time old man Thornton and old man Robins were elected.
Q. When was that? A. In '72 or '72. And he was a member of the National Council, too.

Witness excused.

Eula Jeanes Branson, being sworn, states that she correctly reported the proceedings had in the above and foregoing, on the 5th. day of January, 1907.

Eula Jeanes Branson

Subscribed and sworn to before me, this 7th. day of January, 1907.

Walter W. Chappell
Notary Public.

◇◇◇◇◇

C.F.B.   Cherokee 7279.

DEPARTMENT OF THE INTERIOR,
COMMISSIONER TO THE FIVE CIVILIZED TRIBES.
MUSKOGEE, I. T., JANUARY 7, 1907.

SUPPLEMENTAL PROCEEDINGS in the matter of the application for the enrollment of WILLIAM B. BECK as a citizen by intermarriage of the Cherokee Nation.

APPEARANCES: Applicant appears in person.
                           William Winton appears on behalf of applicant.
                           W. W. Hastings, Attorney for Cherokee Nation.

WILLIAM WINTON, being first duly sworn by John E. Tidwell, Notary Public, testified as follows:

ON BEHALF OF THE COMMISSIONER:

Q What is your name? A William Winton.
Q What is your age? A 55 or 56.
Q What is your post office address? A Peggs, Indian Territory.
Q Do you know a person in the Cherokee Nation by the name of William B. Beck?
      A Yes sir.
Q How long have you known him? A I have knowed[sic] Mr. Beck since I was a boy; it
      must be 35 years.
Q He is a married man, is he? A He is a married man.
Q Did you know him prior to his marriage? A Yes sir.
Q What was his wife's name? A Crittenden.
Q Is she living now? A Yes sir, I think she is living.
Q You knew her before their marriage, did you? A Yes sir.
Q Is she a Cherokee by blood? A She is a Cherokee by blood.
Q Was she so recognized at the time of their marriage? A Well, in the Indian Territory
      she was recognized as a citizen Cherokee by blood.
Q Were they married prior to their marriage in the Nation? A Yes sir
Q Where were they living? A Polk County, Arkansas.
Q When were they married in Arkansas? A I couldn't swear the date; they were married
      before I did.
Q After their marriage in Arkansas, did they remove to the Cherokee Nation?
      A Yes sir.
Q In what year did they remove to the Cherokee Nation? A I do not know exactly, it
      must have been about '67; somewhere in along there.

Q Was his wife, on coming to the Cherokee Nation, recognized as a citizen of the Nation, or was it necessary for her to go before the tribal authorities? A She was readmitted.

Q When? A I dont[sic] know just what date.

Q Soon after she came here with her husband? A Yes sir.

Q After her readmission, did her husband secure a license, and marry her in accordance with the laws of the Cherokee Nation? A He did, but I didn't see the license.

Q Did you witness the marriage? A Didn't witness the marriage.

Q It was generally understood, was it, by those who knew William B. Beck that he was married according to Cherokee law? A Yes sir, in that neighborhood; O[sic] was married first, and when I went to marry he said, 'tell that man Beck to come and get his license, for I am ready for him now.'

Q You didn't see the license? A No sir.

Q Do you know of your own personal knowledge that he has always exercised the rights of a citizen by intermarriage of the Cherokee Nation since his marriage to his wife after they came to the Cherokee Nation? A Yes sir.

The undersigned, being first duly sworn, states that as stenographer to the Commissioner to the Five Civilized Tribes, she correctly recorded the above and foregoing testimony, and that the same is a full, true and correct transcript of her stenographic notes thereof.

Sarah Waters

Subscribed and sworn to before me this 9th day of January, 1907.

John E. Tidwell
Notary Public.

◇◇◇◇◇

F.R.   Cherokee 7279.

DEPARTMENT OF THE INTERIOR,
COMMISSIONER TO THE FIVE CIVILIZED TRIBES,
Muskogee, Indian Territory, Jan. 14, 1907.

In the matter of the application for the enrollment of William B. Beck as a citizen by intermarriage of the Cherokee Nation.

Noah Wisenhunt, being first duly sworn by Frances R. Lane, a Notary Public for the Western District of Indian Territory, testified as follows:

By the Commissioner:

Q What is your name? A Noah Wisenhunt.

Q Your age? A Seventy-three.

Q And your postoffice address? A Oolagah, I. T.

Cherokee Intermarried White 1906
Volume IV

Q Do you know a person in the Cherokee nation by the name of William B. Beck?
A I do.

Q How long have you known him? A I have known him since 1860.

Q He is a married man, is he? A Yes sir.

Q Did you know him before he was married? A Yes, a short time

Q What was his wife's name? A His wife's name was Malinda Crittenden.

Q Is she living at this time? A She is, or was a few days ago

Q Did you know her before she was married to William B. Beck? A I did.

Q Is she a Cherokee by blood? A She is.

Q Was she so recognized at the time of her marriage to William B. Beck? A Yes sir.

Q Were they married prior to that marriage in the Cherokee Nation? A They was.

Q Do you know where they were living before coming to the Cherokee Nation>
A Yes sir; they was living in Polk County, Arkansas.

Q Do you know about what year they moved to the Cherokee Nation? A Along in 1868 I think. I know because he lived with me he lived in the house with me in 1869.

Q Do you know whether or not his wife, on coming to the Cherokee Nation, was recognized as a citizen of the Cherokee Nation the Nation, or was it necessary for her to go before the tribal authorities to be admitted? A No, I don't know.

Q Do you know whether or not William B. Beck and his wife, Matilda[sic] Crittenden, were married under a license of the Cherokee Nation? A I don't know of my own knowledge for certain.

Q You didn't witness the marriage ceremony? A No sir.

Q Was it generally understood by those who knew William B. Beck and his wife that they were remarried accordng[sic] to the Cherokee law? A Yes, that is what I always heard.

Q Who was married first, you or Mr. Beck? A Mr. Beck.

Q Did the Clerk say anything to you at the time you called for your license about Mr. Beck's license? A He did. He told me to tell Mr. Beck that his license or certificate, whatever it was, was ready. He could come and get it, or send and get it any time he wished.

Q That was Judge Thornton told you that? A Yes sir.

Q He was judge of what district at that time? A Going Snake.

Q You didn't see this license of Mr. Becks[sic]? A No, I didn't see it.

Q Do you know of your own personsl[sic] knowledge that Mr. Beck has always exercised the rights of a citizen by intermarriage of the Cherokee nation[sic] since his marriage? A I do.

Q Did you ever see him vote? A I have; I have sat with him on juries.[sic] in the Cherokee nation[sic].

Q Do you know whether or not he has ever held any office in the Cherokee nation? A I don't believe he did.--Yes, he was a member of the Cherokee council. I voted for him.

Q In what years. A Well, I would have to study--about 10 or 12 years ago.

Cherokee Intermarried White 1906
Volume IV

Frances R. Lane upon oath states that as stenographer to the Commissioner to the Five Civilized Tribes she reported the testimony in the above entitled cause and that the foregoing is an accurate transcript of her stenographic notes thereof.

Frances R Lane

Subscribed and sworn to before me this January 16, 1907.

Edward Merrick
Notary Public.

◇◇◇◇◇

F.R.   Cherokee 7279.

DEPARTMENT OF THE INTERIOR,

COMMISSIONER TO THE FIVE CIVILIZED TRIBES.

In the matter of the application for the enrollment of William B. Beck as a citizen by intermarriage of the Cherokee Nation.

D E C I S I O N .

THE RECORDS OF THIS OFFICE SHOW: That February 15, 1901, application was received by the Commission to the Five Civilized Tribes for the enrollment of William B. Beck as a citizen by intermarriage of the Cherokee Nation. Further proceedings in the matter of said application were had at Muskogee, Indian Territory, September 29, 1902, January 5, 1907, January 7, 1907, and January 14, 1907.

THE EVIDENCE IN THIS CASE SHOWS: That the applicant herein, William B. Beck, a white man, was married in accordance with the Cherokee law, in 1871, to his wife Malinda J. Beck, (nee Crittenden), who was at the time of said marriage a recognized citizen by blood of the Cherokee Nation, who is identified on the Cherokee authenticated tribal roll of 1880, Canadian District, No. 1082, as a native Cherokee, and whose name is included in the approved partial roll of citizens by blood of the Cherokee Nation opposite No. 17315. It is further shown that from the time of said marriage, the said William B. Beck and Malinda J. Beck resided together as husband and wife and continuously lived in the Cherokee Nation up to and including September 1, 1902. The said applicant is identified on the Cherokee authenticated tribal roll of 1880, and the Cherokee Census Roll of 1896, as an intermarried citizen of the Cherokee Nation.

IT IS, THEREFORE, ORDERED AND ADJUDGED: That in accordance with the decision of the Supreme Court of the United States, dated November 5, 1906, in the cases of Daniel Red Bird et al., vs. the United States, Nos. 125, 126, 127 and 128, the said applicant, William B. Beck is entitled, under the provisions of Section twenty-one of the Act of Congress approved June 28, 1898 (30 Stats., 495), to enrollment as a citizen by intermarriage of the Cherokee Nation, and his application for enrollment as such is accordingly granted.

Tams Bixby
Commissioner.

Dated at Muskogee, Indian Territory,
this　JAN 21 1907

◇◇◇◇◇

Cherokee 7279

Muskogee, Indian Territory, January 21, 1907.

W. W. Hastings,
　　Attorney for the Cherokee Nation,
　　　　Muskogee, Indian Territory.

Dear Sir:

　　There is enclosed herewith copy of the decision of the Commissioner to the Five Civilized Tribes, dated January 21, 1907, granting the application for the enrollment of William B. Beck as a citizen by intermarriage of the Cherokee Nation.

Respectfully,

Enc I-44　　　　　　　　　　　　　　　　Commissioner.

RPI

◇◇◇◇◇

Cherokee 7279

W.W.HASTINGS. ATTORNEY.　　OFFICE OF　　H.M. VANCE. SECRETARY.

Attorney for the Cherokee Nation,
Muskogee, I. T.　January 21, 1907.

The Commissioner to the Five Civilized Tribes,
　　Muskogee, Indian Territory.

Sir:

　　Receipt is acknowledged of the testimony and of your decision enrolling William B. Beck as a citizen by intermarriage of the Cherokee Nation. Time for protesting said decision is waived and I consent that said person may be placed upon the schedule immediately.

139

Respectfully,

W. W. Hastings
Attorney for the Cherokee Nation.

◇◇◇◇◇

Cherokee 7279

Muskogee, Indian Territory, January 24, 1907.

William B. Beck,
Fawn, Indian Territory.

Dear Sir:

There is enclosed herewith a copy of the decision of the Commissioner to the Five Civilized Tribes, dated January 21, 1907, granting your application for enrollment as a citizen by intermarriage of the Cherokee Nation.

Respectfully,

Encl. H-6   Commissioner.
JMH

Cher IW 118

◇◇◇◇◇

E.C.M.

DEPARTMENT OF THE INTERIOR,

COMMISSIONER TO THE FIVE CIVILIZED TRIBES.

In the matter of the application for the enrollment of

NAPOLEON B. BREEDLOVE

as a citizen by intermarriage of the Cherokee Nation.

CHEROKEE 158.

◇◇◇◇◇

DEPARTMENT OF THE INTERIOR,
COMMISSION TO THE FIVE CIVILIZED TRIBES,
FAIRLAND, I.T. JULY 12, 1900.

In the matter of the application of Napoleon B. Breedlove et als. for enrollment as citizens of the Cherokee Nation, said Breedlove being sworn by Commissioner Needles, testified:

Q What is your name? A Napoleon B. Breedlove.
Q How old are you? A 74.
Q What is your postoffice address? A Tahlequah.
Q Where do you reside? A Tahlequah now.
Q How long have you lived there? A Two years.
Q Where did you reisde[sic] before that? A Delaware district.
Q How long did you live there? A 20 years.
Q You have lived over 20 years continuously in the Cherokee Nation? A Yes sir.
Q Never made you residence at any time outside? A No sir.
Q Are you a Cherokee by blood? A No sir.
Q You apply for citizenship by intermarriage? A Yes.
Q Are you married? A Yes.
Q What was your wife's name? A Emily W Breedlove.
Q How long have you been married? A 43 years. (63)
Q Your name is upon the authenticated roll of '80? A Yes.
Q And hers also? A Yes.
> On 1880 roll, page 220 number 125, N.B. Breedlove.
> On 1880 roll, page 220, number 126 Emily W. Breedlove.
Q Have you any children under 21 years ol[sic] age living with you? A No.
Q You only apply then for admission for your wife and yourself?
> A That's all.
> Napoleon B. Breedlove page 565, number 30, on '96 roll, Delaware district;
> His wife, Emily Walker Breedlove, page 444, number 418, Delaware district, on '96 roll.

The name of Napoleon B. Breedlove and his wife, Emily Breedlove, appearing upon the authenticated rolls of 1880, and they having made satisfactory proof as to legal residence required, and they being identified upon the rolls of 1896 according to the number and page recited in this testimony, they are ordered admitted to Cherokee citizenship and their names will be entered upon the rolls now being made by this Commission of recognized citizens of the Cherokee Nation.

Brown McDonald, being sworn by Commissioner Needles, says as Stenographer to the Commission to the Five Civilized Tribes, he reported in full the testimony of the above named witness, and that the foregoing is a full, true and correct transcript of his testimony.

Brown McDonald

Sworn to and subscribed before me this 16th day of July, at Westville, Indian Territory.

TB Needles
Commissioner.

◇◇◇◇◇

R.
Cher. 158.

Department of the Interior.
Commission to the Five Civilized Tribes.
Tahlequah, I. T., September 30, 1902.

SUPPLEMENTAL TESTIMONY AND PROCEEDINGS in the matter of the application for the enrollment of NAPOLEON B. BREEDLOVE as a citizen by intermarriage of the Cherokee Nation.

NAPOLEON B. BREEDLOVE, being first duly sworn, and being examined, testified as follows:

BY COMMISSION: What is your name? A Napoleon B. Breedlove.
Q How old are you? A Seventy-seven.
Q What is your post office address? A Tahlequah.
Q You are a white man, are you? A Yes sir.
Q Have you heretofore made application to this Commission for enrollment as a citizen by intermarriage of the Cherokee Nation? A Yes sir.
Q What is the name of your wife? A Emily.
Q Full name Emily W.? A Emily Walker Wilson.
Q Is she living? A Yes sir.
Q Are you and she living together? A Yes sir.
Q She is a Cherokee by blood? A Yes sir.
Q Do you claim your right to enrollment by reason of your marriage to her? A Yes sir.
Q When were you married? A In 1857.
Q Have you and she lived together continuously since that time? A Yes sir.
Q Are you living together now? A Yes sir.
Q Have you resided in the Cherokee Nation continuously since the date of your application for enrollment? A Yes sir.
Q Were you ever married before you married her? A No sir.
Q Was she ever married before she married you? A No sir.

This testimony will be filed with and made a part of the record in the matter of the application for the enrollment of Napoleon B. Breedlove as a citizen by intermarriage of the Cherokee Nation, Cherokee straight card field No. 158.

Wm. Hutchinson, being first duly sworn, states that as stenographer to the Commission to the Five Civilized Tribes he correctly recorded the testimony and proceedings in this case, and that the foregoing is a true and complete transcript of the stenographic notes thereof.

Wm Hutchinson

Subscribed and sworn to before me this 30th day of September, 1902.

John O Rosson
Notary Public.

◇◇◇◇◇

CHEROKEE-158.

DEPARTMENT OF THE INTERIOR,
COMMISSIONER TO THE FIVE CIVILIZED TRIBES.
Muskogee, Indian Territory, January 2, 1907.

In the matter of making proof of the marriage of Napoleon B. Breedlove to his Cherokee wife, prior to November 1, 1875.

Napoleon B. Breedlove, being first duly sworn by B. P. Rasmus, a Notary Public, testified as follows:

COMMISSIONER:

Q. What is your name? A. Napoleon B. Breedlove.
Q. What is your age? A. 81.
Q. What is your post office address? A. Tahlequah.
Q. Do you claim to be a citizen by intermarriage of the Cherokee Nation? A. Yes sir.
Q. Through whom do you claim your right to enrollment as a citizen by intermarriage of the Cherokee Nation? A. My wife.
Q. What is her name? A. Emily W. Wilson.
Q. When were you and Emily W. Breedlove married? A. October 1, 1857.
Q. Where were you living at that time? A. In the Choctaw Nation My wife lived in the Cherokee Nation.
Q. Were you married under a license in the Choctaw Nation? A. We were married first in the Choctaw Nation under a preacher, a man by the name of Thomas Mitchell, but in the fall of '68 we moved over from the Choctaw Nation into the Cherokee Nation and we were married there gain.
Q. Under a license? A. Yes sir.
Q. Have you got that license? A No sir, it was destroyed with all of our papers.

143

Q. Have you got a certificate of marriage at the time? A. We had one, but it was destroyed, also.

Q. Where did you get that license? A. The one in the Cherokee Nation?

Q. Yes sir? A. We got it from down in Sequoyah District, before Judge Fortner.

Q. Had you ever been married prior to your marriage to your present wife? A. No sir.

Q. Had she ever been married prior to her marriage to you? A. No sir. I have known her ever since she was a little girl.

Q. You have lived together as husband and wife continuously from the time of your marriage in '57 in the Cherokee Nation up to the present time? A. Yes sir.

Q. Was your wife a Cherokee citizen at the time of your marriage to her in '57? A. Yes sir.

Q. When was the first time she was enrolled as a Cherokee citizen? A. When she was born.

Q. She was a duly recognized citizen of the Cherokee Nation at the time of your marriage to her? A. Yes sir.

Q. Is there anyone here today, besides yourselves, who knows of your marriage to Emily W. Breedlove? A. No, not here. There is one party that lives in Virginia now. She is part Cherokee, and she was at our wedding, and was one of the bridesmaids.

Q. What is her name? A. Her name at that time was Alice Lynd. Now she is Mrs. Dr. Owne[sic].

Q. Do you think you could get a certificate from her as to your marriage? A. Yes sir, I know I could.

Q. I wish you would furnish a statement from Alice Lynd, stating that she was present at your wedding? A. All right.

Q. Is there any one who was present at your second wedding? The one in the Cherokee Nation? A. No, I don't think so. The judge is dead.

Witness excused.

Emily Breedlove, being duly sworn by B. P. Rasmus, a Notary Public, testified as follows:

COMMISSIONER:

Q. What is your name? A. Emily Breedlove.

Q. How old are you? A. I am 71.

Q. Are you the wife of Napoleon B. Breedlove? A. Yes sir.

Q. When were you first married to Napoleon B. Breedlove? A. I believe it was in 1857.

Q. Were you married to Napoleon B. Breedlove a second time, under the Cherokee laws? A. Yes sir.

Q. When was that? A. I don't know when it wa. I don't remember what year it was.

Q. Was it prior to November 1, 1875? A. I think it was.

Q. Do you know? A. No, I don't know.

Q. Can you furnish the Commissioner with evidence of your marriage to Napoleon B. Breedlove under the Cherokee laws prior to November 1, 1875? A. Yes sir.

Q. I wish you would supply that evidence if possible showing that you were married under a license issued by the duly constituted authority of the Cherokee Nation.

(Commissioner -- Applicant is identified upon the 1880 Roll opposite No. 125, as a citizen by intermarriage. His wife is identified on the 1880 Roll opposite No. 126, as a citizen by blood; she is also identified upon the final roll of Cherokee citizens by blood opposite No. 526.)

Witness excused.

Eula Jeanes Branson, being sworn, states that she correctly reported the proceedings had in the above and foregoing on the 2nd. day of January, 1907.

Eula Jeanes Branson

Subscribed and sworn to before me, this 3rd. day of January, 1907

Walter W. Chappell
Notary Public.

◇◇◇◇◇

C. F. B.   Cherokee 158.

DEPARTMENT OF THE INTERIOR,
COMMISSION TO THE FIVE CIVILIZED TRIBES.
Muskogee, Indian Territory, January 9, 1907.

Supplemental proceedings in the Matter of the Application for the Enrollment of Napoleon B. Breedlove as A citizen by intermarriage of the Cherokee Nation.

W. W. Breedlove being first duly sworn by John E. Tidwell, Notary Public, testified as follows:

Q What is your name?   A W. W. Breedlove.
Q What is your age?   A 46 the 12th of this month.
Q What is your post office address?
A Ogeechee.
Q Are you a citizen by blood of the Cherokee Nation?
A Yes sir.
Q What is your father's name?
A Napoleon B. Breedlove.
Q You appear here to-day for the purpose of giving testimony relative to his right to enrollment as a citizen by intermarriage of the Cherokee Nation?
A Yes sir.

Q He is not a Cherokee by blood?

A No sir.

Q Is he living at this time?   A Yes sir.

Q The only claim he makes to the right to enrollment as a citizen by intermarriage of the Cherokee Nation is by virtue of his marriage to your mother?

A Yes sir.

Q Is your mother living?

A Yes sir.

Q What is her name?   A Emily Breedlove.

Q She is a citizen by blood?   A Yes sir.

Q Do you know when your father and mother were first married?

A No sir.

Q Is it your understanding that they were living in the Cherokee Nation when they were married the first time?

A They lived in the Choctaw Nation. Mother lived in the Cherokee Nation and father was working in the Choctaw Nation when they were married and they lived in the Choctaw Nation.

Q Where were you born?   A In the Choctaw Nation.

Q Do you remember when your parents came to the Cherokee Nation?

A No, I don't recollect.

Q Do you remember of your father and mother after their coming to the Cherokee Nation, being married in accordance to the laws of the Cherokee Nation?

A Yes sir.

Q How old was[sic] you?

A About 7 years old; I think it was in '69.

Q You witnessed the marriage, did you?

A Yes sir; and there was two other children present but they are both dead.

Q Since that time, has your father, Napoleon B. Breedlove been recognized by the tribal authorities as a citizen by intermarriage of the Cherokee Nation?

A Yes sir.

Q He has exercised all the rights and enjoyed all the privileges of that class of citizens?

A Yes sir.

Q Do you know of your own personal knowledge that he has voted in the elections?

A Yes sir.

Q Has he ever held office?

A He had charge of the Cherokee Female Seminary at one time for two years.

Q In what district were your parents married in accordance with the Cherokee laws?

A Sequoyah District.

Q In what year?

A In the fall of '68 I think.

Q Are there any people living who were present at that marriage ceremony besides yourself A Yes, I think there is a woman, - my uncle's wife; I think she is living.

Q Why did your father or mother not appear for the purpose of giving testimony in this case?

A They were here the last day of the year I think.

Q They have appeared and given testimony?

A I understand they have. I got a letter from a party telling me that my evidence in this matter would probably be of some help. They live at Tahlequah and I live up above Vinita. I haven't seen them at all.

Q You were not old enough at the time they were married to know about your father securing a license?

A No, I wouldn't have known but he was married by the district judge, Judge Falkner.

Q The Judge is dead?

A Yes, he was an old man then.

The undersigned being first duly sworn states that as stenographer to the Commission to the Five Civilized Tribes, she recorded the testimony taken in this case and that the foregoing is a full, true and correct transcript of the stenographic notes thereof.

Myrtle Hill

Subscribed and sworn to before me this the 14th day of January, 1907.

John E. Tidwell
Notary Public.

◇◇◇◇◇

E.C.M.   Cherokee 158.

DEPARTMENT OF THE INTERIOR,

COMMISSIONER TO THE FIVE CIVILIZED TRIBES.

In the matter of the application for the enrollment of NAPOLEON B. BREEDLOVE as a citizen by intermarriage of the Cherokee Nation.

D E C I S I O N

THE RECORDS OF THIS OFFICE SHOW: That on July 12, 1900, application was received by the Commission to the Five Civilized Tribes for the enrollment of Napoleon B. Breedlove as a citizen by intermarriage of the Cherokee Nation. Further proceedings in the matter of said application were had at Tahlequah, Indian Territory, September 30, 1902, and at Muskogee, Indian Territory, January 2 and 9, 1907.

THE EVIDENCE IN THIS CASE SHOWS: That the applicant herein, Napoleon B. Breedlove, a white man, was married in accordance with Cherokee law in the year 1868 to his wife, Emily W. Breedlove, nee Wilson, who was at the time of said marriage a recognized citizen by blood of the Cherokee Nation, who is identified on the Cherokee

Cherokee Intermarried White 1906
Volume IV

authenticated tribal roll of 1880, Delaware District, Page 220, No. 126, as a native Cherokee, and whose name is included in the approved partial roll of citizens by blood of the Cherokee Nation, opposite No. 526. It is further shown that from the time of said marriage the said Napoleon B. Breedlove and Emily W. Breedlove resided together as husband and wife, and continuously lived in the Cherokee Nation up to and including September 1, 1902. Said applicant is identified on the Cherokee authenticated tribal roll of 1880, and the Cherokee census roll of 1896, as an intermarried citizen of the Cherokee Nation.

IT IS, THEREFORE, ORDERED AND ADJUDGED: That in accordance with the decision of the Supreme Court of the United States, dated November 5, 1906, in the cases of Daniel Red Bird et al. vs. the United States, Nos. 125, 126, 127 and 128, the said applicant, Napoleon B. Breedlove, is entitled, under the provisions of Section 21, of the Act of Congress approved June 28, 1898 (30 Stats., 495), to enrollment as a citizen by intermarriage of the Cherokee Nation, and his application for enrollment as such is accordingly granted.

Tams Bixby
Commissioner.

Dated at Muskogee, Indian Territory,
this   JAN 29 1907

◇◇◇◇◇

Cherokee 158

Muskogee, Indian Territory, January 29, 1907.

W. W. Hastings,
        Attorney for the Cherokee Nation,
                Muskogee, Indian Territory.

Dear Sir:

There is enclosed herewith copy of the decision of the Commissioner to the Five Civilized Tribes, dated January 29, 1907, granting the application for the enrollment of Napoleon B. Breedlove, as a citizen by intermarriage of the Cherokee Nation.

Respectfully,

Enc I-29   Commissioner.

RPI

◇◇◇◇◇

148

Cherokee 158

Muskogee, Indian Territory, January 29, 1907.

The Commissioner to the Five Civilized Tribes,
Muskogee, Indian Territory,

Sir:

Receipt is acknowledged of the testimony and of your decision enrolling Napoleon B. Breedlove, as a citizen by intermarriage of the Cherokee Nation. Time for protesting said decision is waived, and I consent that said person may be placed upon the schedule immediately.

Respectfully,

W. W. Hastings
Attorney for the Cherokee Nation.

◇◇◇◇◇

Cherokee 158

Muskogee, Indian Territory, January 29, 1907.

Napoleon B. Breedlove,
Tahlequah, Indian Territory.

Dear Sir:

There is enclosed herewith copy of the decision of the Commissioner to the Five Civilized Tribes, dated January 29, 1907, granting the application for your enrollment as a citizen by intermarriage of the Cherokee Nation.

You will be advised when your name has been placed upon a schedule of citizens of the Cherokee Nation and approved by the Secretary of the Interior.

Respectfully,

Enc I-30   Commissioner.

RPI

Cher IW 119

◇◇◇◇◇

Cherokee Intermarried White 1906
Volume IV

CFB

DEPARTMENT OF THE INTERIOR,

COMMISSIONER TO THE FIVE CIVILIZED TRIBES.

———————

In the matter of the application for the enrollment of

JAMES C. GARNER

as a citizen by intermarriage of the Cherokee Nation.

———————

CHEROKEE 264.

◇◇◇◇◇

264

DEPARTMENT OF THE INTERIOR,
COMMISSION TO THE FIVE CIVILIZED TRIBES,
WESTVILLE, I. T., JULY 17, 1900.

In the matter of the application of James C. Garner for enrollment as Cherokee citizen, said Garner being sworn by Commissioner Needles testified as follows:

Q What is your name? A James C. Garner.
Q What is your age? A 55.
Q What is your postoffice address? A Westville.
Q Where do you live? A About five miles west of here.
Q In what District? A Goingsnake.
Q How long have you lived there? A 2 years.
Q Where did you live before? A I had no permanent home; I lived in the Cherokee Nation.
Q How long have you lived in the Cherokee Nation? A 32 years.
Q Have you ever lived out of it? A No sir, not permanently.
Q When did you live out of the Cherokee Nation the last time? A In '78.
Q Have you been living here continuously since '78? A Yes,
Q Are you a Cherokee? A No sir.
Q What do you make application for then? A For citizenship in intermarriage.
Q Does your name appear upon the authenticated roll of '80? A I suppose it does.
On '80 roll page 435, number 762 as James Garner, Goingsnake district.
Q Are you married? A No sir.
Q You apply for enrollment of anyone but yourself? A No sir.
Q You have no children? A No sir.

150

The name of James C. Garner appearing upon the authenticated roll of 1880 of the Cherokee Nation, page and number as indicated in this testimony, and he having made sufficient proof of his actual residence, he is ordered enrolled as a Cherokee citizen by intermarriage, and his name will be entered upon the rolls of the Commission now being made.

On '96 roll, page 822, number 81, as James C. Garner, Goingsnake district.

Q When were you first married? A '69.
Q When did you wife die? A '78.
Q Have you married since? A Once, yes.
Q Whom did you marry the last time? A Rosanna Kelly.
Q A white woman? A No sir, Cherokee.
Q You have no[sic] married since '80? A No sir.

Brown McDonald, being sworn by Commissioner Needles, says as Stenographer to the Commission to the Five Civilized Tribes, he reported in full the testimony of the above named witness, and that the foregoing is a full, true and correct transcript of his notes.

Brown McDonald

Sworn to and subscribed before me this 17th day of July, 1900.

T. B. Needles,
Commissioner.

◇◇◇◇◇

264

Department of the Interior,
Commission to the Five Civilized Tribes,
Muskogee, I. T., September 3, 1902.

I, the undersigned, a stenographer to the Commission to the Five Civilized Tribes, hereby certify on my official oath that the foregoing is a true and complete copy of a certified copy on file in the office of the Commission.

Maud Cotner

Subscribed and sworn to before me this the 3rd day of September, 1902.

BC Jones
Notary Public.

◇◇◇◇◇

Statement of Applicant Taken Under Oath.

CHEROKEE BY BLOOD AND ADOPTION.

55th   Date   July 17,   1900.

Name   James C Garner

District   G. Snake   Year   1880   Page   435   No.   762

Citizen by blood   No   Mother's citizenship   U.S.

Intermarried citizen   Yes

Married under what law..Date of marriage...........

License .... Certificate.......................

Wife's name..............

District..Year..............Page ....No. ....

Citizen by blood..............................Mother's citizenship..............

Intermarried citizen..............

Married under what law..Date of marriage..........

License .... Certificate..............

       Names of Children:

Dist.	Year	Page	No.	Age	
Dist.	Year	Page	No.	Age	
Dist.	Year	Page	No.	Age	
Dist.	Year	Page	No.	Age	
Dist.	Year	Page	No.	Age	

#1 on 1880 Roll as James Garner, also on 1896 Roll as James C. Garner

Card #264

◇◇◇◇◇

Card No. _____

Is residence of husband established?   Yes

Is he identified on the rolls of 1880 and 1896?   Yes

Is the marriage of his parents established? _____

If admitted, is his admission satisfactory? _____

If intermarried, is marriage established? _____

Is residence of wife established? _____

Is she identified on the rolls of 1880 and 1896? _____

Is the marriage of her parents established? _____

If admitted, is her admission satisfactory? _____

If intermarried, is marriage established? _____

Were parties for whom application is made all living?   Yes

Are all the children who were living when the roll of 1896 was compiled, and for whom application was made, identified on said roll?

_____

Birth affidavits filed since date of application _____

_____

New-borns enrolled since date of application _____

_____

Do the findings conform to the facts?   Yes

_____

_____

_____

◇◇◇◇◇

DEPARTMENT OF THE INTERIOR.
Commission to the Five Civilized Tribes.
Muskogee, Indian Territory, October 14th, 1902.

_____

In the matter of the application of James C. Garner for the enrollment of himself as a citizen by intermarriage of the Cherokee Nation.

_____

Supplemental to #264.

_____

Cherokee Nation appears by J. C. Starr.

_____

JAMES C. GARNER, being duly sworn, testified as follows:
Examination by the Commissions.
Q. What is your name? A. J. C. Garner.
Q. James C.? A. Yes, sir.
Q. How old are you? A. 57.

Q. What is your post office? A. Long, Indian Territory, my present postoffice. At the time I enrolled I was at Westville.

Q. You are a white man? A. Yes, sir.

Q. You are on the roll of 1880 as an intermarried citizen?
A. Yes, sir.

Q. What was your wife's name in 1880? A. Her name was Rosanna.

Q. Is she dead? A. No, sir.

Q. Are you living together? A. No, sir.

Q. How long did you and your wife continue to live together from 1880?
A. We separated in March, 1880.

Q. Was that before the eighty roll was prepared? A. No, sir.

Q. Was that after? A. Yes, sir; we were enrolled together.

Q. What was the cause of the separation? A. Well, she just simply took her duds and went home to her father.

Q. Did you ever give her any cause to leave you? A. Not that I know of. If I did I didn't do it intentionally.

Q. How long had you been married when she left you? A. About six months.

Q. Has she lived with you since? A. No, sir.

Q. Did you ever try to get her to come back? A. I did at the start but she wouldn't.

Q. Did she give any reason? A. No, sir.

Q. Do you know why she left you? A. Just because we didn't agree.

Q. What did you disagree about? A. It was just a family disagreement.

Q. Did you have any words? A. Not to amount to anything.

Q. Did she tell you she was going to leave you? A. Yes, sir.

Q. What did you say. A. I told her if she was going to leave she would have to go, I couldn't hold her.

Q. How long did you try to get her to come back? A. Oh, I don't know.

Q. She refused to come? A. She refused to come.

Q. Did you get a divorce? A. No, sir.

Q. Did she sue for a divorce? A. I don't know.

Q. Is she married again? A. Yes, sir.

Q. What is her husband's name? A. Her second husband is named Smith.

Q. White man or Cherokee? A. He was a white man.

Q. Are they living together now? A. No, sir; they separated.

Q. Have you ever married again since your separation? A. No, sir.

Q. Have you been living in the Cherokee Nation since 1880? A. Yes, sir.

Q. From 1880 up to this time? A. Yes, sir.

Examination by Mr. Starr.

Q. Where were you living when this separation took place?
A. In Goingsnake.

Q. Near what town? A. Near Cinnatti[sic].

Q. In the Cherokee Nation? A. Yes, sir.

Q. Did you have a place of your own? A. Yes, sir.

Q. How long had you been living on that place? A. 3 or 4 months.

Q. Where did you wife go to? A. To her fathers[sic].

Q. How far from your place? A. About half a mile from the place we lived on.

Cherokee Intermarried White 1906
Volume IV

Q. What was her father's name? A. Kelley.

Q. What was his first name? A. Joel.

Q. Did you go after her? A. Yes, sir.

Q. What did she say about coming back? A. Said she wouldn't live with me any more.

Q. Give any reason? A. Just said she didn't like to live with me.

Q. Where have you lived since that time? A. Lived partly in Goingsnake, partly in Sequoyah, partly in Cooweescoowee.

Q. Whose place were you living on at the time of the separation?

A. It was mine. It was mine and hers together. We bought it together.

Q. What became of the place? A. She sold it afterwards. I stayed there three days and nights after she left and she didn't come back.

Q. Where did you go.[sic] [sic] Eureka Springs and stayed there and worked and then come back.

Q. When did you come back? A. September, 1880.

Q. Have you been living in the Cherokee Nation since September, 1880? A. Yes, sir.

Q. Never been out to live any length of time? A. No, sir.

Q. How long after the separation was it before your wife married this man William Smith? A. I don't remember.

Q. Is he living now? A. I don't know. He went to Texas to his father. At least that is my understanding.

Q. What became of your wife? A. She married again.

Q. Who did she marry the last time? A. Married a man by the name of Joe Mounts.

Q. Where do they live? A. I don't know where they live. He did live, the last time I knew of him, on the Illinois river, across the river from the Berry Crittenden place; somewhere along there.

Q. You say you never sued your wife for a divorce? A. No, sir.

Q. She never brought suit against you? A. If she did I didn't know it. I never was subponaed[sic] to court.

Examination by the Commission.

Q. What is the name of the wife through whom you claim citizenship?

A. Her maiden name was Gatsy L. Parris.

Q. When did you marry her? A. In '69.

Q. How long did you live with her? A. I lived with her until she died.

Q. When did he die? A. She died in '78.

The applicant presents an original license issued by Aaron H. Beck, clerk of the district court of Goingsnake district, in 1869, granting authority for the marriage of one J. C. Garner to G. L. Parris. The certificate of marriage attached shows that the parties named in said license were married on the 18th of July, 1869, by George W. Whitmire, judge of the district court of Goingsnake district.

Jesse O. Carr, being first duly sworn, states that as stenographer to the Commission to the Five Civilized Tribes he reported the above entitled case and that the foregoing is a true and complete transcript of his stenographic notes thereof.

Jesse O. Carr

Subscribed and sworn to before me this 3rd day of January, 1903.

John O Rosson
Notary Public.

<><><><><>

C.F.B.   Cherokee 264.

DEPARTMENT OF THE INTERIOR,
COMMISSIONER TO THE FIVE CIVILIZED TRIBES.
MUSKOGEE, I. T., JANUARY 2, 1907.

In the matter of the application for the enrollment of James C. Garner as a citizen by intermarriage of the Cherokee Nation.

Applicant appears in person.

APPEARANCES:

Cherokee Nation represented by H. M. Vance,
on behalf of W. W. Hastings, Attorney.

JAMES C. GARNER, being first duly sworn by B. P. Rasmus, notary public, testified as follows:

ON BEHALF OF THE COMMISSIONER:

Q What is your name? A James C. Garner.
Q What is your age? A 61 years old.
Q What is your post office address? A Westville.
Q Are you an applicant for enrollment as a citizen by intermarriage of the Cherokee Nation? A Yes sir.
Q You have no Cherokee blood? A None that I know of.
Q The only claim you make to the right to enrollment as a citizen by intermarriage of the Cherokee Nation is by virtue of a marriage to a citizen by blood of the Cherokee Nation, is it? A Yes sir.
Q What is the name of the citizen? A Gatsy L. Garner.
Q Is she living or dead? A She is dead.
Q When were you married to her? A I was married the 18th of July, 1869.
Q Where were you married? A I was married in Going Snake District, Cherokee Nation.
Q Was she a Cherokee citizen by blood at the time you married her.
    A Yes sir, acknowledged as such.
Q Were you ever married prior to your marriage to her.[sic] A No sir.
Q Was she ever married prior to her marriage to you? A No sir.
Q When did she die? A She died the 14th of December, 1878.

Q From the time of your marriage to her did you and she continuously reside together as husband and wife until the time of her death? A We did.

Q And lived in the Cherokee Nation, did you? A Yes sir.

Q Have you married since her death? A Yes sir.

Q What is the name of your present wife? A I have no wife now; we separated; her name was Rosanna Kelley.

Q When did you marry her? A I married her in September, '79.

Q Was she a citizen by blood of the Cherokee Nation? A Yes sir.

Q How long did you and she live together as husband and wife?
    A 6 months, something like that.

Q Did you leave her, or did she leave you? A She left me.

Q Did she secure a divorce? A No sir, not that I know of.

Q Did you secure a divorce? A No sir, I did not.

Q Was there any serious trouble between you and your second wife prior to the time she left you? A No sir.

Q She just left you without any particular cause? A Yes sir, she just pulled up and left.

Q Did she give you any reason for leaving you? A No sir, she just said she was going to leave, and that was all there was to it.

Q Do you know of any reason for her leaving you? A No sir.

Q Since your marriage to your first wife, Gatsy L., have you continuously lived in the Cherokee Nation? A The Cherokee Nation is my home; I have been outside the Cherokee Nation working, but it has been my home.

Q Do you own property here? A No sir, I did at the death of my first wife, but I sold that.

Q What was the longest period of time that you were ever absent from the Cherokee Nation? A Well, I cannot say; I will have to study and see what was the longest period. Five months, during the summer of 1880.

Q That was the longest period of time that you were ever absent from the Cherokee Nation? That was simply a temporary absence, and you considered the Cherokee Nation your home? A Yes sir; I had two children living and they were both here. I considered the Cherokee Nation my home.

There is on file in this case a certified copy of marriage licence[sic] and certificate, showing that in the year 1869 license was granted J. C. Garner, an unmarried citizen of the United States, to marry Miss G. L. Parris, a Cherokee citizen, by Haron[sic] H. Beck, Clerk, District Court, Going Snake District; and that, in accordance with the terms of said license, said parties were united in marriage July 18, 1869, by George W. Whitmire, Judge of the District Court.

BY H. M. VANCE:

Q Is your second wife living? A So far as I know, she is.

Q Where was she living when you last heard of her? A She was living on the Illinois River, Going Snake District, Cherokee Nation.

Q What is her post office address? A I couldn't answer that question.

Q Do you know her present name? A She was living with a man named Joe Mountz when I last heard.

Q Have you married since you and she separated? A No sir.

Q What is her given name? A Rosanna.

ON BEHALF OF THE COMMISSIONER:

The applicant, James C. Garner, is identified on the authenticated Cherokee tribal roll of 1880, Going Snake District, No. 762.

The undersigned, being first duly sworn, states that as stenographer to the Commissioner to the Five Civilized Tribes, she correctly reported the above and foregoing testimony, and that the same is a full, true and correct transcript of her stenographic notes thereof.

Sarah Waters

Subscribed and sworn to before me this 4th day of Jan. 1907.

John E. Tidwell
Notary Public.

◇◇◇◇◇

(The Marriage License and Certificate below typed as given.)

Cherokee Nation)
Goingsnake Dist)

1869

bee it known that authority is hereby granted to any of the Judges and all ministers of all evangical denominations having the care of souls to solemnise the rights of matrimony acording to the cerimonies usually observed in such case between J. C. Garner an unmarried citizen of the United States to Miss G. L. Parris a Cherok Citizen he the said G. L. Garner havin complied with the law in such cases

)
) Haron H Beck Clk Dist Court
)

Cherokee Nation)
Goingsnake Dist)

this will sertify that I have this day performed the duties injoined by matrimony between Mr J. C. Garner to Miss J. L. Parris he the said Garner having complied with the law in such case

July, 18/ 69

) George W. Whitmire
) Judge Dist Court

Department of the Interior,
Commission to the Five Civilized Tribes,
Muskogee, I. T.,-------------------

I, the undersigned, Chief Clerk of the Cherokee Enrollment Division of the Commission to the Five Civilized Tribes and custodian of the records of said Division, do hereby certify that the above and foregoing is a true and correct copy of the original on file in the office of the said Division.

PG Reuter
Chief Clerk Cherokee Division.

Sworn to and subscribed before me this 18th day of October, 1902.

BC Jones
Notary Public.

◇◇◇◇◇

CFB

Cherokee 264.

DEPARTMENT OF THE INTERIOR,

COMMISSIONER TO THE FIVE CIVILIZED TRIBES.

In the matter of the application for the enrollment of JAMES C. GARNER as a citizen by intermarriage of the Cherokee Nation.

D E C I S I O N

THE RECORDS OF THIS OFFICE SHOW: That at Westville, Indian Territory, October 17, 1900, application was received by the Commission to the Five Civilized Tribes for the enrollment of James C. Garner as a citizen by intermarriage of the Cherokee Nation. Further proceedings in the matter of said application were had at Muskogee, Indian Territory, October 14, 1902, and January 2, 1907.

THE EVIDENCE IN THIS CASE SHOWS: That the applicant herein, James C. Garner, a white man, was married in accordance with Cherokee law July 18, 1869, to his wife, Gatsy L. Garner, nee Parris, since deceased, who was at the time of said marriage a recognized citizen by blood of the Cherokee Nation; that the said James C. and Gatsy L. Garner resided together as husband and wife until her death which occurred December

159

14, 1878; that subsequent to the death of the said Gatsy L. Garner said James C. Garner in September, 1879, was married to one Rosanna Kelley, who was at the time of said marriage a recognized citizen by blood of the Cherokee Nation, and who is identified o the Cherokee Authenticated tribal roll of 1880, Going Snake District, page 435, No. 763, as a native Cherokee; that the said James C. and Rosanna Garner resided together as husband and wife for a period of about five months, when the said Rosanna Garner left said James C. Garner without other cause than an apparent dislike for her husband; that although said James C. Garner has attempted to induce said Rosanna Garner to return to him she has not done so, and that since said separation they have lived separate and apart; that said James C. Garner has not remarried, and that he has resided continuously in the Cherokee Nation since July 18, 1869.

Said applicant is duly identified on the Cherokee Authenticated tribal roll of 1880, and the Cherokee Census roll of 1896 as an intermarried citizen of the Cherokee Nation.

In view of the foregoing, it is considered that, following the ruling of the Department in the case of Andrew Brimmer (I.T.B. 3299-02), the right to citizenship in the Cherokee Nation acquired by said applicant by virtue of his marriage to Gatsy L. Parris July 18, 1869, has not been forfeited or lost.

IT IS, THEREFORE, ORDERED AND ADJUDGED: That in accordance with the decision of the Supreme Court of the United States, dated November 5, 1906, in the case of Daniel Red Bird, et al. vs. the United States, Nos. 125, 126, 127 and 128, the said applicant, James C. Garner, is entitled under the provisions of Section 21, of the Act of Congress, approved June 28, 1898 (30 Stats., 495), to enrollment as a citizen by intermarriage of the Cherokee Nation, and his application for enrollment as such is accordingly granted.

Tams Bixby
Commissioner.

Dated at Muskogee, Indian Territory,
this   JAN 29 1907

◇◇◇◇◇

Cherokee 264

Muskogee, Indian Territory, October 21, 1902.

J. C. Garner,
    Westville, Indian Territory.

Dear Sir:-

The marriage license and certificate showing your marriage on July 18, 1869, to Miss G. L. Parris, is herewith returned to you, a copy having been made and retained in the Commission's files.

Respectfully,

Enc. M-103 3/4   Acting Chairman.

◇◇◇◇◇

Cherokee
264

Muskogee, Indian Territory, December 21, 1906.

James C. Garner,
        Long, Indian Territory.

Dear Sir:

November 6, 1906, the United States Supreme Court held that white persons who intermarried with Cherokee citizens according to Cherokee law prior to November 1, 1875, are entitled to enrollment and allotments of land as citizens of the Cherokee Nation.

You are advised that to properly determine your right to enrollment as a citizen by intermarriage of the Cherokee Nation, it will be necessary for you to appear before the Commissioner for the purpose of giving testimony as to the date of your marriage and whether or not your wife, by reason of your marriage to whom you claim the right to enrollment as a citizen of the Cherokee Nation, was a recognized citizen of the Cherokee Nation at the time of your marriage to her, and whether or not you were married to her in accordance with Cherokee laws.

You are therefore directed to appear before the Commissioner at Muskogee, Indian Territory, at 9 o'clock A. M., on Thursday, January 3, 1907, and give testimony as above indicated.

Respectfully,

H.J.C.   Acting Commissioner.

◇◇◇◇◇

Cherokee 264

Muskogee, Indian Territory, January 29, 1907.

W. W. Hastings,
        Attorney for the Cherokee Nation,
                Muskogee, Indian Territory.

Dear Sir:

There is enclosed herewith copy of the decision of the Commissioner to the Five Civilized Tribes, dated January 29, 1907, granting the application for the enrollment of James C. Garner as a citizen by intermarriage of the Cherokee Nation.

Respectfully,

Enc I-422   Commissioner.

RPI

◇◇◇◇◇

Cherokee 264

Muskogee, Indian Territory, January 29, 1907.

The Commissioner to the Five Civilized Tribes,
Muskogee, Indian Territory.

Sir:

Receipt is acknowledged of the testimony and of your decision enrolling James C. Garner as a citizen by intermarriage of the Cherokee Nation. Time for protesting said decision is waived and I consent that said person may be placed upon the schedule immediately.

Respectfully,
W. W. Hastings
Attorney for the Cherokee Nation.

◇◇◇◇◇

Cherokee 264

Muskogee, Indian Territory, January 29, 1907.

James C. Garner,
Long, Indian Territory.

Dear Sir:

There is enclosed herewith copy of the decision of the Commissioner to the Five Civilized Tribes, dated January 29, 1907, granting the application for your enrollment as a citizen by intermarriage of the Cherokee Nation.

You will be advised when your name has been placed upon a schedule of citizens of the Cherokee Nation and approved by the Secretary of the Interior.

Respectfully,

Enc I-24   Commissioner.

RPI

◇◇◇◇◇

23033-1911
Cherokee 264

Muskogee, Oklahoma, August 3, 1911.

Mr. James C. Garner,
     Westville, Oklahoma.

Sir:-

     In compliance with a request made on your behalf by District Agent Charles Wilson, of Westville, there is inclosed herewith your marriage license and certificate, same having been filed in the matter of the application for your enrollment as a citizen of the Cherokee Nation.

Respectfully,

LS-3-5   Commissioner.

Cher IW 120

◇◇◇◇◇

E.C.M.

DEPARTMENT OF THE INTERIOR,

COMMISSIONER TO THE FIVE CIVILIZED TRIBES.

In the matter of the application for the enrollment of

MARY WARD

As a citizen by intermarriage of the Cherokee Nation.

CHEROKEE NO. 367.

◇◇◇◇◇

Cherokee Intermarried White 1906
Volume IV

Department of the Interior,
Commission to the Five Civilized Tribes,
Westville, I.T., July 19, 1900.

In the matter of the application of Daniel M. Ward for enrollment as a Cherokee by blood; being duly sworn and examined by Commissioner Breckenridge[sic], he testified as follows:

Q What is your name? A Daniel M. Ward.
Q What is your age? A I am 27, I am not that old on the roll.
Q What is your post office? A Siloam Spring, Ark.
Q Your district? A Going Snake.
Q For whom do you apply, Mr. Ward? A Myself and my mother.
Q Are you a Cherokee by blood? A Yes, sir.
Q How long have you lived in this district, all your life?
A I have been out fooling around in Cooweescoowee and Delaware Districts.
Q Been making it your home? A Yes, sir.
(On 1880 roll, page 494, No. 2057, Daniel Ward, Going Snake. On 1896 roll, page 806, No. 2386, as Daniel M. Ward, Going Snake district.)

Mr. Ward, you are duly identified on the roll of 1880, and on the roll of 1896, and your residence satisfactorily established, and you will be enrolled as a Cherokee by blood.

---------0---------

Bruce C. Jones, being duly sworn, says that as stenographer to the Commission to the Five Civilized Tribes he reported the testimony of the above named witness, and that the foregoing is a full, true and correct translation of his stenographic notes.

Bruce C. Jones

Sworn to and subscribed before me this the 19th day of July, 1900.

Clifton R Breckinridge
Commissioner.

◇◇◇◇◇

Cherokee Intermarried White 1906
Volume IV

Department of the Interior,
Commission to the Five Civilized Tribes,
Westville, I.T., July 19, 1900.

In the matter of the application for the enrollment of Mary Ward; Daniel M. Ward, being duly sworn and examined by Commissioner Breckenridge[sic], testified as follows:

Q What is your name? A Daniel M. Ward.
Q What is your post office? A Siloam Springs, Ark.
Q What district do you live in? A Going Snake district.
Q How long have you lived in this district? A All my life.
Q You apply now for your mother? A Yes, sir.
Q What is her full name? A Mary Ward.
Q What is her age? A 68 I believe.
Q Is she old and infirm and unable to apply for herself? A Yes, sir.
Q How long has she lived in this district? A I guess ever since she was about 18 or 20.
Q Does she live with you? A Yes, sir.
Q Is she a Cherokee by blood? A No, sir, by adoption.
Q Are sure she wasn't a Cherokee by blood, only by adoption? A Yes, sir.
Q How long has her name been Ward, since 1880? A Yes, sir.
(On 1880 roll, page 494, No. 2056, Mary Ward, Going Snake dist. On 1896 roll, page 833, No. 219, Mary ward, Going Snake dist.)

Your mother is duly identified on the roll of 1880 and likewise on the roll of 1896, her residence satisfactorily established, and she will be enrolled as a Cherokee by adoption.

---------0---------

Bruce D. Jones, being duly sworn, says that as stenographer to the Commission to the Five Civilized Tribes he reported the testimony of the above named witness, and that the foregoing is a full, true and correct translation of his stenographic notes.

Bruce C Jones

Sworn to and subscribed before me this the 19th day of July, 1900.

Clifton R. Breckinridge
Commissioner.

◇◇◇◇◇

H.
Cher. 367.

Department of the Interior.
Commission to the Five Civilized Tribes.
Tahlequah, I. T., October 6, 1902.

SUPPLEMENTAL TESTIMONY AND PROCEEDINGS in the matter of the application for the enrollment of MARY WARD as a citizen by intermarriage of the Cherokee Nation.

MARY WARD, being first duly sworn, and being examined, testified as follows:

BY COMMISSION: What is your name? A Mary Ward.
Q How old are you? A Going on seventy-one years old.
Q What is your post office address? A Siloam Springs, Arkansas.
Q Are you a white woman? A Yes sir.
Q Have you heretofore made application to this Commission for enrollment as a citizen by intermarriage of the Cherokee Nation? A Yes sir.
Q What is the name lf[sic] your husband? A Thomas.
Q Is he living? A No sir, he is dead, he has been dean about twenty-four years.
Q Was he a Cherokee by blood? A Yes sir.
Q When were you and he married? A Married in 1851.
Q Had you lived together continuously from the date of your marriage until the time of his death? A Yes sir.
Q Do you claim your right to enrol,ment[sic] by reason of your marriage to him? A Yes sir.
Q Were you ever married before you married him? A No sir.
Q Was he ever married before he married you? A No sir.
Q Have you resided in the Cherokee Nation continuously since the date of your application for enrollment? A Yes sir.

> This testimony will be filed with and made a part of the record in the matter of the application for the enrollment of MARY WARD as a citizen by intermarriage of the Cherokee Nation, Cherokee straight card field No. 367.

Wm. Hutchinson, being first duly sworn, states that as stenographer to the Commission to the Five Civilized Tribes he correctly recorded the testimony and proceedings in this case, and that the foregoing is a true and complete transcript of the stenographic notes thereof.

Wm Hutchinson

Subscribed and sworn to before me this 9th day of October, 1902.

John O Rosson
Notary Public.

◇◇◇◇◇

Cherokee 367.

Department of the Interior,
Commission to the Five Civilized Tribes,
Tahlequah, I. T., May 29, 1903.

In the matter of the application of Daniel M. Ward for the enrollment of himself and his children, Thomas M. and George Ward, as citizens by blood, and for the enrollment of his mother, Mary Ward, as a citizen by intermarriage of the Cherokee Nation.

Daniel M. Ward, being duly sworn, and examined by the Commission, testified as follows:

Q What is your name? A Daniel M. Ward.
Q How old are you? A Twenty-eight, I believe.
Q What is your postoffice? A Siloam Springs, Arkansas.
Q What is your mother's name? A Mary Ward.
Q Is she living with you? A Yes sir.
Q How old is she? A I believe she is seventy-one or seventy-two.
Q Is she very feeble? A Yes sir.
Q Unable to get around? A Not much, she can't go anywhere except around the house, unable to go anywhere.
Q You have a power of attorney to file for her? A Yes sir.

Witness presents a power of attorney duly executed on May 22, 1903, by Mary Ward, authorizing said Daniel M. Ward to select her allotment of lands in the Cherokee Nation and designate her homestead therein.

From the testimony it appears that Mary Ward is an aged and infirm person and the witness Daniel M. Ward will, therefore, be permitted to select her allotment and designate her homestead.

The undersigned, being duly sworn, states that as stenographer to the Commission to the Five Civilized Tribes he correctly recorded the testimony and proceedings in this case, and that the foregoing is a true and correct transcript of his stenographic notes thereof.

E.G. Rothenberger

Cherokee Intermarried White 1906
Volume IV

Subscribed and sworn to before me this 6th day of July, 1903.

Samuel Foreman
Notary Public.

◇◇◇◇◇

F.R.   Cherokee-367.

DEPARTMENT OF THE INTERIOR,
COMMISSIONER TO THE FIVE CIVILIZED TRIBES.
Mukogee[sic], I. T., January 10, 1907.

In the matter of the application for the enrollment of Mary A. Ward as a citizen by intermarriage of the Cherokee Nation.

Daniel M. Ward being first duly sworn by Frances R. Land[sic], a Notary Public for the Western District of Indian Territory, testified as follows:

By the Commissioner:
Q What is your name? A Daniel M. Ward.
Q What is your age? A I have forgotten my age, but I think about 32 years.
Q What is your postoffice address? A Siloam Springs, Ark.
Q In whose behalf do you appear here today? A Mary Ward's.
Q Mary Ward is your mother? A Yes sir.
Q Does Mary Ward claim citizenship in the Cherokee Nation by intermarriage?
A Yes sir.
Q Through whom does she claim such citizenship.[sic] A Thomas Ward.
Q Is Thomas Ward a citizen of the Cherokee Nation? A Yes.
Q When was your mother, Mary Ward, married to Thomas Ward?
A In 1851.
Q Where were they married? A On Flint Creek, Going Snake District, Cherokee nation.
Q Have you any documentary evidence of that marriage? A No sir.
Q No certificate or anything? A No, I have a witness I supposed would be here today.
Q You say there are certain witnesses who saw the ceremony performed? A Yes sir
Q Is Thomas Ward living at this time? A No sir.
Q When did he die? A He died in 1879 I guess.
Q Is your mother, Mary Ward, Living at this time? A Yes.
Q Is she unable to be here in person? A Yes, she was not able.
Q From the time of the marriage of Mary Ward to Thomas Ward, in 1851, until the death of Thomas Ward in 1877, did they reside continuously together as husband and wife in the Cherokee Nation? A Yes, except during the war; they lived on the line, and in the Territory during all the time of the war.
Q Was Mary Ward ever married prior to her marriage to Thomas Ward? A No sir.
Q Was Thomas Ward ever married prior to his marriage to Mary Ward? A No sir.
Q Has Mary Ward ever married since the death of her husband Thomas Ward?
A No sir.

Q Does she still reside in the Cherokee Nation? A Yes.

Q And has always since the death of her husband Thomas Ward? A Yes sir.

Q Does she still reside in the Cherokee Nation? A Yes.

Q You never knew of any certificate or any record that might have been made covering tge[sic] marriage of Thomas and Mary Ward? A No, I don't.

Q Who was the witness you expected to bring here? A J. P. Chandler; he told me he would be here today; he was getting up affidavits of his own evidence and told me that he would be here. My mother told me this morning when I left home that there was a record of her marriage at Tahlequah that was sent there to be recorded, but I don't know myself.

Q That was the only marriage contract ever entered into between them, was in 1851?

A Yes sir.

The name of the applicant Mary Ward appears on Charokee[sic] Field Card No. 367, and is included in the 1880 authenticated roll of citizen[sic] of the Cherokee Nation, Going Snake District opposite No. 2051.

The name of the applicant also appears on the 1896 roll opposite No. 219, Going Snake District.

Frances R. Lane upon oath states that as stenographer to the Commissioner to the Five Civilized Tribes she reported the testimony in the above entitled cause, and that the foregoing is an accurate transcript of her stenographic notes thereof.

Frances R Lane

Subscribed and sworn to before me this January 11, 1907.

Edward Merrick
Notary Public.

◇◇◇◇◇

C. F. B.   Cherokee 367.

DEPARTMENT OF THE INTERIOR,
COMMISSION TO THE FIVE CIVILIZED TRIBES.
Muskogee, Indian Territory, January 11, 1907.

In the Matter of the Application for the Enrollment of Mary Ward as a citizen by intermarriage of the Cherokee Nation.

M. B. Studivant for Applicant.

APPEARANCES:

Cherokee Nation represented by
W. W. Hastings, Attorney.

Cherokee Intermarried White 1906
Volume IV

M. B. Studivant being first duly sworn by B. P. Rasmus, Notary Public, testified as follows:

Q What is your name?   A M. B. Studivant.
Q What is your age?   A 62.
Q What is your post office address?
A Grove.
Q Do you know a person in the Cherokee Nation by the name of Mary Ward?
A Yes sir.
Q Is she a married woman?   A She was.
Q Her husband is dead?   A Yes sir.
Q What was her husband's name? A Thomas Ward.
Q When was Mary Ward married to Thomas Ward?
A I reckon before I could recollect anything about it.
Q They were married prior to 1870?
A Yes sir; I guess they were.
Q Were they married before the war?
A Yes sir; they were living together in the time of the war.
Q Did they continue to live together until the death of Thomas Ward?
A Yes sir.
Q You don't know when he died?   A No sir.
Q Had Mary Ward married since the death of her husband, Thomas Ward?
A If she has, I never heard of it.
Q Have you known her since the war?
A Yes sir.
Q Has she always lived in the Cherokee Nation?
A Yes sir.

ON BEHALF OF CHEROKEE NATION.

Q Was Thomas Ward living in the Cherokee Nation when he died?
A Yes sir.
Q And that was since the war?   A Yes sir.
Q You don't remember the date?   A No sir.
Q Have you ever heard of either of them being married other than to each other?
A No sir.

J. C. L. Ward being first duly sworn by B. P. Rasmus, Notary Public, testified as follows:

ON BEHALF OF COMMISSIONER:

Q What is your name?   A J. L. C. Ward.
Q What is your age?   A 50 years.
Q What is your post office address?
A Siloam Springs.

Cherokee Intermarried White 1906
Volume IV

Q Do you know a person in the Cherokee Nation by the name of Mary Ward?
A Yes sir.
Q What was Mary Ward's husband's name?
A Thomas Ward.
Q When did you first become acquainted with these parties?
A I can recollect them in tine of the war; '63 I think.
Q Was Thomas Ward a recognized citizen of the Cherokee Nation at the time you became acquainted with him?
A Yes sir.
Q Living in the Cherokee country?
A Yes sir.
Q Thomas Ward and Mary Ward at that time were residing together as husband and wife?
A Yes sir.
Q When did Thomas Ward die?   A I think it was '77.
Q Has Mary Ward married since the death of her husband?
A No sir.
Q Has Mary Ward resided in the Cherokee Nation continuously since you have known her?
A Yes sir; there on the old place.
Q As far as you know were either of these parties married prior to their marriage to each other?
A I don't know whether they were or not.
Q You never heard that they were?
A No sir.

The undersigned being first duly sworn states that as stenographer to the Commission to the Five Civilized Tribes, she recorded the testimony taken in this case and that the foregoing is a full, true and correct copy of the stenographic notes thereof.

Myrtle Hill

Subscribed and sworn to before me this the 14th day of January, 1907.

John E. Tidwell
Notary Public.

◇◇◇◇◇

E. C. M.   Cherokee 367.

DEPARTMENT OF THE INTERIOR,

COMMISSIONER TO THE FIVE CIVILIZED TRIBES.

————————————

In the matter of the application for the enrollment of MARY WARD as a citizen by intermarriage of the Cherokee Nation.

_D_E_C_I_S_I_O_N_

THE RECORDS OF THIS OFFICE SHOW: That at Westville, Indian Territory, July 19th, 1900, application was received by the Commission to the Five Civilized Tribes for the enrollment of Mary Ward as a citizen by intermarriage of the Cherokee Nation. Further proceedings in the matter of said application were had at Westville, Indian Territory, July 19th, 1900, Tahlequah, Indian Territory October 6th, 1902 and May 29th, 1903 and at Muskogee, Indian Territory, January 10th, 1907, and January 11th, 1907.

THE EVIDENCE IN THIS CASE SHOWS: That the applicant herein, Mary Ward, a white woman, was married in 1851 to one Thomas Ward, since deceased, who was at the time of said marriage a recognized citizen by blood of the Cherokee Nation, who died prior to 1880, but whose son, Daniel W. Ward, who acquired his Cherokee citizenship solely through his father, is identified on the Cherokee authenticated tribal roll of 1880, Going Snake District No. 2057, as a native Cherokee.

IT IS, THEREFORE, ORDERED AND ADJUDGED: That in accordance with the decision of the Supreme Court of the United States dated November 5th, 1906 in the cases of Daniel Red Bird et al. vs. the United States, Nos. 125, 126, 127 and 128, the said applicant, Mary Ward is entitled under the provisions of Section Twenty-one of the Act of Congress approved June 28th, 1898 (30 Stats. 495), to enrollment as a citizen by intermarriage of the Cherokee Nation, and her application for enrollment as such is accordingly granted.

                                                          Tams Bixby
                                                               Commissioner.

Dated at Muskogee, Indian Territory,
this   JAN 25 1907

◇◇◇◇◇

Cherokee Intermarried White 1906
Volume IV

Cherokee 367

Muskogee, Indian Territory, January 25, 1907.

W. W. Hastings,
      Attorney for the Cherokee Nation,
         Muskogee, Indian Territory.

Dear Sir:

      There is enclosed herewith copy of the decision of the Commissioner to the Five Civilized Tribes, dated January 25, 1907, granting the application for the enrollment of Mary Ward as a citizen by intermarriage of the Cherokee Nation.

      Respectfully,

Enc I-147   Commissioner.

RPI

◇◇◇◇◇

Cherokee 367

W.W.HASTINGS.   OFFICE OF   H.M. VANCE.
ATTORNEY.   SECRETARY.

Attorney for the Cherokee Nation,
MUSKOGEE, I. T.   January 25, 1907.

The Commissioner to the Five Civilized Tribes,
      Muskogee, Indian Territory.

Sir:

      Receipt is acknowledged of the testimony and of your decision enrolling Mary Ward as a citizen by intermarriage of the Cherokee Nation. Time for protesting said decision is waived and I consent that said person may be placed upon the schedule immediately.

      Respectfully,
           W. W. Hastings
           Attorney for the Cherokee Nation.

◇◇◇◇◇

173

Cherokee 367

Muskogee, Indian Territory, January 25, 1907.

Mary Ward,
　　Siloam Springs, Arkansas.

Dear Madam:

There is enclosed herewith copy of the decision of the Commissioner to the Five Civilized Tribes, dated January 25, 1907, granting the application for your enrollment as a citizen by intermarriage of the Cherokee Nation.

You will be advised when your name has been placed upon a schedule of citizens of the Cherokee Nation and approved by the Secretary of the Interior.

Respectfully,

Enc I-148　　　　　　　　　　　　　　　　　　　Commissioner.

RPI

Cher IW 121

◇◇◇◇◇

F.R.

DEPARTMENT OF THE INTERIOR,

COMMISSIONER TO THE FIVE CIVILIZED TRIBES.

In the matter of the application for the enrollment of

GEORGE BRADLEY

as a citizen by intermarriage of the Cherokee Nation.

Cherokee 962.

Cherokee Intermarried White 1906
Volume IV

◇◇◇◇◇

DEPARTMENT OF THE INTERIOR,
COMMISSION TO THE FIVE CIVILIZED TRIBES,
SALLISAW, I.T., AUGUST 6, 1900.

In the matter of the application of George Bradly[sic] for enrollment of himself, wife and children, as citizens of the Cherokee Nation, said Bradly being duly sworn, testified as follows:

(Sworn and examined by Commissioner Needles.)

Q What is your name? A George Bradly.
Q Your age? A 47.
Q Your postoffice? A Hanson, I.T.
Q Have you been recognized by the Cherokee tribal authorities as a citizen of the Cherokee Nation? A Yes, by adoption.
Q What district do you live? A Sequoyah.
Q How long have you lived there? A About 22 years.
Q What is the name of your father? A He is a non-citizen.
Q What is the name of your mother? A She is also a non-citizen.
Q Are you married? A Yes.
Q Under what law? A Cherokee law.
Q Have you[sic] marriage license or certificate with you? A Yes.
Q Where were you living at time of your marriage? A Tahlequah.
Q What was your wife's name? A Cyntha Ann Sanders.
Q What is her age? A 45.
Q Is she a citizen by blood of the Cherokee Nation? A Yes.
Q Is her name on the authenticated rolls? A Yes.
Q What is the name of her father? A Jesse Sanders.
Q Is he a citizen? A Yes.
Q Is he living? A No sir.
Q Have you any children under 21 years of age? A Yes.
  Applicant on '80 roll, page 682, number 68;
  On '96 roll, page 1111, number 12.
  Appplicant's[sic] wife on '80 roll, page 682, number 69 as Cyntha Ann Bradly.
  On '96 roll, page 1053, number 130;
  On '94 roll, page 937, number 121, as Cynthia Bradly.
Q Now give me the names of your children under 21 years of age?
  A John W., 20 years old.
  On '80 roll, page 682, number 72; as Quincy Bradly.
  On '96 roll, page 1053, number 133;
  On '94 roll, page 937, number 124, as Quincy.
[sic] Next one? A Nora, 18 years old.
  On '96 roll, page 1053, number 134.
  On '94 roll, page 937, number 125, as Noura[sic].

175

Q Next one? A Bertha, 16 years old.

On '96 roll, page 1053, number 135 as Birdie.

On '94 roll, page 937, number 126 as Berthy.

Q Next one? A Robert, 14 years old.

On '96 roll, page 1053, 136;

On '94 roll, page 937, number 127.

Q Next one? A Benjamin, 10 years old.

On '96 roll, page 1053, number 137.

On '94 roll, page 937, number 128;

and

Frederick (twins) 10 years old; on '96 roll, 1053, number 138 as

Fred G.,

On '94 roll, page 937, number 129 as Fredy.

Q Next one? [sic] Walter, 7 years old.

On '96 roll, page 1053, number 139;

On '94 roll, page 937, number 130.

Q Next one? A George, 5 years old.

On '96 roll, page 1053, number 140.

Q Are all these children now living with you? A Yes.

The name of George Bradly appearing upon the authenticated rolls of '80 and census roll of '96, and his wife, Cynthia, name also appearing upon the roll of '80 as well as the rolls of '96 and '94, and his children as named in the testimony, names also appearing upon the census roll of '96 and pay-rolls of '94 respectively, they having made proof of their residence, and they being fully identified, the said Cynthia and his said children are ordered listed by this Commission for enrollment as citizens by blood of the Cherokee Nation, and the said George Bradly ordered listed for enrollment as a citizen by marriage.

Brown McDonald, being duly sworn, says as Stenographer to the Commission to the Five Civilized Tribes, he reported in full the testimony of the above named witness, and that the foregoing is a full, true and correct transcript of his notes.

Brown McDonald

Sworn to and subscribed before me this 16th day of August, 1900, at Muldrow, I.T.

TB Needles
Commissioner.

◇◇◇◇◇

Cher-962

DEPARTMENT OF THE INTERIOR.
Commission to the Five Civilized Tribes,
Muskogee, I.T., October 20, 1902.

In the matter of the application of George Bradley for enrollment as a citizen by intermarriage of the Cherokee Nation, and for the enrollment of his wife Cynthia A., and his children, John Q., Nora, Bertha, Robert, Benjamin, Frederick G., Walker, George and Benjamin as citizens by blood of the Cherokee Nation.

George Bradley, called as a witness, being first duly sworn by the Commission, testified as follows:

Q Your name is George Bradley? A Yes sir.
Q How old are you? A 49 years.
Q What is your postoffice? A Hanson, I. T.
Q Are you a white man? A Yes sir.
Q Is your name on the roll of 1880 as an adopted white citizen? A Yes, it is on the roll; its[sic] on ever[sic] roll that has been made for thirty years.
Q What is your wife's name? A Cynthia Ann.
Q Is she a Cherokee by blood? A Yes sir.
Q Is she the wife through whom you claim your citizenship? A Yes.
Q Was she your wife in 1880? A Yes sir.
Q Have you and your wife Cynthia been living together ever since 1880?
A Yes sir.
Q Your home has been in the Cherokee nation ever since that time? A Yes
Q Have you and your wife ever been separated? A No sir.
Q Are you living together now? A Yes sir.
Q How many children have you by your wife Cynthia? A Ten living; one dead.
Q Which one is dead? The oldest one; it is not on the roll.
Q You have got ten children living? A Yes sir.
Q What is the oldest ones[sic] name? A Jesse.
Q Is Jesse enrolled by himself? A Yes sir.
Q All the other children are living with you? A Yes sir.

Q What is the next ones name? A   John Q.
Q You have had no deaths in your family in the last two and a half years.
A No sir.

-----0----

Frances R. Lane upon oath states that as stenographer to the Commission to the Five Civilized Tribes she correctly recorded the testimony in the above entitled cause, and that the foregoing is an accurate transcript of her notes thereof.

Frances R Lane

177

Subscribed and sworn to before me this 25th day of October, 1902

BC Jones
Notary Public.

◇◇◇◇◇

JAN 21 1907

F.R.   Cherokee 962.

DEPARTMENT OF THE INTERIOR,
COMMISSIONER TO THE FIVE CIVILIZED TRIBES.

In the matter of the application for the enrollment of George Bradley as a citizen by intermarriage of the Cherokee Nation.

George Bradley being first duly sworn by Frances R. Lane, a Notary Public for the Western District of Indian Territory, testified as follows:

By the Commissioner:
Q What is your name? A George Bradley.
Q What is your age? A Fifty-four.
Q What is your postoffice address? A Hanson, Ind. Ter.
Q You are a white man, not possessed of any Indian blood? A Yes sir.
Q Your claim to such right is by virtue of your marriage to a citizen by blood of the Cherokee nation[sic]? A Yes sir.
Q What is the name of such citizen? A Cyntha[sic] A. Bradley.
Q What was her name prior to her marriage to you? A Sanders.
Q When were you married to Cynta A. Bradley, nee Sanders?
A Married in March, 1873; I don't remember the date exactly.
Q Where were you married to her? A Tahlequah District.
Q Who performed the marriage ceremony? A Judge Riley Keys.
Q Was that marriage under a license of the Cherokee Nation? A Yes sir.
Q Have you any documentary evidence showing that marriage?

> Applicant presents certified copy of marriage license issued March 14, 1873, to George Bradley and Cynthia Sanders, and certificate showing that said parties were married by Riley Keys on March 18, 1873.

Q Were you ever married before you married Cyntha A. Sanders[sic]
A No sir.
Q Was Cyntha Sanders ever married before she married you? A No sir.
Q Is Cynths[sic] A. Bradley living at this time? A Yes sir.
Q At the time you were married to Cyntha A. Sanders, was she a recognized citizen of the Cherokee nation[sic]? A Yes sir.

178

Cherokee Intermarried White 1906
Volume IV

Q Have you and Cyntha A. Bradley lived together a husband and wife and continuously live in the Cherokee Nation from time of your marriage until the present time?
A Yes sir.
Q You have never been separated? A No sir.

> The applicant, George Bradley, is identified on the authenticated tribal roll of 1880, Sequoyah District, No. 68, and is also included in the Cherokee census roll of 1896, page 1111, No. 12, Sequoyah District.
> The name of the applicant's wife is also included in the 1880 roll, Sequoyah District, No. 69, and on the 1896 Cherokee Census roll, page 1053/[sic] No. 130, Sequoyah District, and is also included in the approved partial roll of citizen[sic] by blood of the Cherokee Nation, opposite No. 2592.

Frances R. Lane, upon oath, states that as stenographer to the Commission to the Five Civilized Tribes she reported the testimony in the above entitled cause and that the forgoing is an accurate transcript of her stenographic notes thereof.

Frances R. Lane

Subscribed and sworn to before me this January 21, 1907.

Edward Merrick
Notary Public.

◇◇◇◇◇

CERTIFIED COPY.

Cherokee Nation
Flint District.

By the authority in me vested by the laws of the Cherokee Nation I do hereby grant License of Marriage unto George Bradley a citizen of the United States to marry Miss Cynthia Sanders, a Cherokee by birth and a daughter of Jesse & Caroline Sanders. He having been recommended to me by petition as a man of good moral character and industrious habits. I grant him license as he has complied with the law regulating intermarriage with white men. Given from under my hand in office this the 14 day of March, 1873.
License Fee $5.00

(Signed) James W. Adair, Clerk,
Circuit Court, Flint, C. N.

This is to certify that I, Riley Keys, an acting judge of the Cherokee nation[sic], did this day solemnize the rights of matrimony between George Bradley and Cynthia Sanders this the 18 day of March, 1873.

(Signed) Riley Keys,
Chief Justice Supreme Ct., C. N.

I hereby certify that the above license and certificate is correct according to records in my office.

(Signed) J. B. Lynvh[sic],
Clk. Flint C. N.

The undersigned, being first duly sworn states that as stenographer to the Commissioner to the Five Civilized Tribes she made the above and foregoing copy and that the same is a true and correcy[sic] copy of a copy of certain marriage records now on file in this office.

Frances R. Lane

Subscribed and sworn to before me this January 23, 1907.

Edward Merrick
Notary Public.

◇◇◇◇◇

F.R.   Cherokee 962.

DEPARTMENT OF THE INTERIOR,
COMMISSIONER TO THE FIVE CIVILIZED TRIBES.

In the matter of the application for the enrollment of George Bradley as a citizen by intermarriage of the Cherokee Nation.

D E C I S I O N .

THE RECORDS OF THIS OFFICE SHOW: That on August 6, 1900, application was received by the Commission to the Five Civilized Tribes for the enrollment of George Bradley as a citizen by intermarriage of the Cherokee Nation. Further proceedings in the matter of said application were had at Muskogee, Indian Territory, October 20, 1902, and January 21, 1907.

THE EVIDENCE IN THIS CASE SHOWS: That the applicant herein, George Bradley, a white man, was married in accordance with the Cherokee law March 18, 1873, to his wife Cyntha A. Bradley (nee Sanders) who was, at the time of said marriage a recognized citizen by blood of the Cherokee Nation, who is identified on the Cherokee authenticated tribal roll of 1880, Sequoyah District, No. 69, as a native Cherokee, and whose name is included in the approved partial roll of citizens by blood of the Cherokee Nation opposite No. 2592. It is further shown that since said marriage said George

Bradley and Cyntha A. Bradley have resided together as husband and wife, and continuously lived in the Cherokee Nation up to and including September 1, 1902. Said applicant is identified on the Cherokee authenticated tribal roll of 1880, and Cherokee census roll of 1896, as an intermarried citizen of the Cherokee Nation.

IT IS, THEREFORE, ORDERED AND ADJUDGED: That in accordance with the decision of the Supreme Court of the United States, dated November 5, 1906, in the cases of Daniel Red Bird et al., vs. the United States, Nos. 125, 126, 127 and 128, the said applicant, George Bradley is entitled, under the provision of Section 21 of the Act of Congress approved June 28, 1898 (30 Stats., 495), to enrollment as a citizen by intermarriage of the Cherokee Nation, and his application for enrollment as such is accordingly granted.

Tams Bixby
Commissioner.

Dated at Muskogee, Indian Territory,
this   JAN 29 1907

◇◇◇◇◇

Cherokee 962

Muskogee, Indian Territory, January 29, 1907.

W. W. Hastings,
        Attorney for the Cherokee Nation,
                Muskogee, Indian Territory.

Dear Sir:

There is enclosed herewith copy of the decision of the Commissioner to the Five Civilized Tribes, dated January 29, 1907, granting the application for the enrollment of George Bradley as a citizen by intermarriage of the Cherokee Nation.

Respectfully,

Enc I-7   Commissioner.

RPI

◇◇◇◇◇

Cherokee 962

Muskogee, Indian Territory, January 29, 1907.

The Commissioner to the Five Civilized Tribes,
    Muskogee, Indian Territory.

Sir:

Receipt is acknowledged of the testimony and of your decision enrolling George Bradley as a citizen by intermarriage of the Cherokee Nation. Time for protesting said decision is waived and I consent that said person may be placed upon the schedule immediately.

Respectfully,

W. W. Hastings
Attorney for the Cherokee Nation.

◇◇◇◇◇

Cherokee 962

Muskogee, Indian Territory, January 29, 1907.

George Bradley,
    Hanson, Indian Territory.

Dear Sir:

There is enclosed herewith copy of the decision of the Commissioner to the Five Civilized Tribes, dated January 29, 1907, granting the application for your enrollment as a citizen by intermarriage of the Cherokee Nation.

You will be advised when your name has been placed upon a schedule of citizens of the Cherokee Nation and approved by the Secretary of the Interior.

Respectfully,

Enc I-8   Commissioner.

RPI

◇◇◇◇◇

Cherokee
I.W. 121

Muskogee, Indian Territory, April 16, 1907.

George Bradley,
    Hanson, Indian Territory.

Dear Sir:

Your marriage license and certificate filed in connection with your application for enrollment as a citizen by intermarriage of the Cherokee Nation is returned to you herewith, copies of the same being retained in the files of this office.

Respectfully,

Encl. W-20.   Commissioner.
S.W.

Cher IW 122

◇◇◇◇◇

E.C.M.

DEPARTMENT OF THE INTERIOR,

COMMISSIONER TO THE FIVE CIVILIZED TRIBES.

In the matter of the application for the enrollment of

MARGARET CRITTENDEN

As a citizen by intermarriage of the Cherokee Nation.

CHEROKEE NO. 1701.

◇◇◇◇◇

Cherokee Intermarried White 1906
Volume IV

DEPARTMENT OF THE INTERIOR,
COMMISSION TO THE FIVE CIVILIZED TRIBES,
FORT GIBSON, I.T., AUGUST 21, 1900.

In the matter of the application of Margaret Crittenden for enrollment of herself and child as citizens of the Cherokee Nation, said Crittenden being sworn by Commissioner Needles, testified as follows:

Q What is your name? A Margarett Crittenden? Q Your age. A 59.
Q Your postoffice? A Wagoner.
Q Are you a citizen of the Cherokee Nation? A Yes, by adoption.
Q What district do you live in? a Cooweescoowee.
Q How long have you lived in the Cherokee Nation continuously? A About 31 years.
Q Whom do you apply for enrollment for? A Myself, little boy, and one daughter.
Q Your father and mother are both non-citizens? A Yes.
Q Are you married? A Have been; am a widow now.
Q What was your husband's name? A Mose Crittenden.
Q When did you marry him? A In '63 as well as I recollect.
Q Is he living? A No sir.
Q His father and mother dead? A Yes.
Q What children have you to enroll? A Isaac M., 12 years old.
On '96 roll, page 123, number 731.
Q Is this child living and living with you? A Yes.
Applicant on '80 roll, page 417, number 332, as Critdenten[sic].
The name of Margarett Crittenden appearing upon the authenticated roll of '80 as Margaret Critdenten and on the roll of '96 as Crittenden, and her son, Isaac M., name also being found upon the roll of '96, and being fully identified according to page and number as indicated in the testimony, herself and Isaac will be duly listed for enrollment as Cherokee citizens she by intermarriage and her son by blood.

The undersigned, being first duly sworn, states that as stenographer to the Commission to the Five Civilized Tribes, he correctly recorded the testimony and proceedings in this case, and that the foregoing is a full and complete transcript of his stenographic notes thereof.

Brown McDonald

Subscribed and sworn to before me this 7th day of September, 1900.

TB Needles
Commissioner.

◇◇◇◇◇

Cherokee 1701.

DEPARTMENT OF THE INTERIOR,
COMMISSION TO THE FIVE CIVILIZED TRIBES.
Muskogee, I. T., October 17, 1902.

In the matter of the application of Margaret Crittenden for the enrollment of herself as a citizen by intermarriage, and for the enrollment of her son, Isaac M. Crittenden, as a citizen by blood, of the Cherokee Nation.

SUPPLEMENTAL PROCEEDINGS.

MARGARET CRITTENDEN, being sworn, testified as follows:

By the Commission,

Q What is your name? A Margaret Crittenden.
Q How old are you? A About sixty or sixty-one, I don't know just which.
Q What's your postoffice? A Wagoner.
Q Are you a white woman? A Yes, sir.
Q You are claiming as a citizen by intermarriage, are you?
A Yes, sir.
Q What is the name of your husband? A Mose Crittenden.
Q Was he your husband in '80? A Yes, sir.
Q He's the husband through whom you claim citizenship? A Yes, sir.
Q Is he living? A No, sir.
Q When did he die? A Four years ago this coming January.
Q Did you live with your husband up until he died? A Yes, sir.
Q Never separated? A No, sir.
Q How long have you lived in the Cherokee Nation? A About thirty-three years.
Q Altogether? A Yes, sir.
Q You have not lived out of the Cherokee Nation since '80? A No, sir.
Q You are still his widow, are you? A Yes, sir.
Q And have not lived out of the Nation since your husband's death? A No, sir.
Q Have you any children? A Yes, sir.
Q How many? A Two.
Q What are their names? A Isaac and Liza.
Q Is Liza Crittenden married? A No, sir.
Q She is over twenty-one? A Yes, sir.
Q She enrolled herself, did she? A Yes, sir.

Retta Chick, being first duly sworn, states that, as stenographer to the Commission to the Five Civilized Tribes, she recorded the testimony and proceedings in the matter of the foregoing application, and that the above is a true and complete transcript of her stenographic notes thereof.

Retta Chick

Subscribed and sworn to before me this 14th day of November, 1902.

PG Reuter
Notary Public.

◇◇◇◇◇

F.R.   Cherokee 1701.

DEPARTMENT OF THE INTERIOR,
COMMISSIONER TO THE FIVE CIVILIZED TRIBES.
Muskogee, I. T., January 17, 1907.

In the matter of the application for the enrollment of Margaret Crittenden as a citizen by intermarriage of the Cherokee Nation.

Margaret Crittenden, being first duly sworn, by Frances R. Lane, a Notary Public for the Western District of Indian Territory, testified as follows:

By the Commissioner;
Q What is your name? A Margaret Crittenden.
Q Your age? A Sixty-six. Q Your P.O. address? A Wagoner
Q Do you claim to be a citizen by intermarriage of the Cherokee Nation? A Yes sir.
Q You claim such intermarried right by virtue of your marriage to a citizen by blood of the Cherokee nation[sic]? A Yes sir.
Q What is the name of that citizen? A Mose Crittenden.
Q When were you and Mose Crittenden married? A As well as I recollect in 1863.
Q Where were you married? A Polk county[sic], Arkansas.
Q By whom were you married? A A preacher by the name of Edam.
Q Have you any documentary evidence? Papers showing that marriage?
A No, I have not.
Q At the time you married Mose Crittenden was he a recognized citizen by blood of the Cherokee Nation? A Yes sir.
Q Was his home in the Cherokee Nation at that time? A Yes.
Q And he went over into Arkansas and married you? A Yes.
Q How soon after your marriage did you return to the Cherokee Nation? A We was married in 1863 as well as I recollect and we come back in 1869.
Q Is Mose Crittenden living at this time? A No sir.
Q When did he die? A In 1898.
Q Did you and Mose Crittenden live together as husband and wife from the time of your marriage in 1863 until his death in 1898? A Yes sir.
Q Up to the time of your removal to the Cherokee Nation in 1869 did you live continuously in the Cherokee Nation? A Yes, never have been out since.
Q Were you ever married previous to the time you married to Mose Crittenden? A Yes, I had been married before I married him.
Q Gen married how many time? A Onve[sic] before him.
Q Was your first husband living at the time you married him? A No, he was dead.

Cherokee Intermarried White 1906
Volume IV

Q Was Mose Crittenden married before he married you? A Yes sir.
Q How many times? A One time.
Q Was his first wife living at the time he married you? A No, she was dead.
Q You have not married since the death of Mose Crittenden? A No sir.
Q Do you know whether or not Mose Crittenden was readmitted to citizenship upon his return to the Cherokee Nation in 1869? A I don't know that he was; he went out of her in case of sickness, and left his place and everything here and it remained here until he came back.
Q That is, from the time he went to Arkansas to marry you? A Yes sir.
Q He still had property in the Indian Territory while he was in Arkansas? A Yes sir, he didn't take anything with him; it remained here until he came back.
Q He remained in the Cherokee nation[sic] all the time until his death? A Yes sir.

> The Record of Persons admitted to Citizenship in the Cherokee Nation, in the possession of the Commissioner to the Five Civilized Tribes, there appears on page 9 the following entry.
> "Mose Crittenden, Dec. 15, 1869, re-admitted, Unconditional."
>
> On page 24, the following entry is found:
> "Martha Crittenden, April 10, 1879, white with Cherokee husband and is entitled."

Q Is there anyone here who was present at your marriage?
A No, there aint[sic] anyone here, but thees[sic] men that was here in 1870; they wasn't right present there; but there is two in Texas; I can send an get their evidence if it will do. They was right present and saw me married, but to go that far back it is hard to get witnesses that was present. Chief Buffington was there, but he was not reight[sic] present when I was married.

> Applicant is identified on the 1880 roll, Going Snake District, opposite No. 332; and is also identified on the 1896 Cherokee Census roll as Margaret Crittenden, Cooweescoowee District, No. 187.

Thomas M. Buffington, being first duly sworn, by Frances R. Lane, a Notary Public for the Western District of Indian Territory, testified as follows:
By the Commissioner:
Q What is your name? A Thomas M. Buffington.
Q And your age? A Fifty-one.
Q What is your postoffice address? A Vinita, I. T.
Q Do you know Margaret Crittenden? A I do.
Q How long have you known her?
A I have known her ever since I was a small boy.
Q Was she a married woman at the time you first knew her?

A I heard of Margaret Crittenden and her marrying. We were refugees during the war and stopped one winter in Polk county[sic] and while we were there Mose Crittenden and this woman were married.

Q You were not present at the marriage, however? A No, but I saw them pass through the lane, and my attention was called to the fact that they had been just married.

Q It was understood by you that they had been lawfully married? A Yes sir.

Q They held themselves out as husband and wife? A Yes, and I have know them ever since then.

Q They continued to live together as husband and wife? A Yes sir.Q[sic]

Q You have no reason to think that they were not lawfully married? A No sir; they raised quite a large family. I have staid with them all night many a time..

Witness excused.

James R. Garrett, being first duly sworn by Frances R. Lane, a Notary Public for the Western District of Indian Territory, testified as follows:

Q What is your name? A James R. Garrett.

Q Your age? A Fisty[sic]-six.

Q And your postoffice address? A Tahlequah, Indian Ter.

Q Do you know Margaret Crittenden? A Yes sir.

Q Do you appear here to testify relative to her right to enrollment as a citizen by intermarriage of the Cherokee Nation? A Yes sir.

Q How long have you known her? A I have known her--known them both since 1873.

Q They were married at the time you knew them? A They were living together and always claim to be legal man and wife.

Q It was your understanding that they were lawfully married at that time? A Yes sir.

Q Where were they living at that time? A Living at Neescoop Prairie, Going Snake District; lived there until after this Cherokee strip payment and then they moved close to Wagoner.

Q Do you know when Mose Crittenden died? A Not personally. I only just known when I heard it; he died since they went to Wagoner to live.

Q From the time you first knew them in 1873 until they moved about the time of the strip payment, they resided together as husband and wife, and lived continuously in the Cherokee Nation? A Yes, I was there in 1896 and staid all night with them. They was still living together, and he was living at that time.

Frances R. Lane, upon oath states that as stenographer to the Commissioner to the Five Civilized Tribes she reported the testimony in the above entitled cause and that the foregoing is an accurate transcript of the stenographic notes thereof.

Frances R. Lane

Subscribed and sworn to before me this January 18, 1907.

Edward Merrick
Notary Public.

◇◇◇◇◇

E C M   Cherokee 1701.

DEPARTMENT OF THE INTERIOR,

COMMISSIONER TO THE FIVE CIVILIZED TRIBES.

In the matter of the application for the enrollment of MARGARET CRITTENDEN as a citizen by intermarriage of the Cherokee Nation.

D E C I S I O N _ _

THE RECORDS OF THIS OFFICE SHOW: That on August 21st, 1900, application was received by the Commission to the Five Civilized Tribes for the enrollment of Margaret Crittenden as a citizen by intermarriage of the Cherokee Nation. Further proceedings in the matter of said application were had at Muskogee, Indian Territory, October 17th, 1902 and January 17th, 1907.

THE EVIDENCE IN THIS CASE SHOWS: That the applicant herein, Margaret Crittenden, a white woman, married in 1863 in the State of Arkansas one Moses Crittenden, since deceased, who was at the time of said marriage a recognized citizen by blood of the Cherokee Nation, and who is identified on the Cherokee authenticated tribal roll of 1880, Going Snake District No. 331 as a native Cherokee marked "Dead"; that in 1869 said Moses Crittenden and Margaret Crittenden removed to the Cherokee Nation where, on December 15th, 1869, said Moses Crittenden was re-admitted to citizenship in the Cherokee Nation by duly constituted authorities thereof. It is further shown that from the time of said marriage until the death of said Moses Crittenden, which occurred in 1898, the said Moses Crittenden and Margaret Crittendon[sic] resided together as husband and wife and continuously lived in the Cherokee Nation; that since the death of said Moses Crittenden the said Margaret Crittenden has remained unmarried and continuously lived in the Cherokee Nation. Said applicant is identified on the Cherokee authenticated tribal roll of 1880 and the Cherokee census roll of 1896 as an intermarried citizen of the Cherokee Nation.

IT IS, THEREFORE, ORDERED AND ADJUDGED: That in accordance with the decision of the Supreme Court of the United States dated November 5th, 1906, in the cases of Daniel Red Bird, et al. vs. the United States, Nos. 125, 126, 127 and 128, the said applicant, Margaret Crittenden, is entitled, under the provisions of Section Twenty-one of the Act of Congress approved June 28th, 1898 (30 Stats. 495), to enrollment as a citizen by intermarriage of the Cherokee Nation, and her application for enrollment as such is accordingly granted.

                                        Tams Bixby   Commissioner.

Dated at Muskogee, Indian Territory,
this   JAN 29 1907

◇◇◇◇◇

Cherokee 1701

Muskogee, Indian Territory, January 29, 1907.

W. W. Hastings,
    Attorney for the Cherokee Nation,
        Muskogee, Indian Territory.

Dear Sir:

      There is enclosed herewith copy of the decision of the Commissioner to the Five Civilized Tribes, dated January 29, 1907, granting the application for the enrollment of Margaret Crittenden, as a citizen by intermarriage of the Cherokee Nation.

Respectfully,

Enc I-20   Commissioner.

RPI

◇◇◇◇◇

Cherokee 1701

Muskogee, Indian Territory, January 29, 1907.

The Commissioner to the Five Civilized Tribes,
    Muskogee, Indian Territory.

Sir:

      Receipt is acknowledged of the testimony and of your decision enrolling Margaret Crittenden as a citizen by intermarriage of the Cherokee Nation. Time for protesting said decision is waived and I consent that said person may be placed upon the schedule immediately.

Respectfully,
                W. W. Hastings
                Attorney for the Cherokee Nation.

◇◇◇◇◇

Cherokee 1701

Muskogee, Indian Territory, January 29, 1907.

Margaret Crittenden,
    Wagoner, Indian Territory.

Dear Madam:

    There is enclosed herewith copy of the decision of the Commissioner to the Five Civilized Tribes, dated January 29, 1907, granting the application for your enrollment as a citizen by intermarriage of the Cherokee Nation.

    You will be advised when your name has been placed upon a schedule of citizens of the Cherokee Nation and approved by the Secretary of the Interior.

Respectfully,

Enc I-21   Commissioner.

RPI

◇◇◇◇◇

Cherokee
  1701

Muskogee, Indian Territory, January 29, 1907.

John G. Lieber,
    Muskogee, Indian Territory.

Dear Sir:

    There is enclosed herewith copy of the decision of the Commissioner to the Five Civilized Tribes, dated January 29, 1907, granting the application for the enrollment of Margaret Crittenden as a citizen by intermarriage of the Cherokee Nation.

Respectfully,

Enc l-30   Commissioner.

RPI

Cher IW 123

◇◇◇◇◇

F.R.

DEPARTMENT OF THE INTERIOR,
COMMISSIONER TO THE FIVE CIVILIZED TRIBES.

In the matter of the application for the enrollment of

CAROLINE B. FIELDS

as a citizen by intermarriage of the Cherokee Nation.

Cherokee 3715.

◇◇◇◇◇

DEPARTMENT OF THE INTERIOR.
COMMISSION TO THE FIVE CIVILIZED TRIBES.
VINITA, I.T., SEPTEMBER 29th, 1900.

IN THE MATTER OF THE APPLICATION OF Samuel I. Fields, wife and children for enrollment as citizens of the Cherokee Nation, and he being sworn by Commissioner, T. B. Needles, testified as follows:

Q What is your name? A Samuel I. Fields.
Q What is your age? A Sixty two.
Q What is your Postoffice? A South West City.
Q What district do you live in? A Illinois.
Q Are you a recognized citizen of the Cherokee Nation? A Yes sir; I was born and raised here.
Q Are you a citizen? A Yes sir.
Q By blood or intermarriage? A By blood.
Q What degree of blood do you claim? A My father was - some called him a half breed; some five eighths.
Q Do you not know about what degree of blood you have?
A Over three eights, or one fourth.
Q For whom do you apply for enrollment? A Myself, wife and family.
Q What is the name of your wife? A Caroline B. Phillips.

Q When did you marry her? A In 1872.

Q Is she a white person? A Yes sir.

Q What are the names of your children under twenty one years of age?

A There are three of them dead. There are seven in the family: There are two married and two living at home.

Q Are they under twenty one years of age? A Yes sir.

Q What are their names? A Thomas Jefferson Fields.

Q How old is he? A Sixteen.

Q What is the name of the next one? A Isa Cora Fields.

Q How old is she? A About ten years old.

Q Are these children living and living with you at this time? A Yes sir.

Q How long have you lived in the Cherokee Nation?

A Ever since the war.

 (1880 Roll, Page 254, #960, Samuel J. Fields, Delaware D'st)

 (1880 Roll, Page 254, Caroline D. Fields, Delaware D'st)

Q Her name is Caroline "B", is it not? A yes sir.

#1224(1896 Roll, Page 472. (#1234,) Samuel J. Fields, Delaware D'st)

 (1896 Roll, Page 572, #186, Carolina D. Fields, Delaware ")

 (1896 Roll, Page 472, #1227, Thomas J. Fields, Delaware D'st)

 (1896 Roll, Page 472, #1228, Icy Cora Fields, Delaware D'st)

 The name of Samuel I. Fields, and his wife, Caroline B. Fields, appear upon the authenticated roll of 1880, as well as the census roll of 1896: The names of their two children, Thomas J. and Isa Cora appear upon the census roll of 1896.

 They all, being duly identified according to the page and number of the rolls, as indicated in the testimony and having made satisfactory proof of residence, the said Samuel I. Fields, and Children, Thomas J. and Isa Cora will be duly listed for enrollment by this Commission as Cherokee citizens by blood; and his wife, Caroline B. Fields, as a Cherokee citizen by intermarriage.

 The undersigned, being sworn, states that as stenographer to the Commission to the Five Civilized Tribes, he correctly recorded the testimony and proceedings in this case, and that the foregoing is a true and complete transcript of his stenographic notes thereof.

R R Cravens

Subscribed and sworn to before
me this 1st day of October, 1900.

CR Breckinridge COMMISSIONER.

◇◇◇◇◇

JOR.
Cher. 3715.

Department of the Interior.
Commission to the Five Civilized Tribes.
Tahlequah, I. T., October 15, 1902.

SUPPLEMENTAL TESTIMONY AND PROCEEDINGS in the matter of the application for the enrollment of CAROLINE B. FIELDS as a citizen by intermarriage of the Cherokee Nation.

CAROLINE B. FIELDS, being first duly sworn, and being examined, testified as follows:

BY COMMISSION: What is your name? A Caroline B. Fields.
Q How old are you? A Fifty-four. I was born in 1848, November 8th.
Q What is your post office address? A Southwest City, Missouri.
Q Are you a white woman? A Yes sir.
Q Has application been made to this Commission heretofore for your enrollment as a citizen by intermarriage of the Cherokee Nation? A Yes sir.
Q What is the name of your husband? A Samuel Igo Fields.
Q Is he living? A Yes sir.
Q Is he a Cherokee by blood? A Yes sir.
Q Do you claim your right to enrollment by reason of your marriage to him? A Yes sir.
Q When were you and he married? A Married in 1872.
Q Have you filed with the Commission your Cherokee marriage license ad[sic] certificate? A Yes sir.
Q Does your name appear upon the roll of 1880? A Yes sir.
Q Were you ever married before you married your present husband? A No sir.
Q Was eh[sic] ever married before he married you? A No sir.
Q You are his first wife and he is your first husband? A Yes sir.
Q Have you and [sic] lived together continuously since your marriage? A Yes sir.
Q Were you living together on the 1st day of September, 1902? A Yes sir.
Q You have never been separated at all? A No sir.
Q Have you resided in the Cherokee Nation continuously since your marriage?
A Yes sir.
Q Has she also? A Yes sir.
Q How many children have you that your husband made application for? A Two.
Q What are their names? A Thomas and Isacora.
Q Are both of these children living at this time? A Yes sir.

This testimony will be filed with and made a part of the record in the matter of the application for the enrollment of Caroline B. Fields as a citizen by intermarriage of the Cherokee Nation, Cherokee straight card field No. 3715.

Wm. Hutchinson, being first sworn, states that as stenographer to the Commission to the Five Civilized Tribes he correctly recorded the testimony and proceedings in this case, and that the foregoing is a true and complete transcript of the stenographic notes thereof.

Wm. Hutchinson

Subscribed and sworn to before me this 23rd day of October, 1902.

John O Rosson
Notary Public.

◇◇◇◇◇

C. F. B.   Cherokee 3715.

DEPARTMENT OF THE INTERIOR,
COMMISSION TO THE FIVE CIVILIZED TRIBES.
Muskogee, Indian Territory, January 10, 1907.

In the matter of the application for the enrollment of Caroline B. Fields, as a citizen by intermarriage of the Cherokee Nation.

Caroline B. Fields being first duly sworn by B. P. Rasmus, Notary Public, testified as follows:

Q What is your name?   A Caroline B. Fields.
Q What is your age?   A 58 years old.
Q What is your post office address?
A Maysville, Arkansas.
Q Your residence is in the Cherokee Nation?
A Yes sir.
Q You are an applicant for enrollment a a citizen by intermarriage of the Cherokee Nation?
A Yes sir.
Q You have no Cherokee blood?   A No sir.
Q Your only claim to the right to enrollment as a citizen of the Cherokee Nation is by virtue of your marriage to a citizen by blood?
A Yes sir.
Q What is the name of your citizen husband?
A Samuel I. Fields.
Q Is he living?   A Yes sir.
Q When did you marry him?
A In '72; either November or December.
Q Was he living in the Cherokee Nation at that time?
A Yes sir.
Q He was a recognized citizen of the Nation?
A Yes sir.

Q Since your marriage to him in the year 1872, have you and he continuously lived together as husband and wife?
A Yes sir.
Q And have lived all these years in the Cherokee Nation?
A Yes sir.
Q Is he your first husband?   A Yes sir.
Q Are you his first wife?   A Yes sir.
Q By whom were you married to Samuel I. Fields?
A Judge Woodall.
Q Have you any evidence of a documentary character to show that marriage?
A Yes sir.

The applicant presents an affidavit signed by William C. Woodall executed on the 28th day of September, 1900 showing that in the year 1872, said William C. Woodall united in marriage Samuel I. Fields, a Cherokee by blood, and Caroline B. Phillips, a citizen of the United States, in accordance with the laws and customs of the Cherokee Nation. This affidavit will be filed with and made a part of the record in this case.

The applicant, Caroline B. Fields is identified on the Cherokee authenticated tribal roll of 1880, Delaware District, Number 961. Her husband, Samuel I. Fields, is identified on said roll at Number 960 and his name is included in the approved partial roll of citizens by blood of the Cherokee Nation opposite Number 9014.

The undersigned being first duly sworn states that as stenographer to the Commission to the Five Civilized Tribes, she recorded the testimony taken in this case and that the foregoing is a full, true and correct transcript of her stenographic notes thereof.

Myrtle Hill

Subscribed and sworn to before me this the 16th day of January, 1907.

B. P. Rasmus
Notary Public.

◇◇◇◇◇

CERTIFIED COPY.

United States of America,	)
Northern District	)ss.
Indian Territory.	)

Personally came before me, S. F. Parks, a Notary public in and for the above named District and Territory, William C. Woodall who after being by me duly sworn deposes and says: That in the year 1872 he was the duly elected and qualified District Judge of Delaware District, Cherokee Nation; that among other official acts performed by him as District Judge of said District Court he performed the marriage ceremony between Samuel I. Fields, a Cherokee by blood and a recognized citizen of the Cherokee Nation and Miss Caroline B. Phillips, a citizen of the United States, in accordance with the laws and customs of said Cherokee Nation.

(Signed) William C. Woodall

Sworn and subscribed to before me this the 28th day of September, A.D., 1900.

(Signed) S. F. Parks,

(SEAL).   Notary Public.

My Commission expires Sept. 25" 1904.

I, Frances R. Lane, stenographer to the Commissioner to the Five Civilized Tribes, do hereby certify that the above and foregoing is a true and complete copy of the original document now on file in this office.

Frances R Lane

Subscribed and sworn to before me this January 23, 1907.

Edward Merrick
Notary Public.

◇◇◇◇◇

F.R.   Cherokee 3715.

DEPARTMENT OF THE INTERIOR,
COMMISSIONER TO THE FIVE CIVILIZED TRIBES.

In the matter of the application for the enrollment of Caroline B. Fields as a citizen by intermarriage of the Cherokee Nation.

D E C I S I O N .

THE RECORDS OF THIS OFFICE SHOW: That on September 29, 1900, application was received by the Commission to the Five Civilized Tribes for the enrollment of Caroline B. Fields as a citizen by intermarriage of the Cherokee Nation. Further proceedings in the matter of said application were had at Tahlequah, Indian Territory, October 15, 1902, and at Muskogee, Indian Territory, January 10, 1907.

THE EVIDENCE IN THIS CASE SHOWS: That the applicant herein, Caroline B. Fields, a white woman, was lawfully married in 1872 to Samuel I. Fields, who was at the time of said marriage a recognized citizen by blood of the Cherokee Nation, who is identified on the Cherokee authenticated tribal roll of 1880 Delaware District, No. 960, as a native Cherokee, and whose name is included in the approved partial roll of citizen of the Cherokee Nation opposite No. 9014. It is further shown that since said marriage the said Samuel I. Fields and Caroline B. Fields resided together as husband and wife, and continuously lived in the Cherokee Nation up to and including September 1, 1902. Said applicant is identified on the Cherokee authenticated tribal roll of 1880, and Cherokee census roll of 1896, as an intermarried citizen of the Cherokee Nation.

IT IS, THEREFORE, ORDERED AND ADJUDGED: That in accordance with the decision of the Supreme Court of the United States, dated November 5, 1906, in the cases of Daniel Red Bird et al., vs. the United States, Nos. 125, 126, 127 and 128, the applicant, Caroline B. Fields, is entitled, under the provisions of Section 21 of the Act of Congress approved June 28, 1898 (30 Stats., 495), to enrollment as a citizen by intermarriage of the Cherokee Nation, and his[sic] application for enrollment as such is accordingly granted.

Tams Bixby   Commissioner.

Dated at Muskogee, Indian Territory,
this   JAN 29 1907

◇◇◇◇◇

Cherokee Intermarried White 1906
Volume IV

Cherokee 3715.

Muskogee, Indian Territory, January 28, 1907.

W. W. Hastings,
    Attorney for the Cherokee Nation,
        Muskogee, Indian Territory.

Dear Sir:

There is enclosed herewith copy of the decision of the Commissioner to the Five Civilized Tribes, dated January 29, 1907, granting the application for the enrollment of Caroline B. Fields, as a citizen by intermarriage of the Cherokee Nation.

Respectfully,

Enc I-9

Commissioner.

RPI

◇◇◇◇◇

Cherokee 3715

Muskogee, Indian Territory, January 29, 1907.

The Commissioner to the Five Civilized Tribes,
    Muskogee, Indian Territory.

Sir:

Receipt is acknowledged of the testimony and of your decision enrolling Caroline B. Fields, as a citizen by intermarriage of the Cherokee Nation. Time for protesting said decision is waived and I consent that said person may be placed upon the schedule immediately.

Respectfully,
        W. W. Hastings
        Attorney for the Cherokee Nation.

◇◇◇◇◇

199

Cherokee 3715

Muskogee, Indian Territory, January 29, 1907.

Caroline B. Fields,
    Southwest City, Missouri.

Dear Madam:

    There is enclosed herewith copy of the decision of the Commissioner to the Five Civilized Tribes, dated January 29, 1907, granting the application for your enrollment as a citizen by intermarriage of the Cherokee Nation.

    You will be advised when your name has been placed upon a schedule of citizens of the Cherokee Nation and approved by the Secretary of the Interior.

Respectfully,

Enc I-10

Commissioner.

RPI

Cher IW 124

◇◇◇◇◇

E.C.M.

DEPARTMENT OF THE INTERIOR,

COMMISSIONER TO THE FIVE CIVILIZED TRIBES.

In the matter of the application for the enrollment of

JAMES MARTIN

As a citizen by intermarriage of the Cherokee Nation.

CHEROKEE No. 4468.

◇◇◇◇◇

Cherokee Intermarried White 1906
Volume IV

DEPARTMENT OF THE INTERIOR,
COMMISSION TO THE FIVE CIVILIZED TRIBES,
NOWATA, I. T., OCTOBER 16th, 1900.

In the matter of the application of James Martin for the enrollment of himself, wife and child as citizens of the Cherokee Nation; said Martin being sworn and examined by Commissioner T. B. Needles, testified as follows:

Q What is your name? A James Martin.
Q What is your age, Mr. Martin? A I am 67 year old.
Q What is your post office address? A Ruby.
Q What district do you live in? A Cooweescoowee.
Q Are you a recognized citizen of the Cherokee Nation? A By adoption.
Q For whom do you apply for enrollment? A I want to enroll my wife and daughter.
Q Not yourself? A Myself too.
Q What is the name of your wife? A Amanda Martin.
Q What was her name before you married her? A Wlaker[sic].
Q When did you marry her? A '69.
Q Your wife's name would be on the 1880 toll then would it? A Yes, sir.
Q What is the name of your child? A Polly Martin.
Q How old is Polly? A 16.

      1880 enrollment, page 136, #1783, James Martin, Cooweescoowee.
      1880 enrollment; page 136, #1784, Amanda Martin, Cooweescoowee.
      1896 enrollment; page 315, #679, James Martin, Cooweescoowee.
Page 2141896 enrollment; page (212), #3249, Amanda Martin,   "
      1896 enrollment; page 214, #3250, Polly Martin,   "

Q How long have you lived in the Cherokee Nation? A 30 years.
Q You are living here now? A Yes sir.
Q Is Polly alive and living with you at this time? A Yes, sir.

Com'r Needles:--The name os[sic] James Martin and his wife, Amanda, appear upon the authenticated roll of 1880, he as an intermarried white and she as a Cherokee citizen by blood. Their names also appear upon the census roll of 1896, as well as the name of his daughter, Polly. They having been duly identified according to the page and number of the roll, and having made satisfactory proof as to their residence, said James Martin will be duly listed for enrollment as a Cherokee citizen by intermarriage, and his wife, Amanda, and his daughter, Polly, will be duly listed for enrollment as Cherokee citizens by blood.

---oooOOOooo---

J. O. Rosson, being first duly sworn, states that as stenographer to the Commission to the Five Civilized Tribes, he correctly recorded the testimony and proceedings in this case, and that the foregoing is a true and complete transcript of his stenographic notes thereof.

JO Rosson

Subscribed and sworn to before me this 16th day of October, 1900.

CR Breckinridge

Commissioner.

◇◇◇◇◇

Cherokee 4468.

Department of the Interior,
Commission to the Five Civilized Tribes,
Muskogee, I. T., October 6, 1902.

In the matter of the application of James Martin for the enrollment of himself as a citizen by intermarriage, and for the enrollment of his wife, Amanda, and child, Polly, as citizens by blood of the Cherokee Nation: he being sworn and examined by the Commission, testified as follows:

Q What is your name? A James Martin.
Q What is your age? A 69.
Q What is your postoffice? A Ruby.
Q Are you the same James Martin that made application to this Commission for enrollment as an intermarried citizen on October 16, 1900? A Yes sir.
Q What is your wife's name? A Amanda A.
Q Is she a citizen by blood of the Cherokee Nation? A Yes sir.
Q When were you and Amanda A. married? A Married in '70.
Q Were you ever married before you married Amanda A.? A Yes sir.
Q How many times before? A Once.
Q Was your wife living or dead? A Dead.
Q Had she ever been married before she married you? A No sir.
Q She is your second wife? A Yes.
Q You her first husband? A Yes sir.
Q Have you and she lived together a husband and wife since 1880 up to the present time? A Yes sir.
Q Never have been separated? A No sir.
Q You never have been married to any other woman since 1880? A No sir.
Q Were you and she living together as husband and wife on the first day of September, 1902? A Yes sir.
Q Have you and your wife lived in the Cherokee Nation all the time since 1880? A Yes sir.
Q Is this your daughter, Polly, by your wife, Amanda? A Yes sir.
Q Has this child lived in the Cherokee Nation all its life? A Yes sir, born and raised here.

The undersigned, being duly sworn, states that as stenographer to the Commission to the Five Civilized Tribes he correctly recorded the testimony and proceedings in this

202

case, and that the foregoing is a true and correct transcript of his stenographic notes thereof.

E.G. Rothenberger

Subscribed and sworn to before me this 27th day of October, 1902.

BC Jones
Notary Public.

◇◇◇◇◇

F.R. Cherokee-4468.

DEPARTMENT OF THE INTERIOR,
COMMISSIONER TO THE FIVE CIVILIZED TRIBES.
Muskogee, I. T., January 14, 1907.

In the matter of the application for the enrollment of James Martin as a citizen by intermarriage of the Cherokee Nation.

James Martin being first duly sworn by John E. Tidwell, a Notary Public for the Western District of Indian Territory, testified as follows:

By the Commissioner:
Q What is your name? A James Martin
Q What is your age? A Seventy years.
Q What is your postoffice address? A Ruby, Cherokee Nation.
Q You are a white man and do not possess any Cherokee blood? A No sir.
Q You are an applicant for enrollment as a citizen by intermarriage of the Cherokee Nation? A Yes sir.
Q Your only claim to the right of enrollment as a citizen of the Cherokee Nation such nation is by virtue of your marriage to a citizen by blood of that nation? A Yes sir.
Q What is the name of such citizen? A Amanda Walker.
Q Is she living? A Yes sir.
Q When did you marry her? A I married her in 1869 sometime.
Q Was she a recognized citizen of the Cherokee Nation at the time you married her? A Yes sir.
Q She was living in the Cherokee Nation at that time? A Yes.
Q Was she your first wife? A Yes sir.
Q Was you her first husband? A Yes sir.
Q You are still living with her? A Yes sir.
Q And you have lived all these years in the Cherokee Nation.[sic] A Yes, all the time.
Q You have resided as husband and wife and lived continuously in the Cherokee Nation? A Yes, I have never lived out of the nation.
Q That has always been your home? A Yes sir.
Q Did you marry Amanda Walker under a license of the Cherokee Nation? A Yes sir.

Q Have you a copy of that license? A Yes, I have a copy of that record.

Applicant presents a certified copy of the marriage record of Delaware District, Cherokee Nation, showing that James Mason[sic], a white man, was licensed to marry Mandy Walker January 6, 1869 and that same was returned executed January 7, 1869, said parties having been married by T. J. McGhee, clerk of the district court. Said certificate is executed by J. T. Parks, Executive Secretary of the Cherokee Nation under date of September 25, 1900.

The applicant, James Martin, is identified on the Cherokee authenticated roll of 1880, Cooweescoowee District, opposite No. 1783.

His wife, Amanda Walker, is identified on said roll opposite No. 1784, and he name also appears on the approved roll of citizens of the Cherokee Nation opposite No. 10709.

Frances R. Lane upon oath states that as stenographer to the Commissioner to the Five Civilized Tribes she reported the testimony in the above entitled cause and that the foregoing is an accurate transcript of her stenographic notes thereof.

Frances R. Lane

Subscribed and sworn to before me this January 16, 1907.

Edward Merrick
Notary Public.

◇◇◇◇◇

Execuitve[sic] Department,
Cherokee Nation.

Tahlequah, I. T., Sept 25. 1900

I hereby certify that the following is a true and correct copy of the Marriage Record of Delaware District, now on file in this office, in so far as the License and Marriage Certificate of the parties therein named are concerned:-

" This is to certify by me that Jas. Martin, a white man was licenses to marry Mandy Walker on the 6th day of Jan. 1869, and executed return Jan. the 7th 1869, being with according to the Act passed by the National Council, bearing date Oct. 15, 1855, in regard to white men marrying in this Nation".

Cherokee Intermarried White 1906
Volume IV

(Signed) T. J. McGhee
Clk. D. C. D. C. N.

Given under my hand and the seal of the Cherokee Nation on the day written above.

(Signed) J. T. Parks
Executive Secretary
Cherokee Nation.

This certifies that the undersigned, being duly sworn, states that as stenographer to the Commission to the Five Civilized Tribes she made the above and foregoing copy and that the same is a full, true and correct copy of the original instrument now on file in this office.

Subscribed and sworn to before me this 21st day of January, 1907.

Notary Public.

◇◇◇◇◇

E C M   Cherokee 4468.

DEPARTMENT OF THE INTERIOR,

COMMISSIONER TO THE FIVE CIVILIZED TRIBES.

In the matter of the application for the enrollment of JAMES MARTIN as a citizen by intermarriage of the Cherokee Nation.

_D_E_C_I_S_I_O_N_

THE RECORDS OF THIS OFFICE SHOW: That on October 16th, 1900 application was received by the Commission to the Five Civilized Tribes for the enrollment of James Martin as a citizen by intermarriage of the Cherokee Nation. Further proceedings in the matter of said application were had at Muskogee, Indian Territory, October 6th, 1902 and January 14th, 1907.

THE EVIDENCE IN THIS CASE SHOWS: That the applicant herein, James Martin, a white man, was married in accordance with Cherokee law January 7th, 1869 to his wife, Amanda Martin, nee Walker, who was at the time of said marriage a recognized citizen by blood of the Cherokee Nation, who is identified on the Cherokee authenticated tribal roll of 1880, Cooweescoowee District No. 1784 as a native Cherokee and whose name appears on the approved partial roll of citizens by blood of the Cherokee Nation opposite No. 10709. It is further shown that from the time of said marriage the said James Martin and Amanda Martin resided together as husband and wife and continuously lived in the Cherokee Nation up to and including September 1st, 1902. Said applicant is identified on the Cherokee authenticated tribal roll of 1880 and the Cherokee census roll of 1896 as an intermarried citizen of the Cherokee Nation.

IT IS, THEREFORE, ORDERED AND ADJUDGED: That in accordance with the decision of the Supreme Court of the United States, dated November 5th, 1906, in the cases of Daniel Red Bird et al. vs. the United States, Nos. 125, 126, 127 and 128, the said applicant, James Martin is entitled, under the provision of Section Twenty-one of the Act of Congress approved June 28th, 1898 (30 Stats. 495), to enrollment as a citizen by intermarriage of the Cherokee Nation, and his application for enrollment as such is accordingly granted.

Tams Bixby
Commissioner.

Dated at Muskogee, Indian Territory,
this   JAN 29 1907

◇◇◇◇◇

Cherokee 4468

Muskogee, Indian Territory, January 29, 1907.

W. W. Hastings,
    Attorney for the Cherokee Nation,
        Muskogee, Indian Territory.

Dear Sir:

    There is enclosed herewith copy of the decision of the Commissioner to the Five Civilized Tribes, dated January 29, 1907, granting the application for the enrollment of James Martin as a citizen by intermarriage of the Cherokee Nation.

Respectfully,

Enc I-14   Commissioner.

RPI

◇◇◇◇◇

Cherokee 4468

Muskogee, Indian Territory, January 29, 1907.

The Commissioner to the Five Civilized Tribes,
        Muskogee, Indian Territory.

Sir:

Receipt is acknowledged of the testimony and of your decision enrolling James Martin as a citizen by intermarriage of the Cherokee Nation. Time for protesting said decision is waived and I consent that said person may be placed upon the schedule immediately.

Respectfully,
W. W. Hastings
Attorney for the Cherokee Nation.

◇◇◇◇◇

Cherokee 4468

Muskogee, Indian Territory, January 29, 1907.

James Martin,
        Ruby, Indian Territory.

Dear Sir:

There is enclosed herewith copy of the decision of the Commissioner to the Five Civilized Tribes, dated January 29, 1907, granting the application for your enrollment as a citizen by intermarriage of the Cherokee Nation.

You will be advised when your name has been placed upon a schedule of citizens of the Cherokee Nation and approved by the Secretary of the Interior.

Respectfully,

Enc I-15   Commissioner.

RPI

◇◇◇◇◇

Cherokee
I.W. 124.

Muskogee, Indian Territory, April 16, 1907.

James Martin,
Ruby, Indian Territory.

Dear Sir:

Your marriage license and certificate filed in connection with your application for enrollment as a citizen by intermarriage of the Cherokee Nation is returned to you herewith, copies of the same being retained in the files of this office.

Respectfully,

Encl. W-2   Commissioner.
S.W.

Cher IW 125

◇◇◇◇◇

C.E.W.

DEPARTMENT OF THE INTERIOR,

COMMISSIONER TO THE FIVE CIVILIZED TRIBES.

_____

In the matter of the application for the enrollment of

CATHERINE J. WARD

as a citizen by intermarriage of the Cherokee Nation.

_____

CHEROKEE 4665.

◇◇◇◇ ◇

Cherokee Intermarried White 1906
Volume IV

Department of the Interior,
Commission to the Five Civilized Tribes,
Claremore, I. T., October 22, 1900.

In the matter of the application of Catherine Jane Ward for enrollment as a Cherokee by intermarriage; being sworn and examined by Commissioner Needles, she testified as follows:

Q What is your name? A Catherine Jane Ward.
Q What is your age? A 56.
Q What is your post office address? A Pryor Creek.
Q What district do you live in? A I live in Cooweescoowee district.
Q Are you a citizen by blood of the Cherokee Nation? A No, sir.
Q By intermarriage? A Yes, by intermarriage.
Q Who do you want to enroll? A Just myself.
Q What is your husband's name? A Samuel Ward.
Q Is he living? A No, sir, he is dead.
Q When were you married to him? A In 1862.
Q Have you been married since? A No, sir.
Q When did you husband die? A He died during the war, in 1864.
Q Have you always lived in the Cherokee Nation? A Yes, ever since I have been married.
Q Continuously since you were married you have lived in the Cherokee Nation? A Well, I was away four years in Texas a while.
Q How long ago was that? A I came back here in 1867 I believe.
(On 1880 roll, page 342, No. 3054, Jane Ward, Cooweescoowee dist.)
Q You have been living here continuously, I understand, since 1880, 20 years ago? A Yes, I have been here since that.
Q You haven't married since the death of your husband? A No, sir.
(On 1896 roll, page 559, No. 3611, Jane Ward, Delaware district..)

The name of Catherine Jane Ward appears upon the authenticated roll of 1880 and upon the census roll of 1896 as Jane Ward, and she being duly identified, and having made satisfactory proof as to her residence, said Catherine Jane Ward will be duly listed for enrollment as a Cherokee citizen by intermarriage.

------------o------------

Bruce C. Jones, being duly sworn, says that as stenographer to the Commission to the Five Civilized Tribes he correctly recorded the proceedings and testimony in the above case, and the foregoing is a true and complete transcript of his stenographic notes thereof.

Bruce C Jones

Cherokee Intermarried White 1906
Volume IV

Sworn to and subscribed before me this the 22nd of October, 1900.

TB Needles
Commissioner.

◇◇◇◇◇

COOWEESCOOWEE.

Statement of Applicant Taken Under Oath.

CHEROKEE BY BLOOD AND ADOPTION.

Date Oct 2^d 1900.

Name   Pryor Creek I.T.
District ....Year ....Page ....No. ....
Citizen by blood...............Mother's citizenship ....
Intermarried citizen ....
Married under what law..................Date of marriage ....
License ⑤⑥ ....Certificate..............
Wife's name   Catherine J Ward
District   **COOWEESCOOWEE.**   Year 1880 Page 342 No. 3054
Citizen by blood   No   Mother's citizenship..........................
Intermarried citizen   Yes
Married under what law..................Date of marriage.................
License ....Certificate..............

Names of Children:

	Dist.	Year	Page	No.	Age
	Dist.	Year	Page	No.	Age
	Dist.	Year	Page	No.	Age
	Dist.	Year	Page	No.	Age
	Dist.	Year	Page	No.	Age

1 on 1880 roll as Jane Ward

◇◇◇◇◇

Cherokee Intermarried White 1906
Volume IV

DEPARTMENT OF THE INTERIOR.
Commission to the Five Civilized Tribes.
Muskogee, Indian Territory, September 30th, 1902.

In the matter of the application of Catherine J. Ward for the enrollment of herself as a citizen by intermarriage of the Cherokee Nation.

Supplemental to #4665.

Appearances:

Applicant appears in person.
Cherokee Nation by J. C. Starr.

CATHERINE J. WARD, being duly sworn, testified as follows:
Examination by the Commission.

Q. What is your name, please? A. Catherine J. Ward.
Q. What is your age at this time? A. 58.
Q. What is your post office? A. Prior[sic] Creek.
Q. Are you the same Catherine J. Ward for whom application was made for enrollment as an intermarried citizen on October 22nd, 1900? A. I don't remember the date. It was at Claremore.
Q. You claim as an intermarried citizen, do you, Mrs. Ward? A. Yes, sir.
Q. What was your husband's name? A. Samuel Ward.
Q. Is he living or dead? A. Dead.
Q. When did he die? A. September, '64. Not September; it was February, 1864.
Q. 1864 or 1874? A. Sixty.
Q. He died during the war? A. Yes, sir.
Q. When were you and he married? A. September, 1862.
Q. Did you and he live together continuously as husband and wife from the time of your marriage up until the time of his death? A. Yes, sir.
Q. You were never separated during his lifetime? A. No, sir.
Q. Were you his first wife? A. Yes, sir.
Q. And he was your first husband? A. Yes, sir.
Q. Have you ever been married to any other man except Samuel Ward?
A. No, sir.
Q. You have never married since his death? A. No, sir.
Q. You were still a widow on the first of September, 1902? A. Yes, sir.
Q. How long have you lived in the Cherokee Nation?
A. Ever since '68, I think it was we come.
Q. Have you lived here since 1880 all the time? A. Yes, sir.
Q. Haven't lived out since 1880? A. No, sir.

Cherokee Intermarried White 1906
Volume IV

Jesse O. Carr, being first duly sworn, states that as stenographer to the Commission to the Five Civilized Tribes he reported the above entitled case and that the foregoing is a true and complete transcript of his stenographic notes thereof.

Jesse O. Carr

Subscribed and sworn to before me this 18th day of October, 1902.

BC Jones
Notary Public.

◇◇◇◇◇

DEPARTMENT OF THE INTERIOR.
COMMISSION TO THE FIVE CIVILIZED TRIBES.
AUXILIARY CHEROKEE LAND OFFICE.

Muskogee, Indian Territory, March 2, 1905.

In the matter of the allotment of lands to Catherine J. Ward intermarried applicant, Cherokee Card 4665.

Jefferson D. Edmondson, intermarried applicant, Cherokee Card 4661, being sworn, testified as follows:

Examination by the Commissioner Commission:
Q What is your name? A Jefferson D. Ward.
Q How old are you? A 43.
Q What is your post office? A Prior[sic] Creek, Indian Territory.
Q What is the name of your father? A A. V. Edmondson.
Q The name of your mother? A Laura Edmondson.
Q What is your object in appearing at the Land Office today?
A To designate lands as an allotment for Catherine J. Edmondson[sic].
Q What relation are you to Catherine J. Edmondson[sic]? A I am her son-in-law.
Q The husband of her daughter? A Yes sir.
Q What is your wife's name? A Lula Edmondson.

> Note notation made on Cherokee Card No. 4661, the name of Lula Edmondson, wife of Jefferson D. Edmondson appearing as number 2 thereon, Approved Roll No. 26649.

Q State the reasons why Catherine J. Ward does not make personal appearance and selection? A She is old and sick and not able. She is sixty odd years old.
Q Is her condition of health such that she is unable to make appearance at the Land Office? A Yes sir.
Q What is the name of her father? A I do not know.

Cherokee Intermarried White 1906
Volume IV

Q Do you know the name of her mother?: A Her name before she was married was Lear.

Q You do not know the names of her father and mother? A No sir.

It appears on the records of the Commission that the father of Catherine J. Ward is Francis Lear and the name of her mother Elizabeth Lear.

Q Have you written authority from Catherine J. Ward to make these designations? A Yes sir.

Witness offers Power of Attorney executed by Catherine Jane Ward dated Prior Creek, Indian Territory, February 27, 1905, wherein she appoints J. D. Edmondson her attorney to select lands in the Cherokee Nation.

Q Is the Catherine Jane Ward who executed this Power of Attorney identical with the Catherine J. Ward about whom you have been testifying? A Yes sir same person.

Q Are you the same person named in this power of attorney? A Yes sir

Q Are the lands you desire to select for Mrs. Ward suitable for an allotment? A Yes sir.

Q Are there improvements on the land? A Yes sir.

Q Is it her home place? A Yes sir, home place.

Q Do the lands lay west of Grand river? A Yes sir.

Q Has any application been made at either Vinita or Tahlequah for her account? A No sir, this is the first application.

Blanche Ashton upon oath states that as stenographer to the Commission to the Five Civilized Tribes she accurately recorded the testimony in the above entitled cause and that the foregoing is a correct transcript of her notes thereof. Blanche Ashton Subscribed and sworn to before me this 2nd day of March, 1905.

(Name Illegible)
Notary Public.

◇◇◇◇◇

DEPARTMENT OF THE INTERIOR
COMMISSIONER TO THE FIVE CIVILIZED TRIBES
MUSKOGEE, IND. TER.
JAN. 4, 1907

IN THE MATTER OF THE APPLICATION OF CATHERINE J. WARD FOR ENROLLMENT AS A CITIZEN BY INTERMARRIAGE OF THE CHEROKEE NATION.

CENSUS CARD NO. 4665.

Q What is your name? A Catherine J. Ward.

Q How old are you.[sic] A Sixty two.

Q What is your post office address? A Pryor Creek.

Q Do you claim to be a citizen by intermarriage of the Cherokee Nation. A Yes sir.

Q Thru whom do you claim your intermarried rights. A Samuel T. Ward.

Q When was you married to Samuel T. Ward. A Sixty two in September.

Q Where? A It was near Maysville in Delaware District.

213

Cherokee Intermarried White 1906
Volume IV

Q Was Samuel T. Ward a citizen of the Cherokee Nation at the time you married in '62.
A Yes sir.
Q Living in the Cherokee Nation at that time.
A Yes sir he lived there all his live.
Q Is he living. A No sir.
Q When did he die. A He got killed during the war in '64.
Q Have you ever married again since his death. A No sir.
Q Have you got any evidence of your marriage to Samuel T. Ward. A No sir.
Q Is there anyone here today who was present when you was married to Samuel T. Ward. A No sir not that I know of.
Q Have you lived continuously in the Cherokee Nation since your marriage to Samuel T. Ward. A No I lived one year in Texas and about a year and a half in Missouri and I came back and been here ever since.
Q When did you live a year in Texas. A It was in '65.
Q When did you live a year and a half in Missouri. A Sixty six and sixty seven; it was about a year and a half, I dont[sic] know exactly; I've been here ever since.
Q You have been here ever since 1867. A Yes sir.
Q Have you been recognized as a citizen by intermarriage of the Cherokee Nation ever since you returned here in 1867. A Yes sir
Q And been on all the Cherokee rolls prepared since that time[sic] A Yes.
Q Have you held property in the Cherokee Nation.
A No I never had any property.

The applicant is identified on the 1880 Cherokee Roll Delaware District opposite No. 3054.

Q What is the name of the father and mother of your husband.
A James Ward, and Louisa Ward.
Q Has your husband any brothers and sisters living at this time. A He has no sisters, never had any; he has three brothers.
Q Are they living. A Yes sir.
Q What are their names. A Joe Ward; Joseph L. Ward.
Q How old is Joseph L. Ward. A He's about sixty two.
Q Has he a family. A Yes sir.
Q What's his wife's name. A Alice
Q How old is she? A I don't know; I think she's about ten years younger than he is.
Q How many children have they got. A They have three living.
Q What's their names. A Stella Pace she is now; and Pink is the nick name, I think her name is Louisa.
Q What are the names of the other brothers of your husband? A George.
Q Has he got a family. A Yes sir.
Q What is the name of his wife and children?
A His wife's name is Eliza and his oldest daughter is Lela.
Q Has he got any other children. A Yes, James is one of his sons and John the other.
Q What's [sic] name of the other brother of your husband.
A The other brother of George is named Ethel. [sic]

Q What's your husband's other brother's name.

A John.

Q How old is he. A About fifty seven.

Q Has he got a family. A Yes sir /[sic]

Q What is his wife's name. A Liza.

Q What is his children's name.

Q Dora, Lula, Lee and Winnie.

Q Any others.

Q Yes, they call her Dee; I forget her name; and there's one boy named Dennison.

Q What's his other brother's name? A William Ward.

Q How old is William Ward.

Q He's about fifty two or three.

Q What's his post office address? A Claremore.

Q Has he got a family. A Yes.

Q What's his wife's name. A His wife's name is Addie.

Q What's the names of his children? A Lula, Elva, Altie and Maud, four children.

Q Can you get any of the Wards to come in here and testify as to your marriage to their brother. A They are not here; if they were here I could.

Q Have you anybody else here today who knows of your marriage to your husband. A They know of it but they wasn't present at the wedding.

Clara Mitchell Wood being first duly sworn upon her oath states that as stenographer for the Commissioner to the Five Civilized Tribes she reported the above and foregoing proceedings and that this is a correct transcript of her stenographic notes.

Clara Mitchell Wood

Subscribed and sworn to before me this 8th day of January 1907.

B.P. Rasmus
Notary Public.

◇◇◇◇◇

C. F. B.   Cherokee 4665.

DEPARTMENT OF THE INTERIOR,
COMMISSION TO THE FIVE CIVILIZED TRIBES.
Muskogee, Indian Territory, January 7, 1907.

Supplemental proceedings in the Matter of the Application for the Enrollment of Katherine J. Ward as a citizen by intermarriage of the Cherokee Nation.

George D. Ward for Applicant/[sic]

APPEARANCES:

Cherokee Nation represented by H. M. Vance, in behalf of W. W. Hastings, Attorney.

George W. Ward being first duly sworn by John E. Tidwell, Notary Public, testified as follows:

ON BEHALF OF COMMISSIONER.

Q What is your name?   A George D. Ward.
Q What is your age?   A 60 the 4th of next June.
Q What is your post office address?
A Afton.
Q You appear here to-day for the purpose of giving testimony relative to the right to enrollment of Katherine[sic] J. Ward as a citizen by intermarriage of the Cherokee Nation?
A Yes sir.
Q Are you related to her in any way?
A She married by brother.
Q Is your brother a citizen by blood of the Cherokee Nation?
A Yes sir.
Q Was he at the time he married his wife, Katherine J. Ward, a recognized citizen of the Cherokee Nation?
A Yes sir.
Q Living in the Cherokee country, was he?
A Yes sir.
Q Were you present at the ceremony?
A No,
Q When was it performed?
A I think it was in '62.
Q Were you living in the community?
A Yes sir; I was right there at home.
Q But you didn't witness the ceremony?
A No sir, he married about two miles from there.
Q You have every reason to believe that they were married at the time?
A Yes sir.

Q You know of your own personal knowledge that since that time they have resided together as husband and wife?

A Yes sir, until his death.

Q When did he die?

A He was killed during the war.

Q After his death, did she re-marry?

A No sir.

Q She has lived continuously in the Cherokee Nation since his death?

A Well, after the war she went to Missouri and was gone a year or so. I think she came back in '68.

Q Was that the only time she has ever been absent from the Nation for any length of time?

A Yes sir.

Q That absence was in the nature of a visit, was it?

A Yes, she went to her brother's; then she came back and lived with my mother up until her daughter was married and then she has been living with her ever since.

Q Do you know whether during that year she considered the Cherokee Nation her home?

A Yes sir, she did.

W. W. Ward being first duly sworn by John E. Tidwell, Notary Public, testified as follows:

ON BEHALF OF COMMISSIONER.

Q What is your name?   A W. W. Ward.

Q What is your age?   A 52.

Q What is your post office address?

A Claremore, Indian Territory.

Q Do you know a person in the Cherokee Nation by the name of Katherine J. Ward?

A Yes sir.

Q Is she related to you in any way?

A My sister-in-law.

Q What was her husband's name?

A Samuel.

Q He was your brother?

A Yes sir.

Q A citizen of the Cherokee Nation?

A Yes sir.

Q Was he a recognized citizen of the Cherokee Nation at the time he married Katherine J. Ward?

A Yes sir.

Q Do you remember when they were married?

A No sir; I was too small; before the war I think or at the beginning.

Q How long ago can you remember them?

A I can remember them ever since I was about 8 or 9 years old.

Q About that year would that be? A About '63.

Q Do you remember when Katherine J. Ward's husband died?
A He was killed during the war. I believe it was in February.
Q Since his death, has Katherine J. Ward married?
A No sir.
Q She has lived in the Cherokee Nation continuously since then up to and including the present time?
A Yes sir.
Q Never been out except on visits?
A Not to my knowledge.

The undersigned being first duly sworn states that as stenographer to the Commission to the Five Civilized Tribes, she correctly recorded the testimony taken in this case and that the foregoing is a full, true and correct transcript of her stenographic notes thereof.

Myrtle Hill

Subscribed and sworn to before me this the 8th day of January, 1907.

John E Tidwell
Notary Public.

◇◇◇◇◇

C.E.W.   Cherokee 4665.

DEPARTMENT OF THE INTERIOR,

COMMISSIONER TO THE FIVE CIVILIZED TRIBES.

In the matter of the application for the enrollment of CATHERINE J. WARD as a citizen by intermarriage of the Cherokee Nation.

D E C I S I O N

THE RECORDS OF THIS OFFICE SHOW: That at Claremore, Indian Territory, October 22, 1900, application was received by the Commission to the Five Civilized Tribes for the enrollment of Catherine J. Ward as a citizen by intermarriage of the Cherokee Nation. Further proceedings in the matter of said application were had at Muskogee, Indian Territory, September 30, 1902, March 2, 1905, and January 4 and 7, 1907.

THE EVIDENCE IN THIS CASE SHOWS: That the applicant herein, Catherine J. Ward, a white man, was married in accordance with Cherokee law September, 1862, to one Samuel T. Ward, since deceased, who was at the time of said marriage a recognized citizen by blood of the Cherokee Nation; that from the time of said marriage the said Samuel T. Ward and Catherine J. Ward resided together as husband and wife until his death, which occurred about the year 1864; that since the death of the said Samuel T. Ward said Catherine J. Ward has remained unmarried; and that she has resided continuously in the Cherokee Nation since the year 1862. Said applicant is identified on the Cherokee authenticated tribal roll of 1880, and the Cherokee census roll of 1896, as an intermarried citizen of the Cherokee Nation.

IT IS, THEREFORE, ORDERED AND ADJUDGED: That in accordance with the decision of the Supreme Court of the United States, dated November 5, 1906, in the cases of Daniel Red Bird et al. vs. the United States, Nos. 125, 126, 127 and 128, the said applicant, Catherine J. Ward, is entitled, under the provisions of Section 21, of the Act of Congress approved June 28, 1898 (30 Stats., 495), to enrollment as a citizen by intermarriage of the Cherokee Nation, and her application for enrollment as such is accordingly granted.

Tams Bixby
Commissioner.

Dated at Muskogee, Indian Territory,
this   JAN 29 1907

◇◇◇◇◇

Cherokee
4665.

Muskogee, Indian Territory, December 27, 1906.

Catherine J. Ward,
    Pryor Creek, Indian Territory.

Dear Madam:

November 6, 1906, the United States Supreme Court held that white persons who intermarried with Cherokee citizens according to Cherokee law prior to November 1, 1875, are entitled to enrollment and allotments of land as citizens of the Cherokee Nation.

You are advised that to properly determine your right to enrollment as a citizen by intermarriage of the Cherokee Nation, it will be necessary for you to appear before the Commissioner for the purpose of giving testimony as to the date of your marriage and whether or not your husband, by reason of your marriage to whom you claim the right to enrollment as a citizen by intermarriage of the Cherokee Nation, was a recognized Cherokee citizen at the time of your marriage to him.

You are therefore directed to appear before the Commissioner at Muskogee, Indian Territory, at 9 o'clock A. M., on Friday, January 4, 1907, and give testimony as above indicated.

219

Respectfully,

H.J.C.   Acting Commissioner.

◇◇◇◇◇

Cherokee 4665

Muskogee, Indian Territory, January 29, 1907.

W. W. Hastings,
     Attorney for the Cherokee Nation,
          Muskogee, Indian Territory.

Dear Sir:

There is enclosed herewith copy of the decision of the Commissioner to the Five Civilized Tribes, dated January 29, 1907, granting the application for the enrollment of Catherine J. Ward as a citizen by intermarriage of the Cherokee Nation.

Respectfully,

Enc I-25   Commissioner.

RPI

◇◇◇◇◇

Cherokee 4665

Muskogee, Indian Territory, January 29, 1907.

The Commissioner to the Five Civilized Tribes,
     Muskogee, Indian Territory.

Sir:

Receipt is acknowledged of the testimony and of your decision enrolling Catherine J. Ward, as a citizen by intermarriage of the Cherokee Nation. Time for protesting said decision is waived and I consent that said person may be placed upon the schedule immediately.

Respectfully,
               W. W. Hastings
               Attorney for the Cherokee Nation.

◇◇◇◇◇

Cherokee 4665

Muskogee, Indian Territory, January 29, 1907.

Catherine J. Ward,
Pryor Creek, Indian Territory.

Dear Madam:

There is enclosed herewith copy of the decision of the Commissioner to the Five Civilized Tribes, dated January 29, 1907, granting the application for your enrollment as a citizen by intermarriage of the Cherokee Nation.

You will be advised when your name has been placed upon a schedule of citizens of the Cherokee Nation and approved by the Secretary of the Interior.

Respectfully,

Enc I-26

Commissioner.

RPI

Cher IW 126

◇◇◇◇◇

E.C.M.

DEPARTMENT OF THE INTERIOR,

COMMISSIONER TO THE FIVE CIVILIZED TRIBES.

In the matter of the application for the enrollment of

LIZZIE WARD

As a citizen by intermarriage of the Cherokee Nation.

CHEROKEE NO. 4832.

◇◇◇◇◇

Cherokee Intermarried White 1906
Volume IV

Department of the Interior,
Commission to the Five Civilized tribes[sic],
Claremore, I. T. October 23rd, 1900.

In the matter of the application of Thomas F. Ward for the enrollment of himself, wife and children, as Cherokee Citizens. He being sworn before the Commission testified as follows-

Q What is your name? A. Thomas F. Ward.
Q What ids yout[sic] age? A. 50
Q What is your post office address? A. Foyl[sic].
Q What district do you live in? A. Cooweescoowee.
Q Are you a recognized citizen of the Cherokee Nation? A. Yes sir.
Q By blood? A. Yes sir.
Q What degree of blood? A. Cannot say.
Q Who do you want enrolled? A. Myself, wife and family.
Q How many children? [sic] 4.
Q What is your wifes[sic] name? A. Lizzie.
Q Is she a white woman or citizen? A. White woman.
Q When were you married to her? A. In 1873.
Q What is the names of your children? A. James H.
Q What is his age? A. 18 years.
Q What is the next one? A. Bertha M.
Q What is her age? A. 16 years.
Q What is the next one? A. John F. Ward. Q What is his age? A. 14.
Q What is the next one? A. Ella N. [sic] What is her age? A. 11 years.
1880 roll, page 205, No 3351, T. F. Ward, Cooweescoowee, N. C.

1880	205	3352, Lizzie Ward.	"
1896	282	5166 Thomas Ward,	"
1896	330	1122 Lizzie Ward	"
1896	282	5167 James Ward,	"
1896	282	5168 Bertha Ward.	"
1896	282	5169 John Ward	"
1896	282	5170 Ella N. Ward	"

Q How long have you lived in the Cherokee Nation? A. Perty[sic] much all my live.
Q Is Lizzie your first wife? A. Yes sir.
Q Are you her first husband? A. Yes sir.
Q Are you living with her now? A. Yes sir.
Q Are these children all alive and living with you at this time? A. Yes sir.
The name of Thomas F. Ward appears on the authenticated 1880 roll as T. F. Ward and on the 1896 census roll as Thomas Ward. The name of his wife Lizzie appears on the authenticated roll of 1880 and on the census roll of 1896 as an intermarried white. The names of their children: James M.; Bertha M.; John F.; and Ella N. Ward appear on the census roll of 1896. They all being duly identified and having made satisfactory proof as to residence, consequentally[sic] Thomas F. Ward and his said children as enumerated in

the testimony will be duly listed for enrollment as Cherokee by blood. His wife Lizzie will be listed for enrollment as a Cherokee by intermarriage.

Chas. von Weise being duly sworn states as stenographer to the Commission to the Five Civilized Tribes he reported in full all the proceedings in the above cause and that the foregoing is a full, true and complete transcript of his stenographic notes in said proceedings.

Chas von Weise

Subscribed and sworn to before me this the 24th of October, 1900.

MD Green
~~Commissioner.~~
Notary Public.

◇◇◇◇◇

Cher
Supp'l to # 4832

Department of the Interior,
Commission to the Five Civilized Tribes,
Muskogee, I. T., October 15, 1902.

In the matter of the application of THOMAS F. WARD, for the enrollment of himself and his children, JAMES M., BERTHA M., JOHN F. and ELLA N. WARD, as citizens by blood, and his wife, LIZZIE WARD, as a citizen by intermarriage, of the Cherokee Nation:

LIZZIE WARD, being duly sworn and examined by the Commission, testified as follows:

Q What is your name ? A Lizzie Ward. I go by that name now; that's the way I have always been enrolled.
Q How old are you ? A I am forty four.
Q What is your post office ? A Talala.
Q Was it Foil[sic] when you applied before ? A Yes sir.
Q Are you an applicant for enrollment as an intermarried citizen ? A Yes sir.
Q What is your husband's name ? A Thomas F. Ward.
Q Is he a Cherokee by blood ? A Yes sir.
Q When were you married to Thomas F. Ward ? A In 1873.
Q Had you ever been married before you married Thomas F. Ward ?
A No sir.
Q Had he ever been married prior to his marriage to you ?
A No sir.
Q Have you and Thomas F. Ward lived together from the time of your marriage up to the present time ? A Yes sir. Up till about the 22nd of March.
Q March of 1902 ? A Yes sir.

223

Cherokee Intermarried White 1906
Volume IV

Q Have you separated then ? A Yes sir.
Q You haven't been living together since last March ? A No sir.
Q Have you procured a divorce from Mr. Ward A No sir. I haven't got any divorce.
Q So you are yet his wife in the eyes of the law ? A Yes sir.
Q What was the cause of your separation ?
A Well, we just couldn't agree.
Q Where were you living when you separated ? A At Foil[sic].
Q In the town or out in the country ? A Out on the farm.
Q Well, when you separated where did he go ? A He's there.
Q And you left ? A I left him.
Q Did he take you away when you left or did you go alone ? A I taken[sic] myself. That is, the children taken me.
Q Your children took you ? A Yes sir.
Q Have you got all the children with you ?
A All that's under age.
Q You and he were not living together on the first day of September, 1902 ?
A No sir.
Q Have you made any effort to live with him since the separation last spring ?
A No sir.
Q Has he made any effort to get you back ? A Not a bit.
Q What subject caused you to disagree that you couldn't get along after living together that long ?
A I don't know; I just didn't want to take his abuse, his cursing that's all I can tell you.
Q You have never been separated before this time ?
A No sir, we had always lived together until then. I am down on every roll I reckon. The first roll when I was married was '74 or 5 and I know I drawed[sic] bread money.
Q You are on the 1880 roll are you ?
A Yes sir, on every roll since I was married.
Q Have you lived in the Cherokee Nation all the time since 1880 ?
A All the time. I have have lived anywhere else. I have lived here ever since we were married.
Q You were married in 1873 ? A Yes sir.

E. C. Bagwell, on oath states that, as stenographer to the Commission to the Five Civilized Tribes, he correctly recorded the testimony and proceedings had in the above entitled cause, and that the foregoing is an accurate transcript of his stenographic notes thereof.

E.C. Bagwell

Subscribed and sworn to before me this November 17, 1902.

BC Jones
Notary Public.

◇◇◇◇◇

224

Cherokee Intermarried White 1906
Volume IV

Cher
Supp'l to # 4832

Department of the Interior,
Commission to the Five Civilized Tribes,
Vinita, I. T., February 13, 1903.

In the matter of the application of THOMAS F. WARD, for the enrollment of himself, and his children, JAMES M., BERTHA M., JOHN F. and ELLA N. WARD, as citizens by blood, and his wife, LIZZIE WARD, as a citizen by intermarriage, of the Cherokee Nation:

THOMAS M. WARD, being duly sworn, and examined, testified as follows:

Examined by the Commission:
M
Q What is your name ? A Thomas F. Ward.
Q How old are you ? A Twenty one next Monday.
Q Where do you live ? A Talala.
Q Living with your mother ? A Yes sir.
Q Do you remember when your father and your mother separated ? A Yes sir.
Q You are the son of Thomas F. and Eliza Ward, are you ? A Yes sir.
Q How long ago since your parents separated ? A The last of March or first of April.
Q Well, do you know what the cause of this separation was ?
A It was caused by his abusing her.
Q Abused by whom ? A Father.
Q What did he do ? A Why he threatened a time or two to kill her, I believe.
Q You believe, did you hear him ? A Yes sir.
Q What did he say ? A He told her he would take his gun down and kill her. That's been two years ago when he said that, and then she lived on with him until last spring, and he brought up the same subject again, and he said she wasn't decent for the hogs to run with, and all such things as that.
Q How long had this sort of thing been going on ?
A About four years I believe, the best I can remember.
Q Did you ever hear him threaten to kill her more than once ?
A Yes sir, twice or three times.
Q Well, what would he say to her on those occasions, just as near as you can state his language ? A Why I can't, it's been so long now I can't; he cussed right sharply.
Q Threatened to shoot her did he ? A Yes sir, he threatened to shoot her.
Q Would he take down his gun ? A No, he never did take down his gun.
Q Did you ever see him strike your mother ?
A Yes sir I seen him strike her once.
Q Did he strike her and hurt her ? A No sir, he never did hurt her.
Q Did he strike her with his fists his closed fists or with his open hand ? A Yes sir with his fists.
Q What part of her person, her face ? A Yes sir.

Q Did that occur more than once ? A Once is about all I can remember of I believe.

Q Would the quarrel frequently ? A Yes sir right frequently.

Q How often ? A It wasn't so often, about once every two weeks I believe.

Q It would average about once every two weeks ?

A Maybe once a month.

Q You say he would call her names ? A Yes sir.

Q Would that occur pretty often ? A Yes sir, every time he would get one of those spells he would call her names.

Q What was your father's occupation, farmer ? A Farming, yes sir.

Q What were his habits, would he drink any ?

A No sir, he never would drink any only just once in a while he would drink some.

Q Never get drunk would he ? A Never got drunk since I can remember.

Q What sort of a provider was he, give you plenty to eat ?

A Yes sir he give us enough to eat.

Q A comfortable home ? A Yes sir.

Q Plenty to wear ? A Yes sir.

Q How did he conduct himself towards you children ?

A He conducted himself fine towards us children.

Q Did he ever whip you children ? A Yes sir, he whipped us, but I guess we needed it.

Q Do you remember the occasion when they quit living together ? A No sir.

Q Who left home ? A My mother.

Q You remember the time, the occasion, do you ? A Yes sir, I don't remember what day of the week it was.

Q Was there any special trouble between them at all that day ? A Well there wasn't no special trouble that I remember of.

Q Don't you remember why she left ? A She left on account of his abuse.

Q Did he abuse her that day ? A He abused her that morning.

Q What did he do ? A He cussed her that morning.

Q What did he say ? A He called her a damned old bitch, and things like that.

Q Did he say anything else to her ? A That's about all I can remember now.

Q Well, did he ever threaten to leave her ? A He left home three or four different times.

Q How long would he stay away ? A About a week or ten days.

Q He would come back ? A Yes sir.

Q Where did your mother go when she left him ? A We moved to Talala.

Q Take any goods with you, any household stuff ?

A Yes sir we taken[sic] half of what we had as near as we could get.

Q Did you have any talk with your father that day ? A Yes sir I had a talk with him.

Q What did he say ? A Why he said, let her go he didn't care.

Q Did you children go with her ? A Yes sir, all of us, four of us I believe went with her.

Q You went with her at first ? A Yes sir and have stayed with her ever since.

Q Did he ever ask you to stay with him ? A No sir.

Q It was several days before you all moved from there, wasn't it ?

A We moved everything we had away in three days, I believe it was.

Q Did your mother stay around there these three days or did she go right away ? A Se went to father's brother's and stayed.

Q While you were moving the things ? A While I was moving things, yes sir.

Q Do you know whether they have made any attempt to live together since then ?
A No sir I don't think they have.
Q Neither one has seen the other ? A Yes sir once.
Q Have you seen your father since ? A Yes sir.
Q Talk with him ? A Yes sir.
Q Frequently ? A Yes sir.
Q He never asked you if your mother was coming back ?
A No sir, never asked me no questions about it at all.
Q What was your mother's behavior toward your father ? A Why she didn't have any misbehavior at all.
Q Was she kind ? A Yes sir she was kind.
Q Good housekeeper ? A Yes sir good housekeeper, good as any man could ask.
Q Its[sic] only been in the last four or five years this trouble has come up ? A Yes sir, something like that; its[sic] been a long time, but I can't state just how long it was.
Q How did your mother seem to take this abuse from your father ? A She taken it the best she could, she couldn't do otherwise than take it.
Q Would your mother talk back much when he abuse her ? A She talked back once in a while, not very often; she never would talk very harsh to him.
Q She took it all very patiently ? A Yes sir.
Q And she stood that sort of thing pretty well for four years ? A Yes sir.
Q Did she tell you children why she was leaving ? A No sir, only she said she wouldn't live with him and him cuss and abuse her, that she had put up with it as long as she could.
Q And you children preferred to go with your mother rather than stay with your father ?
A Yes sir.

Examined by J. C. Starr:

Q Where were you living at the time this separation took place ?
A Two miles and a half northwest of Foil.
Q Were you there the day the separation occurred ? A Yes sir.
Q What occurred that day ? A Wasn't anything only the abuse he give her that morning, he called her a damned old bitch, and said she wasn't fitten for the hogs to run with.
Q Why did he tell her that ? A He was mad, I guess.
Q What was he mad about ? A That's something I can't tell.
Q When was it he tried to strike her with his fists ?
A Its[sic] been a year ago, I guess, or maybe more.
Q It was long before this separation ? A Yes sir.
Q What did you mother say to him that day of the separation ? A Why I don't remember what she said to him that day, only she told him she was going to leave, and she wanted him to get somebody to divide the stuff; she said he could get somebody to come and divide the stuff that she was going to leave. He said alright, but he wasn't going to get anybody to divide the stuff; and she went and got somebody to come and divide the stuff.
Q Did she take her stuff away ? A Yes sir.
Q He didn't object ? A No sir.

Q What was the cause of this trouble, to start with ?

A The last trouble, there was preaching going on at Grove, and a couple of preachers came down there Sunday to eat dinner, and that was what started the trouble.

Q In what way did the preachers cause the trouble ?

A He didn't like it because the preachers come down there to dinner.

Q What did he say about the preachers ? A He said a whole lot but I don't remember now, but anyway that's what started the trouble when they come down there Sunday.

Q How long before the separation took place ? A The next week after that Sunday.

Q What reason did he give for getting made because the preachers come there ?

A He didn't give no reason for getting mad at all.

Q Who brought the preachers there ? A I did, me and my oldest brother, we was at preaching and we invited them down.

Q What did you father say about the preachers coming there ?

A He didn't like it, because the preachers kinder always talked to him about religion, and he didn't like that any too well. He's like myself, he wasn't no christian[sic], and he didn't want anybody to talk to him about it.

Q What I want to get at now, in what way did the preachers cause trouble ?

A That's what I don't know; he never did say; I don't know.

Q The trouble come up over the preachers ? A Yes sir. And he never did say, and that's the reason I don't know.

Q And a short time after that your mother picked up everything and left him ?

A Yes sir.

Q And left him living there on the place ? A Yes sir.

Q How long did he continue to live on the place ?

A Until December.

Q Where does he live now ? A Claremore.

Q What became of the place ? A A fellow named Cason is living on the place now.

Q Did your father rent it out or sell it ? A Rented it.

Q He has charge of it yet ? A Yes sir.

Q Four or five of the children are going to take allotments there, he has charge of three allotments on the place ? A Yes sir.

Q You are going to take your allotment there ? A Yes sir.

Q He has no object to that has he ? A No sir.

Q How long before this trouble with the preachers since they had had trouble ?

A Two or three weeks.

Q What was the cause of that trouble ? A I don't know, I wasn't there at home when the beginning of it started; I don't remember now just where I was, but I come in though in two or three days.

Q The trouble was all over when you come in ?

A It lasted one night after I got in.

Q You just knew they was having some trouble ? A Yes sir, my youngest brother was telling me that they had had some trouble; I never asked him.

Q The next trouble before that, when did that happen ?

A I don't know just about what time they did happen.

Q Was it very long before this last trouble that you spoke of ?

A No sir, I don't think it was very long; it don't seem to me like it was.

Q What reason do you give for all this trouble that your father and mother have had ?
A I don't know as I could give any reason for it.
Q You don't know anything about the cause of the trouble ? A No sir.
Q You just know that they had trouble, and don't know what the cause of the trouble was when the preachers come there ?
A No sir, I don't know what the cause of the trouble was when the preachers come.

Examined by the Commission:

Q How many preachers were there ?   A Two.
Q What church did they belong to ?   A Baptist.
Q Both of them ? A Yes sir.
Q How long did they stay ? A They stayed until after dinner; one of them stayed all evening I believe and to supper, and went back to church.
Q Didn't stay all night ? A No sir.
Q You were there all the time, yourself ? A No sir, when I got my dinner I went to the barn that evening, and didn't come back till church time that night.
Q Your father didn't belong to the church did he ? A No sir.
Q Did your mother ? A Yes sir.

Examined by J. C. Starr:

Q What were the names of these preachers ? A One was named Adams.
Q What was his first name ? A I don't know.
Q Is he living now ? A Yes sir, he lives at Miami.
Q What is the name of the other one ?
A I have forgot the other one's name; he was just a new preacher there.

E. C. Bagwell, on oath states that, as stenographer to the Commission to the Five Civilized Tribes, he correctly recorded the testimony and proceedings had in the above entitled cause, and that the foregoing is an accurate transcript of his stenographic notes thereof.

E.C. Bagwell

Subscribed and sworn to before me this March 7, 1903.

Samuel Foreman
Notary Public.

◇◇◇◇◇

Cherokee Intermarried White 1906
Volume IV

Cher
Supp'l to #4832

Department of the Interior,
Commission to the Five Civilized Tribes,
Vinita, I. T., February 24, 1903.

In the matter of the application of THOMAS F. WARD, for the enrollment of himself and his children, JAMES M., BERTHA M., JOHN F., and ELLA N. WARD, as citizens by blood, and his wife, LIZZIE WARD, as a citizen by intermarriage, of the Cherokee Nation:

THOMAS F. WARD, being first duly sworn and examined, testified as follows:

Examined by the Commission:

Q State your name ? A Thomas F. Ward.
Q How old are you ? A I am fifty three years old.
Q What is your post office ? A Claremore now.
Q Are you a Cherokee by blood ? A Yes sir.
Q What is your wife's name ? A Elizabeth.
Q Lizzie is it ? A Lizzie is the way we call it.
Q You enrolled her as Lizzie didn't you ? A Ye sir.
Q Was she your wife in 1880 ? A Yes, she was my wife then.
Q She is claiming her citizenship through you is she ? A Yes sir.
Q You are[sic] your wife have separated ? A Yes sir we have separated
Q When did you separate ? A In March, on the 13th day of March.
Q What year ? A 1902.
Q Last March ? A Last March.
Q What was the cause of this separation between you ?
A Well, all the cause I know of, at night, on the 13th of March, I went to bed and went to sleep, and woke up in the night and I had a hard on; I guess you want to know it just as it is; and when I reached over, and waked up in the night sometime, I don't know what time of night it was--
Q Well ? A And I went over and reached over at her, and she jerked my hand away, and I went back the second time, and she done the same thing, and I went back the third time, and she said "For God Almighty's sake get up and leave here".
Q Well, did you get up ? A Not yet I aint[sic]. I said "You had better not call on the Lord, but call on the preachers".
Q What did you mean by that ?
A Well she had just joined the church three weeks before that, and the preacher was there that day and eat dinner; and she said something when I said that, I can't way what it was that she said, she muttered out something, I can't tell it, so I got up and left, and I went off in the other room, and went to bed and slept by myself.
Q Was that the cause of your separation ?
A That is so far as I know.

230

Cherokee Intermarried White 1906
Volume IV

Q How long was it after that before you separated ?
A About three or four days.
Q Did she leave your house ? A Hold on now, and I will tell you just exactly as it was.
Q Well go ahead ? A And so about three days, two or three days, after that, one of my sons, Mosie, asked me one night what was the matter with me, and I told him nothing, and he argues that there was, and I told him it didn't make any difference if there was and he wanted me to go to a doctor and get some medicine, and the next morning I got up and went to the barn to feed the horses, and I met him, and I said "Mosie I will tell you what is the matter I couldn't tell you in the house last night," and he told me he knew all about it, and he told me then that his mamma wanted to divide up and leave, and I told him if she wanted to go she could go.
Q Did you ever have a talk with her then before you actually separated ? A No sir, we lived as friendly as ever up to that time. After that night we didn't have any jawing much about it.
Q Did she leave your house or did you leave ? A She left my house.
Q Did she take the children with her ? A All of them. The girls wanted to go with her, we had two girls, and the boys went with her too, with the exception of this Mosie, I told him he had to go.
Q Where did you wife go ? A Up close to Talala.
Q You never have lived together since that time ?
A I never have spoke to her since.
Q Did you ever ask her to come back ?
A No sir, and I never will.
Q Did she ever ask to come back to you ? A No sir.
Q Is that the only trouble you ever had ?
A Well I can't say its[sic] the only trouble, we might have had some little Jowers before that.
Q That was the cause of the separation ?
A That was the cause of the separation that night.
Q She says in her testimony that you abused her, is that true ?
A Well, I guess every man in this country abuses his wife. I guess there aint[sic] a man with a wife in the country but what abuses her if she calls that abuse.
Q What ? A Why trying to use my tool on her, trying to frig her.
Q Well you don't call that abusing her do you ?
A No sir; well if she calls that abusing her, that's all the abuse I give her. I never layed[sic] the weight of my hand on her to hurt her.
Q Did you ever swear at her ? A Yes I swear sometimes, and do it yet; when I get mad I swear.
Q At her ? A I can't say that I ever swore at her straight out, what I call swearing, in my life. They claim that I have, but I don't know it if I did.
Q You always treated her gith[sic] did you ?
A I always treated her as well as I knowed[sic] how.
Q You made proper provision for her ? A Yes sir.
Q You had been married a good long while ? A Yes sir.

Q You had no trouble all those years ?

A Nothing more than that it might be a little fuss about something. Little disturbances sometimes.

Q Was your wife a delicate woman or was she a healthy woman ?

A She was a healthy woman.

Q How many children have you ? A Six living and two dead.

Q These six children are living with her are they ?

A Four of them, you might say.

Q How old is your wife ? A She is forty five years old.

Q Have either of you ever applied for a divorce ?

A No sir, I never have, she has.

Q She has ? A Yes sir.

Q What did she allege as a ground for a divorce ?

A Well, just as she has put it in here.

Q Abuse ? A Abuse.

Q Cruelty ? A Yes sir.

Q You were never cruel to her were you ? A No sir.

Q Did she tell you at the time she was leaving whey she left you ?

A No sir, she didn't; she just told me she was going to leave. We both set down to the table and she eat breakfast at the same table, and I got up from the table, and she come into the other room where I was, and she said "Tom, I want my part of this stuff and I want to get away from here"; and I says "Alright, you can have it".

Q You were willing that she should leave ?

A Yes sir, if she wanted to go, I was. I asked her to stay. When the arbitrators come, I told her in the presence of those arbitrators I would rather she would stay there, if anybody was to leave I would leave.

Q You never gave her any cause to leave you ?

A No sir, I never did; I never wanted her to leave.

E. C. Bagwell, on oath states that, as stenographer to the Commission to the Five Civilized Tribes, he correctly recorded the testimony and proceedings had in the above entitled cause, and that the foregoing is an accurate transcript of his stenographic notes thereof.

EC Bagwell

Subscribed and sworn to before me this March 31, 1903.

Samuel Foreman
Notary Public.

◇◇◇◇◇

Cherokee Intermarried White 1906
Volume IV

No. 4832

DEPARTMENT OF THE INTERIOR
COMMISSIONER TO THE FIVE CIVILIZED TRIBES
Muskogee, Indian Territory
January 4, 1907

In the matter of the application of Lizzie Ward for enrollment as a citizen by intermarriage of the Cherokee Nation.

The applicant being first duly sworn, testified as follows

Q What is your name? A Lizzie Ward
Q How old are you? A I will be 49 years the 9th day of next April
Q What is your postoffice address? A Foyil
Q You claim to be an intermarried citizen of the Cherokee Nation?
A Yes sir.
Q Through whom do you claim your intermarried right?
A Thomas F. Ward
Q When were you married to Thomas F. Ward? A 26th day of January 1873
Q Where? A Benton County Arkansas
Q How long did you live in Arkansas after your marriage ?
A We didn't live there at all, came right back to the Cherokee Nation?[sic]
Q Was your husband a recognized citizen of the Cherokee Nation at the time you married him in 1873? A Yes sir.
Q Were you ever married before you married him? A No sir.
Q Was he ever married before he married you? A No sir.
Q Have you lived together continuously as husband and wife since 1873?
A All except a little while, we separated about 2 years.
Q When was that? A That was in 1902.
Q What time did you separate in 1902? A In March.
Q Did you leave him or did he leave you? A I left him
Q How long was you away from him ? A About 2 years
Q Where did you live during these 2 years? A Over close to Talala in the Cherokee Nation.
Q Are you living together now as husband and wife? A Yes sir
Q Was Thomas F. Ward a citizen by blood of the Cherokee Nation at the time you married him? A Yes sir.

The applicant is identified on the 1880 Cherokee Roll opposite No. 3352. Her husband, through whom she claims her right is identified on said roll opposite No. 3351. He is also identified on the final roll of citizens by blood of the Cherokee Nation, opposite No. 24688

Witness excused

233

Cherokee Intermarried White 1906
Volume IV

Thomas F. Ward being called as a witness for the applicant and being duly sworn, testified as follows:

Q What is your name? A Thomas F. Ward
Q How old are you? A 56.
Q What is your postoffice address? A Foyil.
Q Do you know Lizzie Ward? A Yes sir
Q What relation are you to Lizzie Ward? A I am her husband.
Q When were you married? A In 1873
Q What time? A 26th of January, 1873
Q Where were you married? A In Benton County, Arkansas
Q Were you a citizen of the Cherokee Nation at the time you married your wife?
A Yes sir
Q How long did you stay in Arkansas? A Just long enough to get back across the line
Q You moved immediately to the Cherokee Nation after your marriage? A Yes sir.
Q Have you lived together continuously in the Cherokee Nation from the time you married to the present time.[sic] A Well most of the time. A little spell there we kinda got cross ways and quit.
Q When was that? A About two years ago
Q Did you quit your wife or did she quit you.[sic] A We both quit
Q Get a divorce, either of you? A No sir
Q Are you living together now as husband and wife? A Yes sir

Witness excused.

Ada C. Foreman being called as a witness for the applicant and being duly sworn, testified as follows:

Q What is your name? A Ada C. Foreman
Q How old are you? A 53
Q What is your postoffice address? A Claremore
Q You are a citizen of the Cherokee Nation ? A Yes, by adoption.
Q Are you acquainted with Thomas F. Ward and Lizzie Ward? A Yes sir
Q How long have you known them. A I really dont[sic] know, ever since they moved up there, about 25 years.
Q Have you always been known as husband and wife in that community?
A Yes sir. They were parted for a short time. Mr. Ward got hurt and got so cranky for a short time that his wife had to quit him for a while.

Witness excused.

George W. Eaton being called as a witness for the applicant and being first duly sworn, testified as follows:

Q What is your name? A George W. Eaton
Q What is your age? A 61

What is your postoffice address? A Claremore
Q Are you acquainted with Thomas F. Ward and his wife Lizzie Ward[sic]
A Yes sir.
Q Are you familiar with the circumstances of their separation?
A Yes sir.
Q Will you state as briefly as possible those circumstances?
A Well, they had always lived together and he got thrown out of a wagon and hurt in the head. For six weeks he didn't know anything and afterwards he was wrong. He left home and I don't know how long they were separated, a year or two years. It was through no fault of his wife--
Q It was through no fault of his wife Lizzie Ward that this separation took place then?
A No, I don't think so.
Q Then whatever abandonment there was in the case was on the part of Thomas Ward?
A Yes sir.

Witness excused.

Gertrude Hanna, being duly sworn, states as stenographer to the Commissioner to the Five Civilized Tribes she reported the proceedings had in the above number case and that the above and foregoing is a true and correct transcript of her stenographic notes taken therein.

Gertrude Hanna

Subscribed and sworn to before me this 5 day of January, 1907

Chas E Webster
Notary Public

◇◇◇◇◇

E C M   Cherokee 4832.

DEPARTMENT OF THE INTERIOR,

COMMISSIONER TO THE FIVE CIVILIZED TRIBES.

In the matter of the application for the enrollment of LIZZIE WARD as a citizen by intermarriage of the Cherokee Nation.

_D_E_C_I_S_I_O_N_

THE RECORDS OF THIS OFFICE SHOW: That on October 23rd, 1900, application was received by the Commission to the Five Civilized Tribes for the enrollment of Lizzie Ward as a citizen by intermarriage of the Cherokee Nation. Further proceedings in the matter of said application were had at Muskogee, Indian Territory,

235

October 15th, 1902, at Vinita, Indian Territory February 13th, 1903 and February 24th, 1903, and at Muskogee, Indian Territory, January 4th, 1907.

THE EVIDENCE IN THIS CASE SHOWS: That the applicant herein, Lizzie Ward, a white woman, was married January 26th, 1873 to one Thomas F. Ward, who was at the time of said marriage a recognized citizen by blood of the Cherokee Nation, and whose name appears upon the approved partial roll of citizens by blood of the Cherokee Nation opposite No. 24688, and who is identified on the Cherokee authenticated tribal roll of 1880, Cooweescoowee District No. 3351, as a native Cherokee; that in March, 1902, on account of cruelty and mistreatment by the said Thomas F. Ward, said Lizzie Ward was compelled to separate from him for a time; that shortly after said separation the said Lizzie Ward returned to live with said Thomas F. Ward; that, with the exception of this period of separation, the said Thomas F. Ward and Lizzie Ward resided together as husband and wife and continuously lived in the Cherokee Nation from the time of said marriage up to and including September 1st, 1902. Said applicant is identified on the Cherokee authenticated tribal roll of 1880 and the Cherokee census roll of 1896 as an intermarried citizen of the Cherokee Nation.

IT IS, THEREFORE, ORDERED AND ADJUDGED: That in accordance with the decision of the Supreme Court of the United States, dated November 5th, 1906, in the cases of Daniel Red Bird et al. vs. the United States, Nos. 125, 126, 127 and 128, the said applicant, Lizzie Ward is entitled, under the provisions of Section Twenty-one of the Act of Congress approved June 28th, 1898 (30 Stats. 495), to enrollment as a citizen by intermarriage of the Cherokee Nation, and her application for enrollment as such is accordingly granted.

Tams Bixby
Commissioner.

Dated at Muskogee, Indian Territory,
this   JAN 29 1907

◇◇◇◇◇

Cherokee 4832

Muskogee, Indian Territory, January 29, 1907.

W. W. Hastings,
    Attorney for the Cherokee Nation,
        Muskogee, Indian Territory.

Dear Sir:

There is enclosed herewith copy of the decision of the Commissioner to the Five Civilized Tribes, dated January 29, 1907, granting the application for the enrollment of Lizzie Ward as a citizen by intermarriage of the Cherokee Nation.

Respectfully,

Enc I-11
RPI

Commissioner.

◇◇◇◇◇

Cherokee 4832

Muskogee, Indian Territory, January 29, 1907.

The Commissioner to the Five Civilized Tribes,
    Muskogee, Indian Territory.

Sir:

    Receipt is acknowledged of the testimony and of your decision enrolling Lizzie Ward as a citizen by intermarriage of the Cherokee Nation. Time for protesting said decision is waived and I consent that said person may be placed upon the schedule immediately.

Respectfully,
W. W. Hastings
Attorney for the Cherokee Nation.

RPI

◇◇◇◇◇

Cherokee 4832

Muskogee, Indian Territory, January 29, 1907.

Lizzie Ward,
    Foyil, Indian Territory.

Dear Madam:

    There is enclosed herewith copy of the decision of the Commissioner to the Five Civilized Tribes, dated January 29, 1907, granting the application for your enrollment as a citizen by intermarriage of the Cherokee Nation.

    You will be advised when your name has been placed upon a schedule of citizens of the Cherokee Nation and approved by the Secretary of the Interior.

Respectfully,

Enc I-13

Commissioner.

237

Cher IW 127

◇◇◇◇◇

> I.W. No 127
>
> Charles H. Allen
>
> Record not in
> Jacket No. 6343

Cher IW 128

◇◇◇◇◇

E.C.M.

DEPARTMENT OF THE INTERIOR,

COMMISSIONER TO THE FIVE CIVILIZED TRIBES.

In the matter of the application for the enrollment of

JOHN P. CHANDLER

As a citizen by intermarriage of the Cherokee Nation.

CHEROKEE NO. 6444

◇◇◇◇◇

_R_R

DEPARTMENT OF THE INTERIOR,
COMMISSION TO THE FIVE CIVILIZED TRIBES,
TAHLEQUAH, I.T., DECEMBER 11th, 1900.

In the matter of the application of John Pink Chandler for the enrollment of himself, wife and children as citizens of the Cherokee Nation; said Chandler being sworn testified as follows:

EXAMINATION BY THE COMMISSION:

Q What is your name? A John Pink Chandler.
Q How old are you? A 63.
Q What is your post office address? A Siloam Springs.
Q Are you a Cherokee by blood? A No, sir.
Q By adoption? A Yes, sir.
Q For whom do you make application? A Susie Beck.
Q Then you apply for yourself wife and five children? A Just four children.
Q How long have you lived in the Cherokee Nation? A Ever since '67.
Q You have always made this your home? since that time? A Yes, sir.
Q What is the name of your father? A David Chandler.
Q What is the name of your mother? A Eliza Chandler.
Q What is the name of your wife? A Susan Beck.
Q How old is she? A She was born in '52.
Q She is a Cherokee by blood? A Yes, sir.
Q What degree of Cherokee blood do you claim for your wife? A Half nearly, I guess.
Q Has she always resided in the Cherokee Nation? A Yes, sir.
Q Always made this her hoje[sic]? A Born and raised right here in the Cherokee Nation.
Q What is the name of her mother? A Cynthia Beck.
Q What is the name of her father? A Joe Beck.
Q Her parents are both dead? A Yes, sir.
Q Now, give me the name of your oldest child, under 21 years of age, at home and living with you? A Lida.
Q How old is she? A She is 21.
    She will ha to apply for herself.
Q Give us the next one? A David.
Q How old? A He is 18.
Q The next child? A Ella Jay.
Q How old is he? A She is 16.
Q What is the name of the next one? A Henry.
Q How old is Henry? A Eight years old.
Q These children are all alive and living with you at home are they? A Yes, sir.
Q They are all children of your present wife, Susan? A Yes, sir.
Q Were you married to her in 1880, 20 years ago? A Oh, yes, we married in 1872.
Q Your name then appears with her's[sic] on the roll of 1880? A Yes, sir.

1880 Roll; page 234, #489, Pink Chandler, Delaware.
Page 567 1896 Roll; page (557), #87, Pink Chandler,   "
1880 Roll; page 234, #490, Susie Chandler,   "
1896 Roll; page 456, #773, Susie Chandler,   "
1896 Roll, page 456, #777, David Chandler,   "
1896 Roll, page 456, #778, Ella J. Chandler,   "
1896 Roll, page 456, #779, Henry Chandler,   "

COMMISSION: The applicant applies for the enrollment of himself as a Cherokee citizen by intermarriage and for the enrollment of his wife and three children as citizens by blood. He is identified upon the authenticated roll of 1880 and the census roll of 1896 as an adopted white. He avers that he was married to his wife in the year 1872, and that neither he nor she were ever previously married. They have living[sic] together continuously since that time as husband and wife. And he will now be listed for enrollment as a Cherokee citizen by intermarriage.

His wife is identified upon the authenticated roll and the census roll of 1896, under the name of her present husband. She has lived in the Cherokee Nation all her life, and will be listed for enrollment as a Cherokee citizen by blood. His three children are identified upon the census roll of 1896, with their mother. They are living and will be listed for enrollment as Cherokee citizens by blood with their mother.

---oooOOOooo---

J. O. Rosson, being first duly sworn, states that as stenographer to the Commission to the Five Civilized Tribes, he correctly recorded the testimony and proceedings in this case, and that the foregoing is a true and complete transcript of his stenographic notes thereof.

_____

Subscribed and sworn to before me this 13th day of December, 1900.

CR Breckinridge
Commissioner.

◇◇◇◇◇

(The above testimony given again.)

◇◇◇◇◇

H.
Cher. 6444.

Department of the Interior,
Commission to the Five Civilized Tribes.
Tahlequah, I. T., October 6, 1902.

SUPPLEMENTAL TESTIMONY AND PROCEEDINGS in the matter of the application for the enrollment of JOHN P. CHANDLER as a citizen by intermarriage of the Cherokee Nation.

JOHN P. CHANDLER, being first duly sworn, and being examined, testified as follows:

BY COMMISSION: What is your name? A John P. Chandler.
Q How old are you? A Sixty-five.
Q What is your post office address? A Siloam Springs, Arkansas.
Q You are a white man, are you? A Yes sir.
Q Have you heretofore made application to this Commission for enrollment as a citizen by intermarriage of the Cherokee Nation? A Yes sir.
Q What is the name of your wife? A Susan.
Q Is she living? A Yes sir.
Q Is she a Cherokee by blood? A Yes sir.
Q When were you and she married? A Married in 1872.
Q Have you and she lived together continuously since that time? A Yes sir.
Q Are you living together now? A Yes sir.
Q Were you ever married before you married her? A Yes sir.
Q What was the name of your former wife? A Eliza Baker.
Q Is she living? A No sir.
Q Did you and she live together up to the time of her death? A Yes sir.
Q Was your present wife ever married before he married you? A No sir.
Q Have you lived in the Cherokee Nation continuously since the date of your enrollment? A Yes sir, never lived anywhere else.

This testimony will be filed with and made a part of the record in the matter of the application for the enrollment of John P. Chandler as a citizen by intermarriage of the Cherokee Nation, Cherokee straight card field No. 6444.

Wm. Hutchinson, being first duly sworn, states that as stenographer to the Commission to the Five Civilized Tribes he correctly recorded the testimony and proceedings in this case, and that the foregoing is a true and complete transcript of the stenographic notes thereof.

Wm Hutchinson

Subscribed and sworn to before me this 8th day of October, 1902.

John O Rosson
Notary Public.

◇◇◇◇◇

CHEROKEE-6444.

DEPARTMENT OF THE INTERIOR,
COMMISSIONER TO THE FIVE CIVILIZED TRIBES.
Muskogee, Indian Territory, January 5, 1907.

In the matter of making proof of the marriage of John P. Chandler to his Cherokee wife, prior to November 1, 1875.

John P. Chandler, after having first been duly sworn by B. P. Rasmus, a Notary Public, testified as follows:

COMMISSIONER:

Q. What is your name? A. John P. Chandler.
Q. What is your age? A. I was born in 1837.
Q. What is your post office address? A. Siloam Springs, Ark.
Q. Do you claim to be a citizen by intermarriage of the Cherokee Nation?
A. Yes sir.
Q. Through whom do you claim your rights? A. I was married the 1st. day of March, 1867 to Eliza Beck, my first wife.
Q. Married under a Cherokee license? A. Yes sir.
Q. Where were you married? A. In Going Snake District.
Q. Have you got your license? A. No, I just went to the Judge and took my papers, and he told me he would send them to me, and he never did.
Q. Did you try to get them? A. Yes sir, but he kept putting me off.
Q. How long did you live with Eliza Beck? A. From '67 to '72.
Q. Was she a recognized citizen by blood of the Cherokee Nation when you married her?
A. Yes sir.
Q. Did she die in '72? A. Yes sir, the 3rd. of April.
Q. Did you remarry after her death? A. Yes sir.
Q. Who did you marry? A. Susie Beck.
Q. Is she any relation to Eliza Beck? A. A cousin.
Q. Is she a citizen? A. Yes sir.
Q. Are you living together now? A, Yes sir.

Q. Were you married to Susie Beck under a Cherokee license? A. No, we were both citizens, and they told me it wasn't necessary.

Q. You have lived in the Cherokee Nation continuously from the time of your marriage to Eliza Beck in '67? A. Yes sir, I am on the same place. Have never moved. Have lived there 35 years.

(Commissioner -- The applicant is identified upon the 1880 Cherokee Roll, opposite No. 489. How[sic] wife, through whom he claims his right to enrollment, is identified upon the same roll, opposite No. 490. She is also identified on the final roll of citizens by blood of the Cherokee Nation, opposite No. 15434.)

Witness excused.

Charles H. Allen, after having first been duly sworn by B. P. Rasmus, a Notary Public, testified as follows:

COMMISSIONER:

Q. What is your name? A. Charles H. Allen.

Q. What is your age? A. 75.

Q. What is your post office address? A. Siloam Springs, Ark.

Q. Are you a citizen by blood of the Cherokee Nation? A. No sir

Q. Are you acquainted with John P. Chandler? A. Yes sir.

Q. Did you know his former wife, Eliza Beck? A. Yes sir.

Q. When were they married? A. I think about 1867. I signed his petition to get his license.

Q. Why were you signing his petition if you were not a citizen by blood? A. At that time, a citizen by adoption could sign them.

Q. Who else signed his petition? A. I don't know.

Q. Were you considered a citizen of the Cherokee Nation at that time? A. Yes sir.

Q. Were you present when he was married to Eliza Beck? A. No sir.

Q. Do you know whether or not he was married under a license? A. Yes sir.

Q. Did you see the license? A. No, I didn't see them, but I saw a man who did see them issued.

Q. What man was it that saw them issued? A. Duckworth for one man.

Q. What is his name? A. L. L. Duckworth.

Q. Was there anybody else that saw them issued? A. I can't think of anybody else now.

Q. How long did John P. Chandler live with Eliza Beck? A. I don't know -- several years. The have several -- 3 or 4 children.

Q. Do you know when she died? A. Not exactly.

Q. Was Eliza Beck a recognized citizen of the Cherokee Nation at the time she married John P. Chandler? A. She was.

Witness excused.

Cherokee Intermarried White 1906
Volume IV

Harris A. Loflin, after having been first duly sworn by B. P. Rasmus, a Notary Public, testified as follows:

COMMISSIONER:

Q. What is your name? A. Harris A. Loflin.
Q. What is your age? A. 66.
Q. What is your post office address? A. Siloam Springs, Ark.
Q. Are you acquainted with John P. Chandler? A. Yes sir.
Q. Did you know his first wife? A. No sir.
Q. Do you know any of the circumstance about his marriage to his first wife? A. No sir.
Q. Do you know whether or not they were married according to the Cherokee law?
A. No sir.
Q. Do you know whether or not he has always been recognized as a citizen by adoption since his marriage to Eliza Beck? A. He has since his second marriage. I never knew him till '74.
Q. You have known him since '74? A. Yes sir.
Q. In what did his recognition as a citizen consist -- how was he recognized?
A. As an adopted citizen.
Q. Did he enjoy the rights of a Cherokee citizen? A. I can't say whether or not ---
Q. Did he hold property, and vote in the elections? A. Yes sir.

Witness excused.

------------------------------ ---

Eula Jeanes Branson, being sworn, states that she correctly reported the proceedings had in the above and foregoing on the 5th. day of January, 1907.

Eula Jeanes Branson

Subscribed and sworn to before me, this the 8th. day of January, 1907.

Walter W. Chappell
Notary Public.

◇◇◇◇◇

Cherokee Intermarried White 1906
Volume IV

C. F. B.   Cherokee 6444.

DEPARTMENT OF THE INTERIOR,
COMMISSION TO THE FIVE CIVILIZED TRIBES.
Muskogee, Indian Territory, January 11, 1907.

Supplemental proceedings in the matter of the application for the enrollment of John P. Chandler as a citizen by intermarriage of the Cherokee Nation.

APPEARANCES:
                    Cherokee Scott for applicant.

                    Cherokee Nation represented by
                    W. W. Hastings, Attorney.

Cherokee Scott being first duly sworn by B. P. Rasmus, Notary Public, testified as follows:

ON BEHALF OF COMMISSIONER.

Q What is your name?   A Cherokee Scott.
Q What is your age?   A 56.
Q What is your post office address?
A Vinita.
Q Do you know a person in the Cherokee Nation by the name of John P. Chandler?
A Yes sir.
Q Is he a white man?   A Yes sir.
Q Is he married?   A Yes sir.
Q What is the name of his wife?
A Susan Beck,- she was.
Q Is she living at this time?   A Yes sir.
Q She is a citizen by blood?   A Yes sir.
Q Do you know when John P. Chandler was married to his wife, Susan Chandler?
A No, I don't know when he was married to Susan Chandler. I know when he was married to Eliza Beck.
Q When did that marriage occur?
A 1st day of March, 1867.
Q Eliza Beck is the person through whom John P. Chandler claims the right to enrollment as a citizen of the Cherokee Nation?
A Yes sir.
Q Was Eliza Beck a recognized citizen of the Cherokee Nation at the time of their marriage?
A Yes sir.
Q And was residing in the Cherokee country?
A Yes sir.
Q Was she John P. Chandler's first wife?
A Yes sir.

Q Was he her first husband?   A Yes sir.

Q You knew them both before their marriage?

A Yes sir.

Q When did Eliza Chandler die?   A In 1871.

Q Did John P. and Eliza Chandler continuously reside together as husband and wife until the death of Eliza Chandler?

A Yes sir.

Q And lived in the Cherokee Nation?

A Yes sir.

Q Since her death, has John P. Chandler married?

A Yes sir.

Q Do you know his present wife?

A Yes sir; Susan Beck; but I don't know when they were married.

Q She is a recognized citizen by blood of the Cherokee Nation?

A Yes sir; always; always lived in the Nation.

Q You were present and witnessed the ceremony when John P. Chandler married Eliza Beck?

A Yes sir.

Q In what district were they married?

A Going Snake District.

Q Did you see the license?

A No sir; I don't remember of seeing it but he got a license. The clerk was right there and the Judge that married them. Judge Thornton married them and his son John Thornton, was the clerk.

Q You have every reason to believe then that he married his deceased wife, Eliza Beck, in accordance with the law of the Cherokee Nation?

A Yes sir.

Q Do you know of your own personal knowledge that since that marriage, John P. Chandler has been recognized as a citizen by intermarriage of the Cherokee Nation?

A Yes sir.

Q He has enjoyed the rights of that class of citizen since then?

A Yes sir; he has always lived in the same place from the time he was first married until now.

The undersigned being first duly sworn states that as stenographer to the Commission to the Five Civilized Tribes, she recorded the testimony taken in this case and that the foregoing is a full, true and correct transcript of the stenographic notes thereof.

Myrtle Hill

Subscribed and sworn to before me this the 14th day of January, 1907.

John E. Tidwell
Notary Public.

◇◇◇◇◇

E C M

Cherokee 6444.

DEPARTMENT OF THE INTERIOR,

COMMISSIONER TO THE FIVE CIVILIZED TRIBES.

In the matter of the application for the enrollment of JOHN P. CHANDLER as a citizen by intermarriage of the Cherokee Nation.

D E C I S I O N

THE RECORDS OF THIS OFFICE SHOW: That on December 11th, 1900 application was received by the Commission to the Five Civilized Tribes for the enrollment of John P. Chandler as a citizen by intermarriage of the Cherokee Nation. Further proceedings in the matter of said application were had at Tahlequah, Indian Territory, October 6th, 1902 and Muskogee, Indian Territory, January 5th, 1907 and January 11th, 1907.

THE EVIDENCE IN THIS CASE SHOWS: That the applicant herein, John P. Chandler, a white man, was married in accordance with Cherokee law March 1st, 1867 to one Eliza Chandler, nee Beck, since deceased, who was at the time of said marriage a recognized citizen by blood of the Cherokee Nation; that from the time of said marriage until the death of said Eliza Chandler, which occurred in the year 1871, the said John P. Chandler and Eliza Chandler resided together as husband and wife and continuously lived in the Cherokee Nation. It is further shown that in the year 1872 the said John P. Chandler was married in accordance with Cherokee law to one Susan Chandler, nee Beck, who was at the time of said marriage a recognized citizen by blood of the Cherokee Nation, who is identified on the Cherokee authenticated tribal roll of 1880, Delaware District No. 490 as a native Cherokee, and whose name is included in the approved partial roll of citizens by blood of the Cherokee Nation opposite No. 15434. It is further shown that from the time of said marriage the said John P. Chandler and Susan Chandler resided together as husband and wife and continuously lived in the Cherokee Nation up to and including September 1st, 1902. Said applicant is identified on the Cherokee authenticated tribal roll of 1880 and the Cherokee census roll of 1896 as an intermarried citizen of the Cherokee Nation.

IT IS, THEREFORE, ORDERED AND ADJUDGED: That in accordance with the decision of the Supreme Court of the United States, dated November 5th, 1906 in the cases of Daniel Red Bird, et al. vs. the United States, Nos. 125, 126, 127 and 128, the applicant, John P. Chandler is entitled, under the provisions of Section Twenty-one of the Act of Congress approved June 28th, 1898 (30 Stats. 495), to enrollment as a citizen by intermarriage of the Cherokee Nation, and his application for enrollment as such is accordingly granted.

247

Tams Bixby
Commissioner.

Dated at Muskogee, Indian Territory,
this   JAN 29 1907

◇◇◇◇◇

Cherokee 6444

Muskogee, Indian Territory, January 29, 1907.

W. W. Hastings,
　　　Attorney for the Cherokee Nation,
　　　　　Muskogee, Indian Territory.

Dear Sir:

　　　There is enclosed herewith copy of the decision of the Commissioner to the Five Civilized Tribes, dated January 29, 1907, granting the application for the enrollment of John P. Chandler as a citizen by intermarriage of the Cherokee Nation.

Respectfully,

Enc I-16

Commissioner.

RPI

◇◇◇◇◇

Cherokee 6444

Muskogee, Indian Territory, January 29, 1907.

The Commissioner to the Five Civilized Tribes,
　　　Muskogee, Indian Territory.

Sir:

　　　Receipt is acknowledged of the testimony and of your decision enrolling John P. Chandler as a citizen by intermarriage of the Cherokee Nation. Time for protesting said decision is waived and I consent that said person may be placed upon the schedule immediately.

Respectfully,

W. W. Hastings
Attorney for the Cherokee Nation.

◇◇◇◇◇

248

Cherokee Intermarried White 1906
Volume IV

Cherokee 6444

Muskogee, Indian Territory, January 29, 1907.

John P. Chandler,
    Siloam Springs, Arkansas.

Dear Sir:

    There is enclosed herewith copy of the decision of the Commissioner to the Five Civilized Tribes, dated January 29, 1907, granting the application for your enrollment as a citizen by intermarriage of the Cherokee Nation.

    You will be advised when your name has been placed upon a schedule of citizens of the Cherokee Nation and approved by the Secretary of the Interior.

Respectfully,

ENCL I-17

Commissioner.

RPI

Cher IW 129

◇◇◇◇◇

E.C.M.

DEPARTMENT OF THE INTERIOR,

COMMISSIONER TO THE FIVE CIVILIZED TRIBES.

In the matter of the application for the enrollment of

REBECCA WILKERSON

as a citizen by intermarriage of the Cherokee Nation.

CHEROKEE 6509

◇◇◇◇◇

249

Cherokee Intermarried White 1906
Volume IV

Department of the Interior.
Commission to the Five Civilized Tribes.
Tahlequah, I. T., December 12, 1900.

In the matter of the application of Rebecca Wilkerson for the enrollment of herself and child as Cherokee citizens, she being sworn and examined by Commissioner T. B. Nedles[sic], testified as follows:

Q What is your name? A Rebecca Wilkerson.
Q What is your age? A 57.
Q What is your postoffice address? A Peggs.
Q What district do you live in? A Tahlequah.
Q Are you a recognized citizen of the Cherokee Nation? A Yes sir.
Q By blood? A No sir.
Q Intermarriage? A Yes sir.
Q Who do you want to enroll; yourself? A Me and my son.
Q What is your son's name? A William D. Wilkerson.
Q How old is he? A 14.
Q Are you married? A My husband is dead.
Q What was his name? A John Wilkerson.
Q What was your name before you were married? A Oglesby.
Q Was that your name in 1880? A Wilkerson in 1880.
Q Have you been married since the death of your husband? A No sir.
Q You always lived in the Cherokee Nation? A Yes sir, ever since I have been married.
1880 roll; page 822, #2596, Rebecca Wilkerson, Tahlequah district
1896 roll; page 1292, #304, Rebecca Wilkerson, Tahlequah district
1896 roll; page 1282, #3831, William Wilkerson, Tahlequah district
Q Is William living with you? A Yes sir.
Q Always lived in the Cherokee Nation? A Yes sir.

Commissioner Needles-
The name of Rebecca Wilkerson appears upon the authenticated roll of 1880 as well as the Census roll of 1896. The name of her son, William D., appears upon the Census roll of 1896 as William Wilkerson. Both being duly identified and having made satisfactory proof as to residence, the said Rebecca Wilkerson will be duly listed for enrollment as a citizen by intermarriage, and her son, William D. Wilkerson will be duly listed for enrollment as a Cherokee citizen by blood.

E. G. Rothenberger, being duly sworn, states that as stenographer to the Commission to the Five Civilized Tribes, he reported in full the testimony and proceedings in the above case, and that the foregoing is a full, true and correct transcript of the stenographic notes in said case.

E.G. Rothenberger

Cherokee Intermarried White 1906
Volume IV

Subscribed and sworn to before me this 18th day of December, 1900.

TB Needles
Commissioner.

◇◇◇◇◇

JOR.
Cher. 6509.

Department of the Interior.
Commission to the Five Civilized Tribes.
Tahlequah, I. T., October 20, 1902.

SUPPLEMENTAL TESTIMONY in the matter of the application for the enrollment of REBECCA WILKERSON as a citizen by intermarriage of the Cherokee Nation.

REBECCA WILKERSON, being first duly sworn, and being examined, testified as follows:

BY COMMISSION: What is your name? A Rebecca J. Wilkerson.

Q How old are you? A Sixty.

Q What is your post office address? A Peggs.

Q You are a white woman? A Yes sir.

Q Have you heretofore made application to this Commission for enrollment as a citizen by intermarriage of the Cherokee Nation?
A Yes sir.

Q What is the name of the husband through whom you claim your citizenship?
A John Wilkerson.

Q Is he living? A No sir.

Q Was he a Cerokee[sic] by blood? A Yes sir.

Q How long has he been dead? A Been dead three years this coming March.

Q When were you and he married? A Married in 1865.

Q Does your name appear upon the roll of 1880? A I reckon ot[sic] does, you can find it all the way through.

Q Have you and your husband John Wilkerson lived together continuously until the time of his death? A Yes sir.

Q Were you living together when he died? A Yes sir.

Q You were never separated? A No sir.

Q Were you eber[sic] married before you married him? A Yes sir.

Q What was the name of your first husband? A Frederick Brown.

Q Was he living at the time you married your first[sic] husband? A No sir.

Q Was that the only time you were ever married before you married your husband John Wilkerson? A Yes sir.

Q Was John Wilkerson ever married before he married you? A Nos sir

Q You were his first wife and he was your second husband? A Yes sir.

Q Have you resided in the Cherokee Nation continuously since you married him?
A Ever since 1868.
Q Did he reside in the Cherokee Nation continuously since o868[sic] until the time of his death? A Yes sir.
Q You have how many minor children? A Just one.
Q Is that child living at this time? A Yes sir.
Q Its name is William? A Yes sir.

This testimony will be filed with and made a part of the record in the matter of the application for the enrollment of Rebecca Wilkerson as a citizen by intermarriage of the Cherokee Nation, Cherokee straight card field No. 6509.

Wm. Hutchinson, being first duly sworn, states that as stenographer to the Commission to the Five Civilized Tribes he correctly recorded the testimony and proceedings in this case, and that the foregoing is a true and complete transcript of the stenographic notes thereof.

Wm Hutchinson

Subscribed and sworn to before me this 30th day of October, 1902.

John O Rosson
Notary Public.

◇◇◇◇◇

Cherokee 6509.

Department of the Interior,
Commission to the Five Civilized Tribes,
Tahlequah, I. T., May 25, 1903.

In the matter of the application of Rebecca Wilkerson for the enrollment of herself as a citizen by intermarriage, and for the enrollment of her child, William D. Wilkerson, as a citizen by blood of the Cherokee Nation.

James Wilkerson, being duly sworn, and examined by the Commission, testified as follows:

Q What is your name? A James Wilkerson.
Q How old are you? A Thirty-two.
Q What is your postoffice? A Peggs.
Q Are you a Cherokee citizen? A Yes sir.
Q Cherokee by blood, are you? A Yes sir.
Q What is your wife's name? A Martha.
Q Who is Rebecca Wilkersn? A My mother.

Q She is a white woman, is she? A Yes sir.
Q What was her husband's name? A John Wilkerson.
Q He is dead, is he? A Yes sir.
Q When did he die? A In 1900.
Q Has your mother married since then? A No sir.
Q She is still the widow of John Wilkerson? A Yes sir.
Q And been living in the Cherokee Nation ever since '80, has she? A Yes sir.

The undersigned, being duly sworn, states that as stenographer to the Commission to the Five Civilized Tribes he correctly recorded the testimony and proceedings in this case, and that the foregoing is a true and correct transcript of his stenographic notes thereof.

EG Rothenberger

Subscribed and sworn to before me this 3rd day of July, 1903.

Samuel Foreman
Notary Public.

◇◇◇◇◇

Cherokee-6509.

DEPARTMENT OF THE INTERIOR,
COMMISSIONER TO THE FIVE CIVILIZED TRIBES.
Muskogee, I. T., January 7, 1907.

In the matter of the application for the enrollment of Rebecca Wilkerson as a citizen by intermarriage of the Cherokee Nation.

George W. Wilkerson , being first duly sworn by Frances R. Lane, a Notary Public for the Western District, Indian Territory, testified as follows:

By the Commissioner:
Q What is your name? A George W. Wilkerson.
Q What is your age? A Thirty-three.
Q What is your postoffice address? A Peggs, I. T.
Q In whose behalf did you appear here today? A Rebecca Wilkerson.
Q Is she living? A Yes sir.
Q Why is she unable to appear in person? A She was struck with Paralysis and one hand cannot be used; she has been sick for eighteen months.
Q Does Rebecca Wilkerson claim citizenship in the Cherokee Nation as an intermarried white? A Yes sir.
Q Through whom does she claim? A John Wilkerson.
Q When was she married to John Wilkerson? A In 1865.

253

Cherokee Intermarried White 1906
Volume IV

Q Where was she married to him? A In the Chickasaw Nation on this side of the river.
Q Have you any documentary evidence of that marriage?--any certificate issued by the judge or the preacher? A No sir.
Q Was there any record made of it at that time? A None at that time. There was no license issued. A man just went before the minister and was married.
Q Do you know when they removed to the Cherokee Nation? A In 1868.
Q Do you know whether or not they re-married when they removed to the Cherokee Nation in accordance with the customs?
Q[sic] No sir. The minister that married them, he come back there and said that there was no use marrying them over; said that the first marriage was sufficient.
Q Your father is not living at this time? A No sir.
Q When did he die? A March 21, 1900.
Q Fom[sic] the time of the removal of Rebecca Wilkerson and her husband to the Cherokee nation[sic] until the death of her husband did they live together continuously as man and wife? A Yes.
Q And were recognized as such in the community? A Yes sir.
Q Has Rebecca Wilkerson remarried since the death of her husband? A No sir.
Q Where is she living at this time? A She is living at my home in Peggs.
Q Do you know anyone who is living at this time who was present at her marriage to John Wilkerson? A She has got a sister who was present.
Q What is her name? A Nancy Bond.
Q What is her postoffice address? A Peggs, I. T.

The name of Rebecca Wilkerson appears on Cherokee Field Card No. 6509, and is included in the authenticated roll of 1880 of Cherokee citizens, Tahlequah District, opposite No. 2596.
Her name is also included in the 1896 roll, opposite No. 304.

Q Was Rebecca Wilkerson ever married prior to her marriage to John Wilkerson?
A Yes, she was married to a fellow by the name of Brown.
Q Was he living at the time of her marriage to John Wilkerson? A No sir.
Q What was the date of her first marriage? A I don't know anything about that.
Q What was the date of the death of her first husband?
A Must have been at the time of the war, or before the war.

Witness excused.

Nancy C. Bond being first duly sworn by Frances R. Lane a Notary Public for the Western District of Indian Territory, testified as follows:

By the Commissioner:
Q What is your name? A Nancy C. Bond.
Q What is your age? A Fifty-three.
Q Your postoffice address? A Peggs, I. T.
Q Are you acquainted with Rebecca Wilkerson? A Yes sir.

Q What relation is she to you? A Sister.

Q Were you present at her marriage to John Wilkerson? A Yes sir.

Q When were they married? A They were married in June, 1865

Q Where were they married? A In the Chickasaw Nation.

Q Do you know by whom they were married? A Mr. Bertholf

Q Was their marriage in accordance with the customs of the Cherokee Nation.[sic]

A I don't know/ a minister married them. He was a Cherokee minister.

Q Do you know whether or not any certificate was issued by the minister?

A No, I don't--there was no license or anything in them days.

Q John Wilkerson was a citizen by blood of the Cherokee Nation? A Yes sir.

Q When did they move to the Cherokee nation[sic]? A It was in 1868.

Q John Wilkerson is now dead? A Yes sir.

Q When did he die? A He died in 1900, March 21st.

Q From the time of the removal of John Wilkerson and his wife in 1868 to the Cherokee nation[sic], until his death, they lived together continuously as man and wife?

A Yes sir.

Q Within the Cherokee nation[sic]? A Yes sir.

Q Rebecca Wilkerson has not married again since the death of her husband, John Wilkerson? A No sir.

Q Was John Wilkerson ever married prevous[sic] to his marriage to Rebecca Wilkerson?

A No sir.

Q Was Rebeca Wilkerson married previous to her marriage to John Wilkerson? A Yes, she had been married before.

Q Was her first husband living at the time she married John Wilkerson? A No, he got killed by a horse.

Frances R. Lane upon oath states that as stenographer to the Commissioner to the Five Civilized Tribes she reported the testimony in the above entitled cause and that the foregoing is an accurate transcript of her stenographic notes thereof.

Frances R Lane

Subscribed and sworn to before me this January 7, 1907.

Edward Merrick
Notary Public.

◇◇◇◇◇

E.C.M.   Cherokee 6593

DEPARTMENT OF THE INTERIOR,

COMMISSIONER TO THE FIVE CIVILIZED TRIBES.

———————————————

In the matter of the application for the enrollment of Rebecca Wilkerson as a citizen by intermarriage of the Cherokee Nation.

D E C I S I O N

THE RECORDS OF THIS OFFICE SHOW: That on December 12, 1900, application was received by the Commission to the Five Civilized Tribes, for the enrollment of Rebecca Wilkerson as a citizen by intermarriage of the Cherokee Nation. Further proceedings in the matter of said application were had at Tahlequah, Indian Territory, October 20, 1902, May 25, 1903, and Muskogee, Indian Territory, January 7, 1907.

THE EVIDENCE IN THIS CASE SHOWS: That the applicant herein, Rebecca Wilkerson, a white woman, married in June, 1865, one John Wilkerson, since deceased, who was, shortly after said marriage admitted to citizenship in the Cherokee Nation, and whose name appears on the Cherokee authenticated tribal roll of 1880, Tahlequah District, No. 2596, as a native Cherokee "Dead". It is further shown that from the time of said marriage until the death of said John Wilkerson, which occurred March 21, 1900, the said John Wilkerson and Rebecca Wilkerson resided together as husband and wife, and continuously lived in the Cherokee Nation; that since the death of said John Wilkerson said Rebecca Wilkerson has remained unmarried, and continuously lived in the Cherokee Nation.   Said Rebecca Wilkerson is identified on the Cherokee census roll of 1896, as an intermarried citizen of the Cherokee Nation.

IT IS, THEREFORE, ORDERED AND ADJUDGED: That in accordance with the decision of the Supreme Court of the United States, dated November 5, 1906, in the cases of Daniel Red Bird et al., vs. the United States, Nos. 125, 126, 127 and 128, the said applicant Rebecca Wilkerson is entitled, under the provisions of Section twenty-one of the Act of Congress approved June 28, 1898 (30 Stat. 495), to enrollment as a citizen by intermarriage of the Cherokee Nation, and her application for enrollment as such is accordingly granted.

Tams Bixby
Commissioner.

Dated at Muskogee, Indian Territory,
this   JAN 29 1907

◇◇◇◇◇

Cherokee 6509

Muskogee, Indian Territory, January 29, 1907.

W. W. Hastings,
    Attorney for the Cherokee Nation,
        Muskogee, Indian Territory.

Dear Sir:

    There is enclosed herewith copy of the decision of the Commissioner to the Five Civilized Tribes, dated January 29, 1907, granting the application for the enrollment of Rebecca Wilkerson as a citizen by intermarriage of the Cherokee Nation.

Respectfully,

Enc I-5
                                    Commissioner.

RPI

◇◇◇◇◇

Cherokee 6509

Muskogee, Indian Territory, January 29, 1907.

The Commissioner to the Five Civilized Tribes,
    Muskogee, Indian Territory.

Sir:

    Receipt is acknowledged of the testimony and of your decision enrolling Rebecca Wilkerson as a citizen by intermarriage of the Cherokee Nation. Time for protesting said decision is waived and I consent that said person may be placed upon the schedule immediately.

Respectfully,
        W. W. Hastings
        Attorney for the Cherokee Nation.

◇◇◇◇◇

Cherokee 6509

Muskogee, Indian Territory, January 29, 1907.

Rebecca Wilkerson,
Peggs, Indian Territory.

Dear Madam:

There is enclosed herewith copy of the decision of the Commissioner to the Five Civilized Tribes, dated January 29, 1907, granting the application for your enrollment as a citizen by intermarriage of the Cherokee Nation.

You will be advised when your name has been placed upon a schedule of citizens of the Cherokee Nation and approved by the Secretary of the Interior.

Respectfully,

Enc I-6   Commissioner.

RPI

Cher IW 130

◇◇◇◇◇

C.E.W.

DEPARTMENT OF THE INTERIOR,

COMMISSIONER TO THE FIVE CIVILIZED TRIBES.

In the matter of the application for the enrollment of

MARY H. NICHOLSON

as a citizen by intermarriage of the Cherokee Nation.

CHEROKEE 7290

◇◇◇◇◇

DEPARTMENT OF THE INTERIOR,
COMMISSION TO THE FIVE CIVILIZED TRIBES,
MUSKOGEE, I.T., FEBRUARY 15th, 1901.

In the matter f[sic] the application of Mary H. Nicholson for enrollment as a citizen of the Cherokee Nation; said Nichlson[sic] being sworn and examined by Commissioner Breckinridge, testified as follows:

Q Give me your full name? A Mary H. Nicholson.
Q How old are you? A 65.
Q What is your post office? A Muskogee.
Q Do you live in the Cherokee Nation? A I do.
Q In what district do you live? A Canadian.
Q Who is it you want to have enrolled? A Just myself.
Q Are you a Cherokee by blood? A No, sir.
Q White woman? A Pure white.
Q How many times have you been married? A Only once.
Q To whom were you married? A David L. Nicholson.
Q Was he a Cherokee by blood? A Yes, sir.
Q Is he dead? A Yes, sir.
Q How long has he been dead? A 22 years.
Q You have never married since his death? A No, sir.

> Tribal Rolls of citizens of the Cherokee Nation examined and applicant's name found thereon as follows:
> 1880 Authenticated Roll; page 37, #1031, M. H. Nicholson, Canadian district.
> 1896 Census Roll; page 91, #212, Mary Nicholson, Canadian district.

Q How long have you lived in the Cherokee Nation? A 27 years.
Q You have lived here continuously for the past 27 years? A Yes, sir.

Com'r Breckinridge:--The applicant is identified on the rolls of 1880 and 1896 as an adopted white. She states she has never remarried since the death of her Cherokee husband, and that she has lived continuously in the Cherokee Nation for 27 years. She will now be listed for enrollment as a Cherokee by adoption.

---oooOOOooo---

J. O. Rosson, being first duly sworn, states that as stenographer to the Commission to the Five Civilized Tribes, he correctly recorded the testimony and proceedings in this case, and that the foregoing is a true and complete transcript of his stenographic notes thereof.

JO Rosson

259

Cherokee Intermarried White 1906
Volume IV

Subscribed and sworn to before me this 18th day of February, 1901.

TB Needles
Commissioner.

<><><><><>

Statement of Applicant Taken Under Oath. Can.

CHEROKEE BY BLOOD AND ADOPTION.

Date   Feb 15   1900.1

Name   Muskogee I.T.

District... Year .... Page .... No. ....

Citizen by blood .... Mother's citizenship ....

Intermarried citizen ....

Married under what law... Date of marriage ....

License .... Certificate...........

Wife's name   Mary H. Nicholson

District..   Can   .Year 1880 Page 37 No. _ 1031

Citizen by blood   No   Mother's citizenship...

Intermarried citizen   Yes

Married under what law... Date of marriage...........

License .... Certificate...........

  Names of Children:

.... Dist............ Year........... Page........... No........... Age.....

.... Dist............ Year........... Page........... No........... Age.....

.... Dist............ Year........... Page........... No........... Age.....

.... Dist............ Year........... Page........... No........... Age.....

.... Dist............ Year........... Page........... No........... Age.....

No 1 on 1880 roll as M. H. Nicholson

<><><><><>

260

Cher-7290.

DEPARTMENT OF THE INTERIOR.
Commission to the Five Civilized Tribes.
Muskogee, I.T., October 20, 1902.

In the matter of the application of Mary H. Nicholson for enrollment as an intermarried citizen of the Cherokee Nation.

Mary H. Nicholson, called as a witness, being first duly sworn by the Commission, testified as follows:

Q Your name is Mary H. Nicholson? A Yes sir.
Q How old are you? A 66.
Q Qhat[sic] is your postoffice address? A Muskogee, I.T.
Q Are you a white woman? A Yes sir.
Q Your name is on the roll of 1880 as an adopted white citizen? A Yes sir
Q What is your husband's name? A David L. Nicholson.
Q Is he living or dead? A He is dead.
Q Was David L. Nicholson your husband in 1880? A Yes sir.
Q Is he the husband through whom you are claiming your right to citizenship?
A Yes sir.
Q When did your husband die? A In 1878.
Q He was not your husband then, in 1880, was he? A Yes, je[sic] is still my husband.
Q He died before 1880, did he? A Yes sir.
Q Have you been married since your husband's death? A No, he was killed.
Q You are still a widow? A Yes sir.
Q Have you been living in the Cherokee nation[sic] from 1880 up to this time?
A Yes sir.
Q You have never lived anywhere else, have you? A No sir.

----oOo-----

Frances R. Lane upon oath states that as stenographer to the Commissioner to the Five Civilized Tribes she correctly recorded the testimony in the above entitled cause, and that the above is an accurate transcript of her stenographic notes thereof.

Frances R Lane

Subscribed and sworn to before me this October 25th, 1902.

BC Jones
Notary Public.

◇◇◇◇◇

Cherokee-7290.

DEPARTMENT OF THE INTERIOR.
COMMISSION TO THE FIVE CIVILIZED TRIBES.
MUSKOGEE, I. T., FEBRUARY 16, 1905.

In the matter of the enrollment of Mary H. Nicholson, as a citizen by intermarriage of the Cherokee Nation, Card No. 7290.

Mary H. Nicholson, having been first duly sworn, testified as follows:

Examination by the Commission:

Q What is your name? A Mary H. Nicholson.
Q What is your postoffice address? A Muskogee.
Q You are a white woman? A Yes sir.
Q You do not claim any right as a Cherokee by blood? A Not a bit.
Q You claim entirely by intermarriage? A Yes sir, by marriage.
Q What is the name of the Cherokee Indian through whom you claim your intermarriage rights? A David L. Nicholson, deceased.
Q When were you married to him? A May 8, '56.
Q Was he your first husband? A First and only.
Q Was you his first wife? A Yes sir; we lived together till he died, at Tahlequah.
Q What year? A '78.
Q You have not married since? A Not at all; never had any idea.
Q You said you were married in '56, were you then living in the Cherokee Nation? A No sir.
Q When did you come to live in the Cherokee Nation? A In '72.
Q You both came together? A Yes sir.
Q From where? A Alabama.
Q And since that time, where have you lived? A Down here on the Arkansas River, about 10 miles east of this place.
Q In the Cherokee Nation? A Yes sir.
Q You lived in the Cherokee Nation, from the time you came here about 1872, up to and including September 1, 1902? A Yes sir; right there I have lived.

(Witness excused).

Josie Davies, having been first duly sworn, states: That as stenographer to the Commission to the Five Civilized Tribes, she reported all proceedings had in the above entitled cause on the 16th day of February, 1905, and that the above and foregoing is a full, true and complete transcript of her stenographic notes thereof.

Josie Davies

Cherokee Intermarried White 1906
Volume IV

Subscribed and sworn to before me this 16th day of February, 1905.

(Illegible) H. Sawyer
Notary Public.

◇◇◇◇◇

C. F. B.   Cherokee 7290.

DEPARTMENT OF THE INTERIOR,
COMMISSION TO THE FIVE CIVILIZED TRIBES.
Muskogee, Indian Territory, January 8, 1907.

In the Matter of the Application for the Enrollment of Mary H. Nicholson as a citizen by intermarriage of the Cherokee Nation.

APPEARANCES:

Applicant appears in person.

Cherokee Nation represented by
W. W. Hastings, Attorney.

Mary H. Nicholson being first duly sworn by John E. Tidwell, Notary Public, testified as follows:

ON BEHALF OF COMMISSIONER:

Q What is your name?   A Mary H. Nicholson.
Q What is your age?   A 71.
Q What is your post office address?
A Muskogee.
Q You are an applicant for enrollment as a citizen by intermarriage of the Cherokee Nation?
A Yes sir.
Q You have no Cherokee Blood?
A None at all.
Q Your only claim to the right to enrollment as a citizen of the Cherokee Nation is by virtue of your marriage to a Cherokee by blood?
A Yes sir.
Q What is the name of the citizen through whom you claim that right?
A David L. Nicholson.
Q Is he living or dead?   A Dead.
Q When did he die?   A '78.
Q When were you married to him?   A '56.
Q Was he living in the Cherokee Nation at that time?
A No sir; in the old Nation. He was raised here, then went back and married me and then came back here.
Q Where were you married?   A In Alabama.

263

Cherokee Intermarried White 1906
Volume IV

Q But he had been a citizen of the Cherokee Nation prior to the time of your marriage?
A Yes sir.
Q Were you his first wife?   A Yes sir.
Q Was he your first husband?   A Yes and last.
Q How long was it after you and he were married before you came to the Cherokee Nation for the purpose of making this your permanent home?
A We were married in '56 and came here in '72.
Q On coming to the Cherokee Nation, was your husband recognized as a citizen of the Cherokee Nation or was it necessary for him to go before the authorities and be re-admitted?
A He was re-admitted.
Q Do you remember the date of his re-admission?
A Fall of '73.
Q Soon after you came here?
A Yes sir; the first time Council met after we came here.
Q Who married you?   A Judge Estes.
Q Did he give you a certificate?
A I think we had a certificate but in moving, it was lost. It is on record in the Court there.
Q From the time you married your husband did you and he continuously live together until his death?
A Yes sir.
Q Since his death, have you re-married?
A No sir.
Q You have lived continuously in the Cherokee Nation up until the present time?
A Yes sir.

The applicant Mary H. Nicholson is identified on the Cherokee authenticated tribal roll of 1880, Canadian District, at No. 1031.

The undersigned being first duly sworn states that as stenographer to the Commission to the Five Civilized Tribes, she recorded the testimony taken in this case and that the foregoing is a full, true and complete transcript of her stenographic notes thereof.

Myrtle Hill

Subscribed and sworn to before me this the 12th day of January, 1907.

Chas E Webster
Notary Public.

◇◇◇◇◇

(Below is handwritten on the microfilm.)

An Act readmitting David L. Nicholson wife and minor children to citizenship

_____ _____

Be it enacted by The National Council

That David L. Nicholson a Cherokee Indian together with his wife and minor children be and the same are hereby readmitted to all the rights and privileges of Cherokee citizenship

Nov 21st 1874
Geo O *(Illegible)*   Daul B Bird
Clerk of Council   Speaker of Council

Nov 27, 1874 *(Illegible)*
DB Bird   Charley Thompson
(Illegible)   *(Illegible)*
        Approved
                                             Will.P. Ross

<><><><><>

AN ACT READMITTING DAVID NICHOLSON, WIFE AND MINOR CHILDREN
TO CITIZENSHIP.

Be it enacted by the National Council:--
                        That David Nicholson together with his wife
and minor children, be and the same are hereby readmitted to all the rights and privileges
of Cherokee Citizenship.
                        November 27th, 1874.
                                        Approved:
                                             Will P. Ross."
                        Executive Department, Cherokee Nation,
                        Tahlequah, Indian Territory, Jan. I0th, I907.
I, A.B. Cunningham, Executive Secretary of the Cherokee Nation, do hereby certify that the above and foregoing is a true and correct copy of an act of the National Council, entitled,

265

"An act readmitting David Nicholson, wife and minor children to Citizenship"

As of record in this office.

In testimony whereof, I hereunto set my hand and affix the seal of the Cherokee Nation, this day and date above written.

A B Cunningham

Executive Secretary.

◇◇◇◇◇

(The Marriage License and Certificate below typed as given.)

OFFICE OF
JUDGE OF PROBATE,
DEKALB COUNTY.

JAS. A. CROLEY, JUDGE.   P. C. HALE, CLERK.

FORT PAYNE, ALA.

State of Alabama   )

Dekalb County   )

To any Judge, minister of the gospel, or Justice of the Peace for said county; your are hereby legally authorized to celebrate and solemnize the rites of matrimony between David L. Nicholson and Mary H. Beeson; and this shall be your warrent for so doing.

May 7 1856.   R. Estes

Judge of Probate.

Executed 8 day of May 1856.

R. Estes,

Judge of Probate.

State of Alabama   )

Dekalb County   )   I, J. A. Croley Judge of Probate, in and for said county, in said State, do hereby certify that the above and foregoing is a true and correct copy as is shown in marriage record A page 481. I futher certify that my office is the proper office for the keeping of marriage records.

Given under my hand and seal of court, this the 11 day of January 1907.

J.A. Croley

Judge of Probate.

◇◇◇◇◇

C.E.W.   Cherokee 7290.

DEPARTMENT OF THE INTERIOR,

COMMISSIONER TO THE FIVE CIVILIZED TRIBES.

In the matter of the application for the enrollment of MARY H. NICHOLSON as a citizen by intermarriage of the Cherokee Nation.

D E C I S I O N

THE RECORDS OF THIS OFFICE SHOW: That at Muskogee, Indian Territory, February 15, 1901, application was received by the Commission to the Five Civilized Tribes for the enrollment of Mary H. Nicholson as a citizen by intermarriage of the Cherokee Nation. Further proceedings in the matter of said application were had at Muskogee, Indian Territory, October 20, 1902, February 16, 1905, and January 8, 1907.

THE EVIDENCE IN THIS CASE SHOWS: That the applicant herein, Mary H. Nicholson, a white woman, married, in the State of Alabama, May 8, 1856, one David L. Nicholson, who was at the time of said marriage a recognized citizen by blood of the Cherokee Nation, and removed to the Indian Territory in the year 1872, and in the year 1874 was readmitted as a citizen by blood of the Cherokee Nation by an Act of the Cherokee National Council entitled, "An act readmitting David Nicholson, wife and minor children to citizenship." It is further shown that from the time of said marriage the said David L. Nicholson and Mary H. Nicholson resided together as husband and wife, and from the time of their admission to citizenship in the Cherokee Nation continuously resided therein until the death of the said David L. Nicholson, which occurred in the year 1878. It is further shown that since the death of said David L. Nicholson said Mary H. Nicholson has remained unmarried; and that she has continuously lived in the Cherokee Nation since 1872. Said applicant is identified on the Cherokee authenticated tribal roll of 1880, and the Cherokee census roll of 1896, as an intermarried citizen of the Cherokee Nation.

IT IS, THEREFORE, ORDERED AND ADJUDGED: That in accordance with the decision of the Supreme Court of the United States, dated November 5, 1906, in the cases of Daniel Red Bird et al. vs. the United States, Nos. 125, 126, 127 and 128, the said applicant, Mary H. Nicholson, is entitled, under the provisions of Section 21, of the Act of Congress approved June 28, 1898 (30 Stats., 495), to enrollment as a citizen by intermarriage of the Cherokee Nation, and her application for enrollment as such is accordingly granted.

Tams Bixby
Commissioner.

Dated at Muskogee, Indian Territory,
this   JAN 29 1907

◇◇◇◇◇

Cherokee Intermarried White 1906
Volume IV

DEPARTMENT OF THE INTERIOR.
COMMISSIONER TO THE FIVE CIVILIZED TRIBES.

CHIEF CLERK,
CHEROKEE LAND OFFICE.

DEAR SIR:

The records of this office show   **Mary H. Nicholson**

listed on Cherokee card No.   **7290**
to be prima facie entitled to enrollment as   **Intermarried**   of the Cherokee Nation for the
following reason, viz: **Is on Schedule for Departmental Approval**

Respectfully,

Commissioner.

Dated   Feb 8 1907

◇◇◇◇◇

COMMISSIONERS:
HENRY L. DAWES,
TAMS BIXBY,
THOMAS B. NEEDLES,
C. R. BRECKINRIDGE.

ALLISON L. AYLESWORTH,
SECRETARY.

ADDRESS ONLY THE
COMMISSION TO THE FIVE CIVILIZED TRIBES.

DEPARTMENT OF THE INTERIOR,
COMMISSION TO THE FIVE CIVILIZED TRIBES.

Cherokee No. 7290

Muskogee, Indian Territory,   **September 26th**   1902

Mary H. Nicholson,
Muskogee, Indian Territory.

Dear Madam:

The Act of Congress, approved July 1, 1902, and entitled "An Act To provide
for the enrollment of the lands of the Cherokee Nation, for the disposition of town sites
therein, and for other purposes," (Public No. 241), provides that "the roll of citizens of the
Cherokee Nation shall be made as of September first, nineteen-hundred and two."

268

In accordance with said provision, you are hereby notified that the Commission to the Five Civilized Tribes will be at its offices at Muskogee, Indian Territory, until Friday, October 31, 1902, inclusive, for the purpose of affording you an opportunity to show that you have not, between the date of the original application for your enrollment and Sept 2, 1902, forfeited your right as a citizen by intermarriage of the Cherokee Nation.

This evidence should be introduced immediately, as it is necessary in determining your right to share in the allotment of the lands of the Cherokee Nation, and until the same is furnished no further action can be taken looking toward your final enrollment as an intermarried citizen.

Yours truly,

Tams Bixby
Acting Chairman.

◇◇◇◇◇

Cherokee
7290

Muskogee, Indian Territory, December 26, 1906.

Mary H. Nicholson,
Muskogee, Indian Territory.

Dear Madam:

November 6, 1906, the United States Supreme Court held that white persons who intermarried with Cherokee citizens according to Cherokee law prior to November 1, 1875, are entitled to enrollment and allotments of land as citizens of the Cherokee Nation.

You are advised that to properly determine your right to enrollment as a citizen by intermarriage of the Cherokee Nation, it will be necessary for you to appear before the Commissioner for the purpose of giving testimony as to the date of your marriage and whether or not your husband, by reason of your marriage to whom you claim the right to enrollment as a citizen by intermarriage of the Cherokee Nation, was a recognized Cherokee citizen at the time of your marriage to him.

You are therefore directed to appear before the Commissioner at Muskogee, Indian Territory, at 9 o'clock A. M., on Saturday, January 5, 1907, and give testimony as above indicated.

Respectfully,

GHL   Acting Commissioner.

◇◇◇◇◇

Cherokee 7290

Muskogee, Indian Territory, January 29, 1907.

W. W. Hastings,
    Attorney for the Cherokee Nation,
        Muskogee, Indian Territory.

Dear Sir:

There is enclosed herewith copy of the decision of the Commissioner to the Five Civilized Tribes, dated January 29, 1907, granting the application for the enrollment of Mary H. Nicholson, as a citizen by intermarriage of the Cherokee Nation.

Respectfully,

Enc I-18   Commissioner.

RPI

◇◇◇◇◇

Cherokee 7290

Muskogee, Indian Territory, January 29, 1907.

The Commissioner to the Five Civilized Tribes,
    Muskogee, Indian Territory.

Sir:

Receipt is acknowledged of the testimony and of your decision enrolling Mary H. Nicholson as a citizen by intermarriage of the Cherokee Nation. Time for protesting said decision is waived and I consent that said person may be placed upon the schedule immediately.

Respectfully,
                                W. W. Hastings
                                Attorney for the Cherokee Nation.

◇◇◇◇◇

Cherokee 7290

Muskogee, Indian Territory, January 29, 1907.

Mary H. Nicholson,
     Muskogee, Indian Territory.

Dear Madam:

There is enclosed herewith copy of the decision of the Commissioner to the Five Civilized Tribes, dated January 29, 1907, granting the application for your enrollment as a citizen by intermarriage of the Cherokee Nation.

You will be advised when your name has been placed upon a schedule of citizens of the Cherokee Nation and approved by the Secretary of the Interior.

Respectfully,

Enc I-19

Commissioner.

RPI

Cher IW 131

◇◇◇◇◇

COPY

Department of the Interior
Commission to the Five Civilized Tribes,
Tahlequah, I.T., December 12, 1900.

In the matter of the application of Richard Riley for the enrollment of himself and wife as Cherokee citizen[sic]; being sworn and examined by Commissioner Breckinridge he testified as follows:

Q Give me your full name? A Richard Riley.
Q Have you a middle name? A No sir.
Q How old are you? A I was 66 years old 4th of this month.
Q What is your post-office? A Vera.
Q In what district do you live? A Cooweescoowee.
Q Who do you want to enroll, yourself and family? A I have no family but me and my old lady.
Q Are you a Cherokee by blood? A Yes sir.
Q Is your wife a Cherokee by blood? A No sir, she is part Choctaw.

Q How long have you lived in the Cherokee Nation? A My first trip to the Cherokee Nation was in February 1835,

Q How long have you been living here now? A I come back here in 1876.

Q You have been living here ever since? A No sir, I come back here last winter; I was out awhile on the Strip.

Q How long had you been living out before you came back here last winter? A About 5 or 6 years.

Q Where were you during that time? A I was on the Strip and in Oklahoma when they sold it

Q Did you come from the Strip back here? A Yes sir.

Q How long did you stay on the Strip? A I staid on her about 10 years.

Q Right along? A Yes sir.

Q And after that where did you live? A I lived on Grand River

Q In the Cherokee Nation? A Yes sir.

Q Did you draw money in 1894? A Yes sir.

Q Did they deduct what you got out on the Strip, did they take that away from what they give you? A Yes sir, took 112 dollars out of me.

Q When you were out there after Oklahoma was organized did you vote? A No sir. I couldn't vote; there was one election there and the tickets were printed, and every man that didn't have learning enough to make out the vote couldn't vote, and that's the reason I couldn't vote.

Q You tried to vote? A No sir, I didn't make no effort to vote.

Q You would have voted if you could have made out your ticket?

A No, I don't know that I would; I had no right to vote there.

Q You said the reason you wouldn't vote was because you couldn't make out your ticket?

A No, I had no right to vote; I told them no.

Q When did you and your wife marry? A August 16, 1861.

Q What is your wife's name? A Polly Ann Simpkins, was her first name.

Q You have lived together ever since 1861? A Yes sir.

Q How old is your wife? A She was 65 years old 3rd day of last September.

1880 roll page 801 #1923 Richard Riley Tahlequah native

1880 roll page 801 #1924 Polly Riley Tahlequah adopted white

1896 roll examined for applicants and names not found

Q Were you admitted to enrollment in 1896? A My list was made up and sent here by J. W. Jordon, and never was attended to I understand.

1894 roll page page[sic] 15 #45 Richard Riley Reservator pay, $153.70.

Com'r Breckinridge: The applicant appliers for the enrollment of himself and his wife; he is identified on the rolls of 1880 and 1894 as a native Cherokee; he is not identified on the roll of 1896, and on the 1894 roll he is identified as a reservator, and received a diminished amount of the Cherokee Strip payment; he will be listed as a Cherokee upon a doubtful card, and the Commission will consider the question of residence in Oklahoma Territory as set forth in the testimony;

His wife is a white woman; she is identified with him on the authenticated roll of 1880, they have lived together ever since their marriage in 1861; she will now be listed for enrollment on a doubtful card as a Cherokee by adoption, to await the decision of the rights of her husband; she is not identified on the roll of 1896.

M. D. Green, being first duly sworn, states that as stenographer to the Commission to the Five Civilized Tribes he correctly recorded the testimony and proceedings in this case and that the foregoing is a true and complete transcript of his stenographic notes thereof.

M.D. Green

Subscribed and sworn to before me this December 13, 1900.

T. B. Needles.

Endorsement.

DEPARTMENT OF THE INTERIOR,
COMMISSION TO THE FIVE CIVILIZED TRIBES.
FILED
DEC 13 1900

Tams Bixby, Acting Chairman.

◇◇◇◇◇

Statement of Applicant Taken Under Oath.

CHEROKEE BY BLOOD AND ADOPTION.

(66)

Date DEC 12 1900   1900.

Name **Richard Riley**   Vera, I.T.

District **TAHLEQUAH**   Year 1880   Page 801   No. 1923

Citizen by blood **Yes**   Mother's citizenship

Intermarried citizen

Married under what law   Date of marriage

License   Certificate

Wife's name **Polly A. Riley**

District **TAHLEQUAH**   Year 1880   Page 801   No. 1924

Citizen by blood **No**   Mother's citizenship

Intermarried citizen **Yes** ~~Choctaw~~

Married under what law   Date of marriage

License   Certificate

Names of Children:

Doubtful

Dist	Year	Page	No.	Age

273

Cherokee Intermarried White 1906
Volume IV

No 2 on 1880 roll as Polly Riley

◇◇◇◇◇

R.

C.   D-946.

Department of the Interior.
Commission to the Five Civilized Tribes.
Muskogee, Indian Territory I. T., March 13, 1902.

SUPPLEMENTAL TESTIMONY AND PROCEEDINGS in the matter of the application of Richard Riley for the enrollment of himself and wife as citizens of the Cherokee Nation.

The applicant was notified by registered letter February 25, 1902 that his application for the enrollment of himself and wife as citizens of the Cherokee Nation would be taken up for final consideration by the Commission at its offices in Muskogee, I. T., on the 13th day of March, 1902. Receipt has been acknowledged of the Commission's letter, and the applicant this day, to-wit: the 13th day of March, 1902, appears in person and by his attorney, N. A. Gibson, Muskogee, I. T.

RICHARD RILEY, being first duly sworn, and being examined, testified s follows:

BY MR. GIBSON OF MR. RILEY: State your name. A. Richard Riley.
Q. Where do you live? A. Cooweescoowee District.
Q. You are the principal applicant in this case, are you?
A. Yes sir.
Q. State whether or not you ever made any effort to vote in any election in Oklahoma during the time you lived there, subsequent to the opening of the Cherokee Strip.
A. No sir, I never voted there.
Q. Ever try to vote? A. No sir.
Q. When did you first locate in the Strip? A. As well as I recollect, it was in 1890. In January or February, I don't recollect exactly which.
Q. State when you returned to the present Cherokee Nation from Oklahoma to live.
A. Along in this month, it is two years ago, I don't recollect exactly what date.
Q. March, 1900? A. Yes sir.
Q. During the time when you lived in the Strip, state whether or not you had any property in the Cherokee Nation of any kind.
A. No sir, I didn't, had no property in the Cherokee Nation
Q. You had a farm prior to going out there? A. I had a farm, but before I went I let another man have it.

274

Q. Did you retain the title to the place until it was paid for? A. There was nothing said about that. I was to make a bill of sale for it when he paid for it.

Q. Has he ever paid for it? A. No sir.

Q. State whether or not he still is upon the place.

A. No sir, he sold it.

BY MR. HASTINGS: That strip was made a part of Oklahoma, was it not, in September, the 16th, 1893? A. September 16th, 1893, I think it was.

Q. You never tried to get this farm back from this fellow? The one that you sold it to?

A. No sir. I came back and bought me a farm in the Nation.

MR. GIBSON: When did you by the farm in the Cherokee Nation?

A. Two years ago, along about in this month.

Q. In what District is that located? A. Cooweescoowee.

Q. State whether or not you are residing on this farm at this time? A. Yes sir.

Q. Is your wife residing there with you? A. Yes sir.

The attorney for the applicant and the representative of the Cherokee Nation submit the case and the same is deemed completed and will be reported to the Commission for final decision based upon the evidence now of record.

The attorney for the applicant requests and will be granted, fifteen days in which to file brief in this case, one copy with the Commission, and one with the representative of the Cherokee Nation.

I, Wm. Hutchinson, do hereby certify that as stenographer to the Commission to the Five Civilized Tribes, I correctly recorded the proceedings in this case, and that the foregoing is a true and complete transcript of the stenographic notes thereof.

Wm Hutchinson

◇◇◇◇◇

Cherokee Intermarried White 1906
Volume IV

Cherokee D-946.

Department of the Interior,
Commission to the Five Civilized Tribes,
Muskogee, I. T., October 17, 1902.

In the matter of the application of Richard Riley for the enrollment of himself as a citizen by blood, and for the enrollment of his wife, Polly A. Riley, as a citizen by intermarriage of the Cherokee Nation; said Polly A. Riley being sworn and examined by the Commission, testified as follows:

Q What is your name? A Polly A. Riley.
Q How old are you? A Sixty-six years old.
Q What is your postoffice? A Vera.
Q Are you a white woman? A Yes sir.
Q You are on the roll of 1880 as an adopted white citizen? A Yes sir.
Q What is your husband's name? A Richard Riley.
Q Was he your husband in 1880? A He was my husband and all the husband I ever have had.
Q Have you and your husband, Richard Riley, been living together in the Cherokee Nation since 1880? A We have lived together about forty-one years last August.
Q Have you ever been separated? A Never was, no sir.
Q Living together now? A Living together now and will be living together until we have to separate.
Q Have you and your husband been living in the Cherokee Nation all that time? A We lived out on the strip a while until they sold it.
Q How long had you been living on the strip? A We lived there ten years; we lived there until they sold it; it was Cherokee lands and we went on it.
Q Have you any children? A Four.
Q They are all grown up? A Grown and married.
Just me and my old man is all there is in the family.

Richard Riley, being sworn and examined by the Commission, testified as follows:
Q What is your name? A Richard Riley.
Q How old are you? A I was sixty-seven years old the fourth day of last December.
Q Are you the husband of Polly A. Riley who has just testified? A Yes sir.
Q I want to ask you, Mr. Riley, whether you have been living in the Cherokee Nation since 1880? A Yes sir, all only except the time I was out yonder.
Q When did you go out to Oklahoma or the Cherokee Strip? A We went out there I think it was about the year '90 or '91.
Q How long did you live out there? A Ten years.
Q Then you came back in 1900, two years ago? A Three years ago last March.
Q Your wife was with you all this time? A Yes sir.
Q Did you own any land out there? A Yes sir, I bought a piece of land, eighty acres.
Q Did you make your home out there? A I made it my home until it was sold.
Q You had no property back here in the Cherokee Nation? A Nothing only a claim.

Q All your household effects were out with you in the Cherokee strip? A Yes sir.

Q Did you ever vote out there? A No sir, never voted out there.

Q You didn't live in the Cherokee Nation from 1890 up until about three years ago?
A Three years ago last March.

Q Is that the only time you have been out of the Cherokee Nation since 1880?
A Yes sir, that is to stay any length of time.

Q Did you ever vote in the Cherokee Nation during that ten years you were out?
A Yes sir, in the Cherokee Nation.

Q Did you come back to the Cherokee Nation? A Yes sir, that belonged to the Cherokee Nation; we were allowed to vote.

Q It didn't belong to the nation after '94? A I know that.

Q Did you vote in the Cherokee Nation between 1894 and the time you came back?
A No sir.

Q Did you ever vote out there in Oklahoma? A No sir, I did not.

J. C. Starr: When did you say you went to the strip? A About the year '90 or '91, somewhere along there.

Q Took an allotment out there? [sic] No sir.

Q Did you buy a place out there? A Yes sir.

Q When did you by the place? A I bought it just before the payment of the strip.

Q Do you own that place yet? A No sir.

Q When did you sell it? A I sold it in about three years ago, just before I come back.

Q Who did you sell it to? A Taylor.

Q What Taylor? A Frank Taylor.

Q What is his postoffice? A Dixie, Oklahoma.

Q Is that place located near Dixie? A Yes sir.

Q Where were you living in the year 1898? A I was living on Grand River, Saline District.

Q When did you say you returned to the Cherokee Nation to live from the strip?
A About three years ago last March.

Q March 1899? A Yes sir.

Q Then you lived in Oklahoma from 1891 until 1899? A I think I lived, as well as I recollect, ten years; that is my recollection.

Q Then you were living in Oklahoma during the year 1898? A Yes.

Q You were mistaken about living on Grand River in 1898? A I thought you said 1880.

Q I said 1898? A I was in Oklahoma then.

Q Where were you on June 28, 1898? A I guess I was in Oklahoma, out in that strip country. I never left the Cherokee Nation at all; they sold it off.

Q You remained in the strip after it became a part of Oklahoma until March 1899, is that a fact? A Yes, I guess I did.

Commission: Was it your intention to make your home there? A No sir, not after they sold it. I only bought that piece of land because I had improvements on it; I didn't want to throw it away.

Q Was it your intention to go out there and leave the Cherokee Nation?
A No sir, that belonged to the Cherokee Nation.

Q You lived there five years after it was sold; did you intend to make your home out there? A No sir, I was just trying to get rid of what I have; I couldn't throw it up and have to work for a living all the time.

The undersigned, being duly sworn, states that as stenographer to the Commission to the Five Civilized Tribes he correctly recorded the testimony and proceedings in this case, and that the foregoing is a true and complete transcript of the stenographic notes thereof.

E.G. Rothenberger

Subscribed and sworn to before me this 17th day of November, 1902.

BC Jones
Notary Public.

◇◇◇◇◇

COPY

Cherokee D-946.

DEPARTMENT OF THE INTERIOR,

COMMISSION TO THE FIVE CIVILIZED TRIBES.

In the matter of the application for the enrollment of Richard Riley as a citizen by blood of the Cherokee Nation, and for the enrollment of his wife, Polly A. Riley, as a citizen by intermarriage of the Cherokee Nation.

D E C I S I O N .

The record in this case shows that on December 12, 1900, Richard Riley appeared before the Commission at Tahlequah, Indian Territory, and made personal application for the enrollment of himself as a citizen by blood of the Cherokee Nation, and for the enrollment of his wife, Polly A. Riley, as a citizen by intermarriage of the Cherokee Nation. Further proceedings in the matter of said application were had at Muskogee, Indian Territory, on March 13, 1902, and October 17, 1902.

The evidence shows that the said Richard Riley is a Cherokee by blood; that he married Polly Ann Simpkins, a Choctaw Indian, in 1861, and that they have lived together as husband and wife ever since that time. They are both identified on the 1880 authenticated tribal roll of the Cherokee Nation. Said Richard Riley is identified on the 1894 pay roll of the Cherokee Nation as a Reservator.

The evidence further shows that the said Richard Riley lived in the Cherokee Nation from 1880 until 1890; that in 1890 he removed to that portion of the Cherokee Nation known as the Cherokee Outlet, which was ceded to the United States in 1893 and became part of Oklahoma Territory; that the said Richard Riley and his wife, Polly A. Riley,

Cherokee Intermarried White 1906
Volume IV

continued to reside in the Cherokee Outlet until 1900, when they returned to the Cherokee Nation as now constituted, and have continuously resided therein since that time.

In a case entitled, Daisy Lee Jordan, et al., vs. Cherokee Nation, it appears the the said Daisy Lee Jordan made application, with others, to the Commission to the Five Civilized Tribes under an Act of Congress approved June 10, 1896 (29 Stats., 321), for admission to citizenship in the Cherokee Nation, which application was duly acted upon by the Commission and rejected. Appeal was taken to the United States Court for the Northern District, Indian Territory, sitting at Muskogee, which court, by its judgment, reversed said decision of the Commission and admitted said Daisy Lee Jordan to citizenship in said Nation.

In said case the question as to whether the residence of Daisy Lee Jordan in the Cherokee Outlet as above described, deprived her of citizenship in the Cherokee Nation, was considered by the Court, and among other things, the court held:

"This court is of the opinion that the residence of the parties named in the Territory of Oklahoma, under the facts and circumstances set forth in the Master's report, does not deprive them of citizenship in the Cherokee Nation. They took their lands in the Territory by virtue of the treaty between the Cherokees and the United States, and they were recognized by the treaty as Cherokees and entitled to a pro rata share of the Strip payment, and the value of the lands which they took in the Strip was deducted from their Strip money. They have not left the Cherokee Nation or removed their property out of the Nation. The Nation has simply ceded to the United States that part of its area upon which these persons were permitted to reside."

It is, therefore, the opinion of this Commission that Richard Riley should be enrolled as a citizen by blood of the Cherokee Nation, and that his wife, Polly A. Riley, should be enrolled as a citizen by intermarriage of the Cherokee Nation, in accordance with the provisions of section twenty-one of the Act of Congress approved June 28, 1898 (30 Stats., 495), and it is so ordered.

COMMISSION TO THE FIVE CIVILIZED TRIBES

Tams Bixby,
Chairman.

TB Needles,
Commissioner.

C. R. Breckinridge,
Commissioner.

Dated at Muskogee, Indian Territory,
this   MAR 2 1903

◇◇◇◇◇

Refer in reply to
the following:
Land   DEPARTMENT OF THE INTERIOR,
59574--1903.

Office of Indian Affairs,
Washington, Sept. 24, 1903.

The Honorable,
    The Secretary of the Interior.

Sir:

The office is in receipt of Department letter of September 16, 1903 (I.T.D. 6400, 5064), returning the record relative to the application of Richard Riley, et al., for enrollment as citizens of the Cherokee Nation, which was forwarded to the Department informally in accordance with its request. The office is directed to submit the case for the Department's consideration as early as practicable. The record in the case is enclosed herewith. It was transmitted by the Commission March 4, 1903.

Richard Riley applied for the enrollment of himself as a citizen by blood of the Cherokee Nation and for the enrollment of his wife, Polly A. Riley, as a citizen by intermarriage. The record shows that Richard Riley is a Cherokee by blood; that in 1861 he married Polly Ann Riley nee Simpkins, a Choctaw Indian; that his name appears on the 1880 tribal roll and on the 1894 payroll as a reservator. It is also shown that Richard Riley resided in the Cherokee Nation from 1880 until 1890, when he removed to that part of the Cherokee Nation known as the Outlet which was ceded to the United States by the act of March 3, 1893 (27 Stats., 612); that he continued to reside in the Outlet until 1900, when he returned to what is now the Cherokee Nation; and that he has resided there since that time. The Commission, in its decision of March 2, 1903, favorable to the applicants, invites attention to the holding of the United States Court for the Northern District of the Indian Territory in the Daisy Lee Jordan case.

The records of this office show that Richard Riley, in accordance with the provisions of the act of March 3, 1893, was allotted the S/2 of the SE/4 of Sec. 31, T. 21, R. 9, containing 80 acres, which is a part of what was originally known as the Cherokee Outlet. Prior to the time that Richard Riley removed to the Outlet he owned a farm in the Cherokee Nation. During his residence in the Outlet he did not vote. The Assistant Attorney General, in an opinion dated April 18, 1903, held that a citizen of the Cherokee Nation could only expatriate his citizenship by removal and the removal of his effects beyond the limits of the nation and becoming a citizen elsewhere. It is necessary therefore that three concurrent conditions take place before expatriation. It is not shown that this applicant became a citizen of any other country and it is believed by the office that Richard Riley is entitled to enrollment as a citizen of the Cherokee Nation.

It is therefore respectfully recommended that the decision of the Commission in so far as it relates to the enrollment of Richard Riley be approved.

Very respectfully,

W. A. Jones,

Commissioner.

GAW-S

◇◇◇◇◇

J.P.

DEPARTMENT OF THE INTERIOR.   FHE
Washington.

I.T.D. 6916-1903.   September 29, 1903.

L.R.S.

Commission to the Five Civilized Tribes,
    Muskogee, Indian Territory.

Gentlemen:

March 2, 1903, you rendered a decision in the case involving the application of Richard Riley, for enrollment as a citizen by blood of the Cherokee Nation, and for the enrollment of his wife, Polly A. Riley, as an intermarried citizen of said Nation, holding that the parties were entitled to enrollment under Section 21 of the act of June 28, 1898 (30 Stat., 495), against which decision the Cherokee Nation protests.

It appears that Richard Riley is a Cherokee by blood, and was married in 1861 to Polly Ann Simpkins, and that both of them are identified on the 1880 authenticated tribal roll of the Cherokee Nation; that Richard Riley lived in the Cherokee Nation from 1880 until 1890, when he removed to that portion of the Cherokee Nation known as the Cherokee Outlet, which was ceded to the United States in 1893 and became a part of Oklahoma; that he and his wife continued to reside in the Cherokee Outlet until 1900, when they returned to the Cherokee Nation as now constituted, and have continuously resided there since that time.

The Nation contends that Riley's residence in the Cherokee Nation prior to its annexation to Oklahoma affects his citizenship in the Cherokee Nation, and as he did not return to the Cherokee Nation prior to June 28, 1898, he is not entitled to enrollment.

You held that by the residence of the applicants in Oklahoma they did not forfeit their citizenship.

Reporting in the matter September 24, 1903, the Commissioner of Indian Affairs stated that prior to the time Richard Riley removed to the Outlet he owned a farm in the Cherokee Nation, and that during his residence in the Outlet he did not vote. Referring to the opinion of the Assistant Attorney General of April 18, 1903, holding that a citizen of the Cherokee Nation could only forfeit his citizenship y removal of himself and his effects beyond the limits of the Nation, and by becoming a citizen elsewhere, he recommended that your decision be affirmed, so far as it relates to the enrollment of Richard Riley.

The Department concurs in the recommendation, and your decision to that extent is hereby affirmed.

The question of the right of his wife to enrollment will be determined after the Court of Claims has passed upon the question of the rights of persons intermarried to Cherokee citizens.

A copy of the Commissioner's letter is inclosed.

Respectfully,

1 inclosure.   Thos Ryan, Acting Secretary.

◇◇◇◇◇

COPY   COPY
D.C. 52894-1906

DEPARTMENT OF THE INTERIOR   Y.P.
I.T.D. 6916-1903.

WASHINGTON.   FHE.

November 28, 1906.

L.R.S.

Commissioner to the Five Civilized Tribes,
      Muskogee, Indian Territory.

Sir:

In letter of September 29, 1903, to the Commission to the Five Civilized Tribes, the Department, in the Cherokee enrolment[sic] case of Richard Riley, et al., advised the Commission that it would pass upon the claim of Riley's wife, Polly Ann Riley, to enrolment[sic] as an intermarried citizen of the Cherokee Nation.

The Supreme Court of the United States, on November 5, 1906, rendered a decision in the cases of Daniel Red Bird, et al., vs. the United States, Nos. 125, 126, 127 and 128, appealed from the Court of Claims.

It is shown in the record in the case of Richard Riley et al, that Polly Ann Riley is a Choctaw Indian, and was married to Riley in 1861. Her name is found on the 1880 roll of the Cherokee Nation.

The Indian Office, in letter of September 24, 1903, recommended that the decision of the Commission of May 2, 1903, in favor of Polly Ann Riley, be affirmed.

Finding no reason to disturb the decision of the Commission, it is accordingly affirmed.

The papers in the case have been returned to the Indian Office.

                Respectfully,
                (Signed) Thos. Ryan,
                     First Assistant Secretary

Through the Commissioner
      of Indian Affairs.
3 inc. for Ind. of.

◇◇◇◇◇

Cherokee Intermarried White 1906
Volume IV

Cherokee
D 936.

Muskogee, Indian Territory, December 12, 1906.

Polly A. Riley,
Vera, Indian Territory.

Dear Madam:

You are hereby advised that the decision of the Commission to the Five Civilized Tribes, dated March 2, 1903, granting your application for enrollment as a citizen by intermarriage of the Cherokee Nation was affirmed by the Secretary of the Interior November 28, 1906.

You are further advised that you will not be permitted to make an allotment selection until your name has been placed upon a schedule of citizens of the Cherokee Nation and approved by the Secretary of the Interior, of which action you will be duly notified.

Respectfully,

S.W.   Commissioner.

◇◇◇◇◇◇

Cherokee
D 946.

Muskogee, Indian Territory, December 12, 1906.

N. A. Gibson,
Attorney for Polly A. Riley,
Muskogee, Indian Territory.

Dear Sir:

You are hereby advised that the decision of the Commission to the Five Civilized Tribes, dated March 2, 1903, granting the application for the enrollment of Polly A. Riley as a citizen by intermarriage of the Cherokee Nation was affirmed by the Secretary of the Interior November 28, 1906.

For your information there is enclosed herewith a copy of Departmental decision referred to.

Respectfully,

Encl. W-100   Commissioner.
S.W.

◇◇◇◇◇◇

Cherokee
D 946.

Muskogee, Indian Territory, December 12, 1906.

W. W. Hastings,
Attorney for the Cherokee Nation,
Muskogee, Indian Territory.

Dear Sir:

You are hereby advised that the decision of the Commission to the Five Civilized Tribes, dated March 2, 1903, granting the application for the enrollment of Polly A. Riley as a citizen by intermarriage of the Cherokee Nation was affirmed by the Secretary of the Interior November 28, 1906.

For your information there is enclosed herewith a copy of Departmental decision referred to.

Respectfully,

Encl. W-200   Commissioner.
  S.W.

Cher IW 132

◇◇◇◇◇

C.E.W.

DEPARTMENT OF THE INTERIOR,

COMMISSIONER TO THE FIVE CIVILIZED TRIBES.

In the matter of the application for the enrollment of

DIOPHANTUS D. THORNTON

as a citizen by intermarriage of the Cherokee Nation.

CHEROKEE 77.

◇◇◇◇◇

285

Cherokee Intermarried White 1906
Volume IV

DEPARTMENT OF THE INTERIOR.
COMMISSION TO THE FIVE CIVILIZED TRIBES.
FAIRLAND, I. T., JULY 10th, 1900.

IN THE MATTER OF THE APPLICATION OF D. D. Thornton for enrollment as a citizen of the Cherokee Nation, and he being sworn by Commissioner, C. R. Breckenridge[sic], testified as follows:

Q What is your name? A D. D. Thornton.
Q What are you commonly called? A Dorcas, or D. D.; either will do
Q What is your age? A I was born in 1821.
Q That makes you about seventy-nine or eighty? A Yes sir.
Q What is your Postoffice address? [sic] Grove, when I live with Mrs. Bates.
Q Is Mrs. Bates your daughter? A Yes sir.
Q And you are living with her now? A Yes sir.
Q In what District is that? A Delaware.
Q How long have you lived in that District? A I believe I moved there in 1870, but I have been living in this Nation -- I moved here in 1847,
Q Where did you come from? A Tennessee.
Q Were you born in Tennessee? A Yes sir.
Q Have you lived in this Nation continually for the last ten? A Yes sir, except the time of the war I lived here fifty three or fifty four years., except during the war.
Q Never changed your residence at all? A No sir.
Q Are you a Cherokee? A Yes sir.
Q By blood? A No sir, an adopted citizen.
Q Neither your father nor mother are on the Rolls as Cherokee citizens? A No sir.
Q You belong to Delaware District, do you? A Yes sir.
Q Have you ever been enrolled by the Cherokee Tribal Authorities; are you on any of the Cherokee Rolls? A Yes sir, when they took the census two years ago, I was taken on the Roll then.
Q Are you on the Roll of 1880? A I can not answer that; I reckon I am.
    (On consulting the Roll of 1880, authenticated roll of citizens of the Cherokee Nation, your name is found as D. D. Thornton - Page 328, #2701.)
Q Are you married? A I have been; my wife is dead.
Q Have you any children under twenty one years of age?
A None of my own.
Q Then you make application only for yourself? A Yes sir.
Q You said you were not married, did you? A Not now sir, I have been married.
Q When did you wife die? A She died in 1888 I believe, or 1889.
Q That was the only time you were ever married? A No sir, I was married before that.
Q When did you marry your last wife? A 1863.
Q And you were ; -- you have never been married since the death of that wife you were living with at that time? A No sir.
Q What is your name in full? A Diophantus Dewit Thornton.
(The name of D. D. Thornton is recorded on the Roll of 1896 as Diophantus D. Thornton, and being properly enrolled on the official records of the Tribe, he is identified as the

same person whose name has been so enrolled and he is enrolled by this Commission as an inter-married citizen.

(On the roll of 1880, D. D. Thornton, and being identified as the same person whose name has been enrolled as just stated; he is hereby enrolled by this Commission as an inter-married citizen.[sic]

Q Give me your wife's name and the name under which she was enrolled in 1880? A her name was Susan.

Q Susan Thornton? A Yes sir.

Q Susan A.? A Susan A. I believe.

Name found on Page 228, #2702.

Q Have you any minor children who have died since 1880? A No sir.

Q Was Mary L. Thornton a child of yours? A Yes sir; I guess Mrs Gossett died since then.

Q Is her husband living? A Yes sir.

Q An inter-married citizen? A Yes sir.

Q Any other children that have died since 1880? A No sir.

Q Do you know anything about Mary L. Thornton? A Yes sr.

Q Who was she? A My daughter.

Q Is she dead? A No sir.

R. R. Cravens, being first duly sworn by Commissioner, C. R. Breckenridge[sic] states that he reported the foregoing case, and that the foregoing and above is a true, full and correct transcript of his stenographic notes in said case.

R R Cravens

Sworn to and subscribed before me this 10th day of July, 1900.

Clifton R Breckinridge
COMMISSIONER.

◇◇◇◇◇

Cherokee Intermarried White 1906
Volume IV

Statement of Applicant Taken Under Oath.

CHEROKEE BY BLOOD AND ADOPTION.

79   Date   **JUL 10 1900**   1900.

Name   Diophantus D. Thornton   ------ Grove, I.T.

District   Delaware   Year   1880   Page   328   No. 2701

Citizen by blood   ———   Mother's citizenship   U. S. Citiz.

Intermarried citizen   Yes

Married under what law..Date of marriage.........................

License ....Certificate.........................

Wife's name.........................

District...................................Year...............Page.................No. ....

Citizen by blood.................Mother's citizenship........................

Intermarried citizen................

Married under what law..................................Date of marriage..................

License ....Certificate.................

    Names of Children:

...............................Dist...........Year...........Page........No.........Age........
...............................Dist...........Year...........Page........No.........Age........
...............................Dist...........Year...........Page........No.........Age........
...............................Dist...........Year...........Page........No.........Age........
...............................Dist...........Year...........Page........No.........Age........

On 1880 Roll as D. D. Thornton

◇◇◇◇◇

JOR.
Cher. 77.

Department of the Interior.
Commission to the Five Civilized Tribes.
Tahlequah, I. T., October 10, 1902.

SUPPLEMENTAL TESTIMONY AND PROCEEDINGS in the matter of the application for the enrollment of DIOPHANTUS D. THORNTON as a citizen by intermarriage of the Cherokee Nation.

DIOPHANTUS D. THORNTON, being first duly sworn, and being examined, testified as follows:

BY COMMISSION: What is your name? A Diophantus Dewitt Thornton.
Q How old are you? A I am eighty-two, I was born in 1821.
Q What is your post office address? A My post office address would be Grove.
Q You are a white man, are you? A Yes sir.

288

Q Have you heretofore made application to this Commission for enrollment as a citizen by intermarriage of the Cherokee Nation? A Yes sir, at Fairland.

Q What is the name of your wife? A First wife Elizabeth Brown.

Q The wife through whom you claim your citizenship? A Susan Delano

Q Is Susan Delano living? A No sir.

Q Was she a Cherokee by blood? A Yes sir.

Q Do you claim your right to enrollment by reason of your marriage to her? A Yes sir.

Q When were you and she married? A We were married about 1863.

Q Where were you married to her in 1863? A I was married in Texas the time of the war, then married again, married over again.

Q Married her again according to Cherokee law? A Yes sir.

Q When did you married[sic] the second time? A We were married in 1872 according to Cherokee law.

Q Does you name appear upon the roll of 1880? A Yes sir, iI[sic] guess it is.

Q How long has your wife been dead? A She has been dead ten or twelve years.

Q Did you and she live together continuously until the time of her death? A Yes sir.

Q You never separated? A No sir.

Q Have you married since she died? A No sir.

Q You have lived as a single man since she died? A Yes sir.

Q Were you ever married before you married her? A I married my first wife Lizzie Brown, I married a Brown as first wife.

Q Was that the first wife you ever had, Lizzie Brown? A Yes sir.

Q Was she living at the time you married your second wife?
A No sir, she was dead.

Q Was that the only time you were ever married before you married Susan Delano?
A Yes sir.

Q You have been married twice? A Yes sir, only been married twice.

Q Was Susan Delano ever married before she married you? A She married Delano, a white man. He died here at Tahlequah, and then she married me after Delano died.

Q Delano was dead when you and your wife married? A Yes sir.

Q Was that the only time she was ever married before she married you?
A Yes sir, I think so.

Q Have you resided in the Cherokee Nation continuously since you and your wife Susan were married? A Yes sir.

This testimony will be filed with and made a part of the record in the matter of the application for the enrollment of Diophantus D. Thornton as a citizen by intermarriage of the Cherokee Nation, Cherokee straight card field No. 77.

Wm. Hutchinson, being first duly sworn, states that as stenographer to the Commission to the Five Civilized Tribes he correctly recorded the testimony and proceedings in this case, and that the foregoing is a true and complete transcript of the stenographic notes thereof.

Wm Hutchinson

Subscribed and sworn to before me this 17th day of October, 1902.

John O Rosson
Notary Public.

◇◇◇◇◇

Department of the Interior,
COMMISSION TO THE FIVE CIVILIZED TRIBES.

In the matter of the death of **Danophantus**[sic] **D Thornton**   a citizen of
the   **Cherokee**   Nation, who formerly resided at or near   **Dodge**   , Ind. Ter., and
died on the **6**[th]   day of   **August** , **1904**

AFFIDAVIT OF RELATIVE.

UNITED STATES OF AMERICA,
   INDIAN TERRITORY,
Northern   District.

I, **Pauline Williams nee Bates**   , on oath state that I am   **50**   years of age
and a citizen by **Blood**   , of the   **Cherokee**   Nation; that my postoffice address is
Dodge   , Ind. Ter.; that I am   **a Daughter**   of   **Danophantus D Thornton**
who was a citizen, by   **Intermarriage**   , of the   **Cherokee**   Nation and that said
Danophantus D Thornton   died on the   **6**[th]   day of **August**   , **1904**

nee Bates
Pauline Williams

Witnesses To Mark:

Subscribed and sworn to before me this   **7**[th]   day of   **January**   , 190 **7**

T. S. Remsen
Notary Public.

AFFIDAVIT OF ACQUAINTANCE.

UNITED STATES OF AMERICA,
   INDIAN TERRITORY,
Northern   District.

I,   **L Alice Thornton**   , on oath state that I am   **27**   years of age, and a
citizen by **Blood**   of the   **Cherokee** Nation; that my postoffice address is   **Grove**
Ind. Ter.; that I was personally acquainted with   **Danophantus D Thornton**   who
was a citizen, by   **Intermarriage**   , of the   **Cherokee**   Nation; and that said
Danophantus D Thornton   died on the   **6**[th]   day of August   , **1904**

L Alice Thornton

Witnesses To Mark:

{

Subscribed and sworn to before me this   **7th**   *day of*   **January**   *, 190* **7**

T. S. Remsen
Notary Public.

◇◇◇◇◇

F.R.   Cherokee - 77

DEPARTMENT OF THE INTERIOR,
COMMISSIONER TO THE FIVE CIVILIZED TRIBES.
Muskogee, I. T., January 10, 1907.

In the matter of the application for the enrollment of Diophantus D. Thornton as a citizen by intermarriage of the Cherokee Nation.

Pauline Williams, nee Bates, being first duly sworn by Frances R. Lane, a Notary Public for the Western District of Indian Territory, testified as follows:

By the Commissioner:
Q What is your name? A Pauline Williams, nee Bates.
Q What is your age? A Fifty.
Q What is your postoffice address? A Grove, Indian Ter.
Q In whose behalf do you appear here today? A My father, Diophantus D. Thornton.
Q Did Diophantus D. Thornton claim to be a citizen of the Cherokee nation[sic] by intermarriage? A Yes sir.
Q Through whom? A My mother was a citizen, Elizabeth Brown, and he married Susan Delano the second time.
Q When was he married to Elizabeth Brown? A That was in 1845.
Q Was she a citizen of the Cherokee nation? A Yes sir.
Q When did they remove to the Cherokee nation? A To this country?
Q Yes? A I don't know. I wouldn't swear to that; that was before I was born.
Q Where were you born? A Down here close to Fort Smith, Ark in the Cherokee nation.
Q So they have been living in the Cherokee nation over fifty years? A Yes sir.
Q Do you know whether or not they were married in accordance with the laws of the Cherokee nation, when they removed to such nation? A Yes, Brother said they was.
Q Were they married prior to November 1, 1875? A I don't know; that was in the old country.
Q But when they were married in the Cherokee nation the second time? A Yes, I reckon--I don't know.
Q Have you any record of that Cherokee marriage? A No, it is on record about the last one, Susan Delano.

Q I am talking about your mother. A No, I suppose it is all lost. They was married before the war, and I suppose the records are all lost.

Q You don't know whether or not they were married under Cherokee laws, under a Cherokee license, do yoi[sic]?

A No, I don't; I can't swear to that; broth said they was

Q When did your mother die? A My mother died just the beginning of the war in 1861.

Q When did D. D. Thornton marry again? A In 1871.

Q Was Susan Delano a citizen of the Cherokee nation? A Yes sir.

Q When did D. D. Thornton marry her? A In 1872.

Q Where? A On Cowskin prairie[sic] near Grove, Indian Territory

Q Do you know whether this marriafe[sic] to the Delano woman was under a license of the Cherokee nation? A Yes sir.

Q Have you any record of it? A Yes, it is on record. Mr. McGhee issued the license and Coffey Woodall was judge; he married them.

Q That was in Delaware District was it? A Yes sir.

> In marriage record S, Delaware District, now in the possession of this office, there appears a certificate showing that D. D. Thornton, a white man, was licensed to marry Susan Delano, on February 1, 1872.
> That said license was returned executed February 4, 1872, being in accordance with an act passed by the National Council October 15, 855 in regard to white men marrying in the Cherokee nation.

Q Is this wife to whom he was married in 1872 living at this time? A No, she is dead.

Q When did she die? A She has been dead about-- I can't swear exactly--something over ten years though.

Q From the date of her marriage in 1872 up until the time of her death did they reside continuously in the Cherokee nation as husband and wife? A Yes sir.

Q Did D. D. Thornton marry again after the death of his second wife? A No sir.

Q He is still living in the Cherokee nation, and has been ever since her death?

A Yes, after she died he lived with me

A Is he living at this time? A No, he is dead now.

Q Was Susan Delano ever married previous to her marriage to D. D. Thornton in 1872?

A No, she was a widow lady when papa married her.

Q Then she had been married before? A Yes, her maiden name was Vann, I think.

Q Do you know whether her first husband was living at the time she was married to D. D. Thornton? A No, he was dead

Q Delano was dead at the time of her marriage to D. D. Thornton? A Yes sir.

Q Do you remember the date of the death of your father? A He died, it will be two years ago last August, he died August 6, 1904.

> The name of the applicant, Diophantus D. Thornton appears on Cherokee Field Card No. 77, and is listed on the 1880 authenticated roll of Cherokee by blood of the Cherokee Nation, Delaware District, opposite No. 2701.
> Applicant's name also appears on the 1896 roll opposite No. 524, Delaware District.

Cherokee Intermarried White 1906
Volume IV

Frances R. Lane upon oath states that as stenographer to the Commissioner to the Five Civilized Tribes she reported the testimony in the above entitled cause and that the foregoing is an accurate transcript of her stenographic notes thereof.

Frances R. Lane

Subscribed and sworn to before me this January 11, 1907.

Edward Merrick
Notary Public.

◇◇◇◇◇

C.E.W.   Cherokee 77.

DEPARTMENT OF THE INTERIOR,

COMMISSIONER TO THE FIVE CIVILIZED TRIBES.

In the matter of the application for the enrollment of DIOPHANTUS D. THORNTON as a citizen by intermarriage of the Cherokee Nation.

D E C I S I O N

THE RECORDS OF THIS OFFICE SHOW: That at Fairland, Indian Territory, July 10, 1900, application was received by the Commission to the Five Civilized Tribes for the enrollment of Diophantus D. Thornton as a citizen by intermarriage of the Cherokee Nation. Further proceedings in the matter of said application were had at Tahlequah, Indian Territory, October 10, 1903, and at Muskogee, Indian Territory, January 10, 1907.

THE EVIDENCE IN THIS CASE SHOWS: That the applicant herein, Diophantus D. Thornton, a white man, was married in the year 1845, to one Elizabeth Thornton, nee Brown, since deceased, an alleged Cherokee; that subsequent to her death, which occurred in the year 1861, the said Diophantus D. Thornton, in February 1872, was married in accordane[sic] with Cherokee law to one Susan Thornton, nee Delano, who was at the time of said marriage a recognized citizen by blood of the Cherokee Nation, and who is identified on the Cherokee authenticated tribal roll of 1880, Delaware District, page 328, No. 2702, as a native Cherokee. It is further shown that from the time of said marriage the said Diophantus D. Thornton and Susan Thornton resided together as husband and wife and continuously lived in the Cherokee Nation until the time of her death, which occurred about the year 1891; that since the death of said Susan Thornton the said Diophantus D. Thornton has remained unmarried and continuously lived in the Cherokee Nation since the year 1872. Said applicant is identified on the Cherokee authenticated tribal roll of 1880, and the Cherokee census roll of 1896 as an intermarried citizen of the Cherokee Nation.

IT IS, THEREFORE, ORDERED AND ADJUDGED: That in accordance with the decision of the Supreme Court of the United States, dated November 5, 1906, in the cases of Daniel Red Bird et al., vs. the United States, Nos. 125, 126, 127 and 128, the said applicant Diophantus D. Thornton, is entitled, under the provisions of Section 21 of the Act of Congress approved June 28, 1898 (30 Stats., 495) to enrollment as a citizen by intermarriage of the Cherokee Nation and his application for enrollment as such is accordingly granted.

Tams Bixby   Commissioner.

Dated at Muskogee, Indian Territory,
this   JAN 30 1907

◇◇◇◇◇

(The letter below is handwritten and typed as given.)

Dodge I.T. March 2^d 1903

To the Commissioner of the Cherokee Land Office
Vinita I.T.

Dear Sir

    I hereby revoke the Power of Attorney given William I. Thornton, my son.

    Authrizeing him to select and file on an allotment for me and forbid him or any one else fileing for me until further notice is given your Honorable Body

Yours Truly
D.D. Thornton

Witnessed
by A B Hampton
    Pauline Williams

◇◇◇◇◇

Cherokee
77

Muskogee, Indian Territory, December 22, 1906.

Diophantus[sic] D. Thornton,
    Dodge, Indian Territory.

Dear Sir:

    November 6, 1906, the United States Supreme Court held that white persons who intermarried with Cherokee citizens according to Cherokee law prior to November

1, 1875, are entitled to enrollment and allotments of land as citizens of the Cherokee Nation.

You are advised that to properly determine your right to enrollment as a citizen by intermarriage of the Cherokee Nation, it will be necessary for you to appear before the Commissioner for the purpose of giving testimony as to the date of your marriage and whether or not your wife, by reason of your marriage to whom you claim the right to enrollment as a citizen of the Cherokee Nation, was a recognized citizen of the Cherokee Nation at the time of your marriage to her, and whether or not you were married to her in accordance with Cherokee laws.

You are, therefore, directed to appear before the Commissioner at Muskogee, Indian Territory, at 9 o'clock A. M., on Wednesday, January 2, 1907, and give testimony as above indicated.

Respectfully,

J.M.H.   Acting Commissioner.

◇◇◇◇◇

Cherokee
77

Muskogee, Indian Territory, January 30, 1907.

W. W. Hastings,
        Attorney for the Cherokee Nation,
                Muskogee, Indian Territory.

Dear Sir:

There is inclosed herewith a copy of the decision of the Commissioner to the Five Civilized Tribes, dated January 30, 1907, granting the application for the enrollment of Diophantus D. Thornton as a citizen by intermarriage of the Cherokee Nation.

Respectfully,

Incl. GL-86.   Commissioner.
    GHL

◇◇◇◇◇

Cherokee
77

Muskogee, Indian Territory, January 30, 1907.

Pauline William,
Grove, Indian Territory.

Dear Madam:

There is enclosed herewith a copy of the decision of the Commissioner to the Five Civilized Tribes, dates January 30, 1907, granting the application for the enrollment as a citizen by intermarriage of the Cherokee Nation of your father, Diophantus D. Thornton.

You will be advised when his name has been placed upon a schedule of citizens of the Cherokee Nation, and approved by the Secretary of the Interior.

Respectfully,

Incl. GL-85   Commissioner.
GHL

◇◇◇◇◇

W.W.HASTINGS.   OFFICE OF   H.M. VANCE.
ATTORNEY.   SECRETARY.
Attorney for the Cherokee Nation,
Cherokee 77   MUSKOGEE, I. T.   January 30, 1907.

Commissioner to the Five Civilized Tribes,
Muskogee, Indian Territory.

Sir:

Receipt is acknowledged of the testimony and of your decision enrolling Diophantus D. Thornton as a citizen by intermarriage of the Cherokee Nation. Time for protesting said decision is waived, and I consent that said person may be placed upon the schedule immediately.

Respectfully,
W. W. Hastings
Attorney for Cherokee Nation.

Cher IW 133

◇◇◇◇◇

F.R.

DEPARTMENT OF THE INTERIOR,

COMMISSIONER TO THE FIVE CIVILIZED TRIBES.

In the matter of the application for the enrollment of

WILLIAM R. QUARLES

as a citizen by intermarriage of the Cherokee Nation.

Cherokee 250.

◇◇◇◇◇

DEPARTMENT OF THE INTERIOR.
COMMISSION TO THE FIVE CIVILIZED TRIBES.
WESTVILLE, I. T., JULY 17th, 1900.

IN THE MATTER OF THE APPLICATION OF William R. Quarles et al, for enrollment as citzens[sic] of the Cherokee Nation, and he being sworn by Commissioner, T. B. Needles, testified as follows:

Q What is your name? A William R. Quarles.
Q What is your age? A Fifty eight.
Q What is your Postoffice address? A Babtist[sic].
Q Where do you live? A Babtist.
Q How long have you lived there? A Thirty years.
Q In the Cherokee Nation? A Yes sir.
Q Lived in the Cherokee Nation the last thirty years continuously? A Yes sir.
Q Are you a Cherokee? A No sir.
Q Make application as a citizen by inter-marriage? A Yes sir.
Q Is your name on the authenticated Roll of 1880? A Yes sir.
(Identified on the Roll of 1880 as William Quarles, Page 464, #1347)
(Identified on the Roll of 1896 as William R. Quarles, Page 827, #1166, Going Snake District)
Q Are you married? A Yes sir.
Q Under what law were you married? A Cherokee law.

Q Have you a marriage liscence[sic] or certificate? A No sir.
Q Is your wifes[sic] name on the Roll of 1880? A Yes sir.
Q What is your wifes[sic] name? A Carrie E. Quarles.
(Identified on the Roll of 1880 as Carrie Quarles, Page 464, #1348)
Q How long has your wife been living in the Cherokee Nation? A Ever since 1848.
Q She has not lived out of it? A No sir.
(Identified on the Roll of 1896, Page 780, #1672, as Carrie E. Quarles)
Q Is her father living? A No sir.
Q When did he die? A 1842.
Q Neither is her mother living, I suppose? A No sir, she died in 1874; her mother did.
Q What is your District? A Going Snake.
Q Have you any children at home living with you under twenty one years of age?
A Yes sir.
Q What are their names? A They are adopted children; they are not my children at all.

The name of William R. Quarles, and his wife, Carrie E. Quarles appearing on the authenticated Rolls of 1880; also upon the census roll of 1896, identified as per page and number in this testimony; and the testimony showing that they have resided in the Cherokee Nation a sufficient length of time to entitle them to citizenship; they are hereby ordered to be enrolled as citizens; William R. Quarles as a citizen by inter-marriage; Carrie E. Quarles as a citizen by blood.; and their names will be placed on the rolls now being made by this Commission.

R. R. Cravens, being sworn, states that as stenographer to the Commission to the Five Civilized Tribes, he reported the foregoing case, and that the above and foregoing is a true, full and correct transcript of his stenographic notes in said case.

R R Cravens

Sworn to and subscribed before me this 18th day of July, 1900.

T B Needles COMMISSIONER.

Commissioner Breckinridge: It is found in Cherokee Straight Case 250, entitled William R. Quarles and others, that Carrie E. Quarles is shown by her enrollment card to have been 62 years of age at the time of her application.

It is ordered that a copy of this statement be attached to each copy of the testimony in her case.

Arthur G. Croninger, being duly sworn, states that as stenographer to the Commission to the Five Civilized Tribes he took in full the preceding statement and order, and that the foregoing is a true and complete transcript of his stenographic [sic]

Arthur G. Croninger

Subscribed and sworn to before me this 17th day of October, 1901.

C.R. Breckinridge
Commissioner.

◇◇◇◇◇

R.
Cher. 250.

Department of the Interior.
Commission to the Five Civilized Tribes.
Tahlequah, I. T., September 29, 1902.

SUPPLEMENTAL TESTIMONY AND PROCEEDINGS in the matter of the application for the enrollment of WILLIAM R. QUARLES as a citizen by intermarriage of the Cherokee Nation.

WILLIAM R. QUARLES, being first duly sworn, and being examined, testified as follows:

BY COMMISSION: What is your name? A William Robert Quarles.
Q How old are you? A I am sixty in December.
Q What is your post office address? A Baptist.
Q Are you a white man? A Yes sir.
Q Have you heretofore made application for enrollment as a citizen by intermarriage of the Cherokee Nation? A Yes sir.
Q What is the name of your wife? A Carrie E. Quarles. Her maiden name was Bushyhead.
Q Is she living? A Yes sir.
Q Are you and she living together now? A Yes sir.
Q Have you lived together continuously since the date of your marriage? A Yes sir, twenty-six years.
Q Do you claim your right to enrollment by reason of your marriage to her? A Yes sir.
Q Were you married to her according to the Cherokee laws? A I suppose I was. My first wife died, the one I brought from Georgia to this country. She was a Cherokee also, and after she died I married Miss Bushyhead. Then I was the same as any other Indian and didn't have to get a license.
Q Were you married to your first wife according to the customs of the Cherokees? A Yes sir. I have got a certificate a certificate[sic] at home, but could not find it. I had it before the Dawes Commission at Westville.
Q Have you and your wife lived together in the Cherokee Nation since you made your application for enrollment? A Yes sir.

299

This testimony will be filed with and made a part of the record in the matter of the application for the enrollment of William R. Quarles as a citizen by intermarriage of the Cherokee Nation, Cherokee straight card fidld[sic] No. 250.

Wm. Hutchinson, being first duly sworn, states that as stenographer to the Commission to the Five Civilized Tribes he correctly recorded the testimony and proceedings in this case, and that the foregoing is a true and complete transcript of the stenographic notes thereof.

Wm Hutchinson

Subscribed and sworn to before me this 29th day of September, 1902.

John O Rosson
Notary Public.

◇◇◇◇◇

C. F. B.   Cherokee 250.

DEPARTMENT OF THE INTERIOR,
COMMISSION TO THE FIVE CIVILIZED TRIBES.
Muskogee, Indian Territory, January 12, 1907.

In the matter of the application for the enrollment of William R. Quarles as a citizen by intermarriage of the Cherokee Nation.

William R. Quarles, Applicant.

APPEARANCES:

Cherokee Nation represented by
W. W. Hastings, Attorney.

William R. Quarles being first duly sworn by B. P. Rasmus, Notary Public, testified as follows:

ON BEHALF OF COMMISSIONER.

Q What is your name?   A William Robert Quarles.
Q What is your age?   A 64.
Q What is your post office address?
A Baptist.
Q You are an applicant for enrollment as a citizen by intermarriage of the Cherokee Nation?
A Yes sir.
Q You have no Cherokee blood?   A No sir.

Cherokee Intermarried White 1906
Volume IV

Q Your only claim to the right to enrollment as a citizen of the Cherokee Nation is by virtue of your marriage to a citizen by blood of the Nation?

A Yes sir.

Q What is the name of the citizen through whom you claim that right?

A Sarah C. Morris.

Q Is she living or dead?   A Dead.

Q When did you marry her?

A '71. I married her in '67 in the state of Georgia and when I came to this country, I married her in '71.

Q You and she were married then in the state of Georgia?

A Yes sir.

Q On coming to the Cherokee Nation, was your wife recognized as a citizen of the Nation or was she admitted to citizenship by the Cherokee authorities?

A By the Cherokee authorities after she came here.

Q After that re-admission, did you re-marry her?

A Yes sir; in August, '71.

Q Did you secure a license?

A They didn't give anything like that when I was married.

Q In what district were you married?

A Going Snake District.

Q By whom were you married?   A Judge Thornton.

Q Was he Judge of Going Snake District at that time?

A Yes sir.

Q Was Sarah C. Quarles your first wife?

A Yes sir.

Q Were you her first husband?   A Yes sir.

Q When did she die?   A March, '75.

Q Did you and she live together continuously as husband and wife until she died?

A Yes sir.

Q Have you married since her death?

A Yes sir.

Q What is the name of your second wife?

A Caroline Bushyhead.

Q Is she living at this time?   A Yes sir.

Q She is a Cherokee by blood?   A Yes sir.

Q And so recognized by the Cherokee authorities when you married her?

A Yes sir.

Q Since you came to the Cherokee Nation from Georgia in the year 1871, have you continuously lived in the Nation up to the present time?

A Yes sir; never been out of the territory, three weeks at a time, since that time.

Q Your first wife you say died before the 1880 roll was made?

A Yes sir.

Q You say she was admitted to citizenship after she came here from Georgia?

A Yes, in the Spring of '71.

Q Have you any certificate of admission?

A No sir.

Cherokee Intermarried White 1906
Volume IV

Q Did your first wife ever receive any certificate of admission?

A No sir.

Q Are any members of her family enrolled by the Cherokee authorities on the 1880 roll or on the final roll that this office is engaged in preparing?

A Yes sir; they are on all the rolls.

Q Can you name some of them?   A Yes sir.

Q Name some of them and tell the relationship.

A Silar Morris and Charlie Morris, brothers; Mary Morris, sister; or it might be Mary Sloan on some of the rolls. Fanny Buffington is a sister; she is the widow of John Buffington.

ON BEHALF OF CHEROKEE NATION.

Q Did these parties, whose names you mention, come here at the same time you did with your first wife?

A Yes sir; all came together.

Q Was your first wife admitted to citizenship along with them in '71?

A Yes sir.

Q By Act of Council?

A No sir; citizenship court was going on at that time.

ON BEHALF OF COMMISSIONER.

Q Those brothers and sisters of your first wife are on the final roll?

A Yes sir.

Q Living at this time?

A Yes sir.

The applicant, William R. Quarles, is identified on the Cherokee authenticated tribal roll of 1880, Going Snake District, No. 1347.

Q You present an affidavit executed by Emily Watts the 27th day of December, 1906, relative to the time of your marriage, which states that said Emily Watts was present and witnesses[sic] the marriage ceremony. Will it be possible for you to have Emily Watts appear before the Commission in person and testify in your case?

A No sir, I think not. I don't think she is able to get here.

Q Her physical condition will not permit her to come and give testimony?

A No sir; she is about 86 years old and very feeble. She is crippled up with rheumatism and can only get around on crutches.

The undersigned being first duly sworn states that as stenographer to the Commission to the Five Civilized Tribes, she recorded the testimony taken in this case and that the foregoing is a full, true and correct transcript of her stenographic notes thereof.

Myrtle Hill

Subscribed and sworn to before me this the 14th day of January, 1907.

John E. Tidwell
Notary Public.

◇◇◇◇◇

United States of America.

Northern District.

Indian Territory.

On this the 27th day of December 1906, personally appeared before me, W. M. Jeffries, a Notary Public within and for the Northern District Indian Territory, duly commission qualified acting, and authorized to administer oaths, ~~Ave Thornton~~ Emily Watts, and being first duly sworn on oath deposes and says, that she is acquainted with William R. Quarles, and that she has known him for thirty five years, that she was present on the 1st day of August 1871 at her house, when the said William R. Quarles was married to Sarah Morris by her husband officiating, under the laws of the Cherokee Nation,

Deponent further states that she is a fullblood Cherokee Indian, and has been in the Indian Territory, and a resident thereof for more than forty years.

That she has known said William R. Quarles continually since 1871, at the time of his marriage, and that after the death of Mrs. Sarah Quarles, who was a citizen of the Cherokee Nation by blood, said William R. Quarles married Carrie E. Bushyhead, a Cherokee Indian by blood, and that said Carrie E. Quarles, nee Bushyhead is still living, and that said William R. Quarles has never forfeited his citizenship in the Cherokee Nation since his first marriage to Sarah Morris,

her
Emily x Watts
mark

Subscribed and sworn to before me this the 27th, day of December, 1906.

W.M. Jeffries
Notary Public.

Commission expires April 23, 1910.

My commission expires_____

Witness to her mark { Mary Knight
Delilah Starr

◇◇◇◇◇

CERTIFIED COPY.

Executive Department
Cherokee Nation.
Tahlequah, Indian Territory.

I, A. B. Cunningham, Executive Secretary of the Cherokee Nation, do hereby certify that the records of "Applicants for Citizenship, Supreme Court Cases, Admitted" shows that Francis E. Morris and Children were admitted to citizenship, February 6th, 1871, entitled as Cherokees.

In testimony whereof, I hereunto set my hand and affix the seal of the Cherokee Nation, this that[sic] 12th, day of January, 1907.

(Signed) A. B. Cunningham,
Executive Secretary.

(SEAL).

I, Frances R. Lane, Stenographer to the Commissioner to the Five Civilized Tribes, hereby certify that the above is a true and complete copy of an instrument now on file with the records of this office.

Frances R. Lane

Subscribed and sworn to before me this January 26, 1907.

Edward Merrick
Notary Public.

◇◇◇◇◇

F.R.   Cherokee 250.

DEPARTMENT OF THE INTERIOR,
COMMISSIONER TO THE FIVE CIVILIZED TRIBES.

In the matter of the application for the enrollment of William R. Quarles as a citizen by intermarriage of the Cherokee Nation.

D E C I S I O N

THE RECORDS OF THIS OFFICE SHOW: That at Westville, Indian Territory, July 17, 1900, application was received by the Commission to the Five Civilized Tribes for the enrollment of William R. Quarles as a citizen by intermarriage of the Cherokee Nation. Further proceedings in the matter of said application were had at Tahlequah, Indian Territory, September 29, 1902, and at Muskogee, Indian Territory, January 12, 1907.

THE EVIDENCE IN THIS CASE SHOWS: That the applicant herein, William R. Quarles, a white man, was lawfully married in the State of Georgia in 1867, to one Sarah C. Quarles (nee Morris), since deceased. It is further shown that the said William R. Quarles and Sarah C. Quarles removed to the Cherokee Nation in the year 1871, and that the said Sarah C. Quarles was admitted to citizenship therein by the duly constituted authorities of said nation on February 6, 1871.   That subsequent to the admission of said Sarah C. Quarles to citizenship, and in the year 1871, the said William R. Quarles and Sarah C. Quarles were re-married according to Cherokee law. It is also shown that from the time of said marriage in 1871 until the death of said Sarah C. Quarles, which occurred in March, 1875, the said William R. Quarles and Sarah C. Quarles resided together as husband and wife and continuously lived in the Cherokee Nation.   It is further shown that said William R. Quarles continued to live in the Cherokee Nation until his marriage to Caroline Quarles (nee Bushyhead), who was at the time of said marriage a recognized citizen by blood of the Cherokee Nation, and who is identified on the Cherokee authenticated tribal roll of 1880, Going Snake District, No. 1348, as a native Cherokee. It is further shown that from the time of said marriage the said William R. Quarels[sic] and Caroline Quarles resided together as husband and wife and continuously lived in the Cherokee Nation up to and including September 1, 1902. Said applicant is identified on the Cherokee authenticated tribal roll of 1880, and on the Cherokee census roll of 1896 as an intermarried citizen of the Cherokee Nation.

IT IS, THEREFORE, ORDERED AND ADJUDGED: That in accordance with the decision of the Supreme Court of the United States, dated November 5, 1906, in the cases of Daniel Red Bird et al., vs. the United States, Nos. 125, 126, 127 and 128, the said applicant William R. Quarles is entitled, under the provision of Section 21 of the Act of Congress approved June 28, 1898 (30 Stats., 495), to enrollment as a citizen by intermarriage of the Cherokee Nation, and his application for enrollment as such is accordingly granted.

Tams Bixby
Commissioner.

Dated at Muskogee, Indian Territory,
this   JAN 30 1907

◇◇◇◇◇

Cherokee
250.

Muskogee, Indian Territory, January 30, 1907.

W. W. Hastings,
      Attorney for the Cherokee Nation,
            Muskogee, Indian Territory.

Dear Sir:

There is inclosed herewith a copy of the decision of the Commissioner to the Five Civilized Tribes, dated January 30, 1907, granting the application for the enrollment of William R. Quarles as a citizen by intermarriage of the Cherokee Nation.

Respectfully,

Incl. GL-82

Commissioner.

◇◇◇◇◇

W.W.HASTINGS. ATTORNEY.   OFFICE OF   H.M. VANCE. SECRETARY.

Attorney for the Cherokee Nation,

Cherokee 250.   MUSKOGEE, I. T.   January 30, 1907.

The Commissioner to the Five Civilized Tribes,
      Muskogee, Indian Territory.

Sir:

Receipt is acknowledged of the testimony and of your decision enrolling William R. Quarles as a citizen by intermarriage of the Cherokee Nation. Time for protesting said decision is waived and I consent that said person may be placed upon the schedule immediately.

Respectfully,
W. W. Hastings
Attorney for the Cherokee Nation.

◇◇◇◇◇

Cherokee
250.

Muskogee, Indian Territory, January 30, 1907.

William R. Quarles,
    Baptist, Indian Territory.

Dear Sir:

    There is inclosed herewith a copy of the decision of the Commissioner to the Five Civilized Tribes, dated January 29, 1907, granting your application for enrollment as a citizen by intermarriage of the Cherokee Nation.

    You will be advised when your name has been placed upon a schedule of citizens of the Cherokee Nation and approved by the Secretary of the Interior.

Respectfully,

Incl. GL-51.
GHL

Commissioner.

Cher IW 134

◇◇◇◇◇

F.R.

DEPARTMENT OF THE INTERIOR,

COMMISSIONER TO THE FIVE CIVILIZED TRIBES.

In the matter of the application for the enrollment of

ARGYLE QUESENBURY

as a citizen by intermarriage of the Cherokee Nation.

Cherokee 960.

Cherokee Intermarried White 1906
Volume IV

◇◇◇◇◇

DEPARTMENT OF THE INTERIOR,
COMMISSION TO THE FIVE CIVILIZED TRIBES,
SALLISAW, I.T., AUGUST 6, 1900.

In the matter of the application of Argyle Quesenbury for enrollment of himself, wife and children, as citizens of the Cherokee Nation, said Quenenbury[sic] being duly sworn, testified as follows:

Q What is your name? A Argyle Quesenbury.
Q Your age? A 60.
Q Your postoffice? A Sallisaw.
Q Have you been recognized by the Cherokee tribal authorities as a citizen of the Cherokee Nation? A Yes as an adopted citizen.
Q Have you ever been enrolled by the Cherokee tribal authorizes as a citizen of the Cherokee Nation? A Yes.
Q What district do you live in? A Sequoyah.
Q How long have you lived in that district? A About 28 or 29 years.
Q Have you lived continuously in the Cherokee Nation for that time?
A No sir, was absent about a year.
Q How long have you lived there continuously? A 23 years.
Q What is the name of your father? A Thomas Quesenbury.
Q Is he a citizen? A No sir.
Q What is the name of your mother? A Mary Quesenbury.
Q Is she living? A No sir.
Q Are you married? A Yes.
Q Under what laws? A Was first married under law of the State of Arkansas and afterwards under Cherokee law.
Q What was your wife's name before you married her? A Harriett B. Wheeler.
Q Is she living? A Yes
Q Is she a citizen? A Yes.
Q Is her name on the roll of '80? A Yes.
Q What was her father's name? A John F. Wheeler.
Q Is he a citizen? A Yes.
Q Is he living? A Yes.
Q What is your[sic] mother's name? A Nancy.
Q Is he[sic] a citizen? A Yes.
Q Have you any children under 21 years of age living with you?
    A No sir.
        Applicant on '80 roll, page 714, number 1014.
        On '96 roll, page 1117, number 142.
        Applicant's wife on '80 roll, page 714, number 1015;
        On '96 roll, page 1092, number 1138
        On '94 roll, page 985, number 1088.

Applicant's daughter, Lucy Quesenbury, aged 23 years,
on '80 roll, page 714, 1020;
On '96 roll, page 1092, number 1141;
On '94 roll, page 985, number 1091.

Q She lives at home with you? A Yes.
Q She has been a resident of the Cherokee Nation since her birth?
A Yes.

The name of Argyle Quenesbury[sic] and his wife, Harriett B., and his daughter, Lucy, names appearing upon the authenticated roll of '80 as well as upon the census roll of '96 and the pay-roll of '94, respectively, and they being fully identified, and having made satisfactory proof as to their residence, they are ordered listed for enrollment by this Commission as Cherokee citizens by blood, with the exception of Argyle Quesenbury, who is ordered listed for enrollment as a Cherokee citizen by marriage.

Brown McDonald, being duly sworn, says as Stenographer to the Commission to the Five Civilized Tribes, he reported in full the testimony of the above named witness, and that the foregoing is a full, true and correct transcript of his notes.

Brown McDonald

Sworn to and subscribed before me this 16th day of August, 1900, at Muldrow, I.T.

TB Needles
Commissioner.

◇◇◇◇◇

Cherokee 960.

Department of the Interior,
Commission to the Five Civilized Tribes,
Muskogee, I. T., October 7, 1902.

In the matter of the application of Argyle Quesenbury for the enrollment of himself as a citizen by intermarriage, and for the enrollment of his wife, Harriet B. and child, Lucy Quesenbury, as citizens by blood of the Cherokee Nation; he being sworn and examined by the Commission, testified as follows:

Q What is your name? A Argyle Quesenbury.
Q What is your age at this time? A Next birthday I will be 63.
Q What is your postoffice? A Sallisaw.
Q Are you the same Argyle Quesenbury that made application to this Commission for enrollment as an intermarried citizen on August 6, 1900? A Yes sir.
Q What is your wife's name? A Harriett B.
Q Is she a citizen by blood of the Cherokee Nation? A Yes sir.
Q Is she living at this time? A Yes sir.
Q When were you and your wife, Harriett B., married? A In '66.

Q Were you ever married prior to your marriage to this wife? A No sir.

Q Was she ever married prior to her marriage to you? A No sir.

Q You are her first husband and she your first wife? A Yes sir.

Q Have you and your wife, Harriett B., lived together as husband and wife all the time since 1880 up until the present time? A Yes sir.

Q You have never separated since 1880? A No sir.

Q And you have never married any other woman since 1880? A No sir.

Q Were you and your wife, Harriett B., living together as husband and wife on the first day of September, 1902? A Yes sir.

Q Have you and your wife, Harriet B., lived in the Cherokee Nation since 1880 up until the present time? A Yes sir.

Q Never lived out of the Cherokee Nation since '80? A No sir.

Q Your daughter, Lucy, yours and your wife's child? A Yes sir.

Q Is she living at this time? A Yes sir.

Q Has she lived in the Cherokee Nation all her life? A Yes sir.

The undersigned, being duly sworn, states that as stenographer to the Commission to the Five Civilized Tribes he correctly recorded the testimony and proceedings in this case, and that the foregoing is a true and correct transcript of his stenographic notes thereof.

E.G. Rothenberger

Subscribed and sworn to before me this 31st day of October, 1902.

BC Jones
Notary Public.

◇◇◇◇◇

Cherokee No. 960.

DEPARTMENT OF THE INTERIOR.
COMMISSIONER TO THE FIVE CIVILIZED TRIBES.

Muskogee, Indian Territory, January 3, 1907.

In the matter of the application for the enrollment of Argyle Quesenbury as a citizen by intermarriage of the Cherokee Nation.

Argyle Quesenbury, being first duly sworn and examined, testifies as follows:

BY THE COMMISSIONER:

Q What is your name? A Argyle Quesenbury.

Q How old are you? A 67.

Q Where do you live? A Sallisaw.

Q Do you claim to be an intermarried citizen of the Cherokee Nation? A Yes, sir.

Q Through whom do you claim your intermarried rights?

A Through my wife, Harriet B. Wheeler.

Q When were you married to Harriet B. Wheeler? A In 1866, in the state of Arkansas.

Q When were you married the second time? A In 1870?[sic]

Q Married under a Cherokee licence[sic] the second time? A Yes, sir.

Q Have you got that licence with you? A No, sir.

Q Where is the licence now? A I was married in the district where I lived and I never got them. I was married by the Judge.

Q Is that Judge living at this time? A No, sir.

Q You have never had the licence since you were married? A No, sir.

Q Were you ever married before? A No, sir.

Q Was she? A No, sir.

Q Have you lived together continuously in the Cherokee Nation since you[sic] second marriage? A Yes, sir.

Q Was your wife a citizen at the time you married her? A Yes, sir. Second time, not the first time.

Q When was she first admitted to citizenship? A In 1869.

Q Have you got a copy of that act? A No, sit[sic].

Q Can you get a copy of that act and furnish this office with it? A I don't know.

Q Is there any body here to-day that knows about that? A Yes, sir, W. W. Wheeler.

The applicant is identified on the 1880 Cherokee Roll, Sequoyah District, opposite No. 1014. His wife through whom he claims his right is identified on said roll opposite No. 1015. She is also identified on the final roll of citizens by blood of the Cherokee Nation opposite No. 2589.

WITNESS EXCUSED.

W. W. Wheeler, being first duly sworn and examined, testifies as follows:

BY THE COMMISSIONER:

Q What is your name? A W. W. Wheeler.

Q How old are you? A 59.

Q Where do you live? A Sallisaw.

Q Are you a citizen by blood of the Cherokee Nation? A I am.

Q Are you acquainted with Harriet B. Quesenbury? A She is my sister.

Q When was she first admitted to Cherokee citizenship? A Well since the war, I think it was in '69.

Q Was she admitted by an act of the Cherokee Council? A Yes, sir.

Q Were you admitted at the same time? A Yes, sir.

Q Have you got a copy of that act of the Council? A I have not.

Q When was she first enrolled as a citizen? A We are on the rolls clear back. During the troubles of 1845 my father left this country on account of the assassination of our people and he moved to Arkansas. At the close of the war we came back and we have been living there ever since.

Q Did you draw any movey[sic] during the '70's? A I think so, yes, sir. I think it was in '76 we drew some money.

WITNESS EXCUSED.

F. Elma Lane, upon oath, states that she reported the proceedings in the above entitled cause and that the foregoing is a true and correct transcript of her stenographic notes taken therein.

F. Elma Lane

Subscribed and sworn to before me this 4th day of January 1907.

Chas E Webster
Notary Public.

◇◇◇◇◇

C. F. B.   Cherokee 960.

DEPARTMENT OF THE INTERIOR,
COMMISSION TO THE FIVE CIVILIZED TRIBES.
Muskogee, Indian Territory, January 14, 1907.

Supplemental proceedings in the matter of the application for the enrollment of Argyle Quesenbury as a citizen by intermarriage of the Cherokee Nation.

The applicant, Argyle Quesenbury, presents a certified copy of an Act by the National Council, admitting certain persons to citizenship in the Cherokee Nation, passed at Tahlequah, Indian Territory Cherokee Nation, December 12, 1870, which shows that among others, Harriet B. Quesenbury, wife of applicant, was admitted by said decree, to the enjoyment of the rights and privileges of said decree, to the enjoyment of the rights and privileges of citizenship in the Cherokee Nation.

W. W. Wheeler being first duly sworn by B. P. Rasmus, Notary Public, testified as follows:

Q[sic]

Q What is your name?   A W. W. Wheeler.

Q What is your age?   A Past 59.

Q What is your post office address?

A Salisaw[sic], Indian Territory.

Q Do you know a person by the name of Argyle Quesenbury?

A Yes sir; have known him all my life.

Q He is an applicant for enrollment as a citizen by intermarriage of the Cherokee Nation?

A Yes sir; he marred my sister.

Q Your sister, Harriett B. Quesenbury now, formerly Harriett B. Wheeler, was a recognized citizen of the Cherokee Nation at the time she married Argyle Quesenbury?

A Yes sir; according to the Cherokee law.

Q He married her prior to the time he married her according to the laws of the Cherokee Nation?

A Yes sir.

Q Where did he marry her the first time?

A In Fort Smith.

Q But not in accordance with the laws of the Cherokee Nation?

A No; not until afterwards.

Q After this marriage, was Harriet B. Quesenbury admitted to citizenship in the Cherokee Nation?

A Yes sir.

Q And after that act of admission, Argyle Quesenbury remarried her in accordance with the laws of the Cherokee Nation?

A Yes sir; just about before the close of the year 1870.

Q In what district did he secure his license?

A Sequoyah District.

Q Did you see his license? A Yes sir; but I didn't read it particularly.

Q You saw his petition?

A Yes sir; I noticed a few of the names on the petition.

Q You have every reason to believe that he complied with the laws of the Cherokee Nation?

A I feel positive that he did.

Q Were you present at the marriage ceremony?

A Yes sir; I was present,- there at Cottonwood.

Q Since that time have Argyle Quesenbury and Harriett B. Quesenbury resided together as husband and wife?

A Yes sir.

Q And have continuously lived in the Cherokee Nation?

A Yes sir; if they have ever been out of it, I don't know it.

Q Was Argyle Quesenbury, Harriett B. Quesenbury's first husband?

A Yes sir.

Q And she was his first wife? A Yes sir.

Q Since the marriage of these parties in accordance with the law of the Cherokee Nation, has Argyle Quesenbury to your own personal knowledge, been recognized as a citizen by intermarriage of the Cherokee Nation the Nation?

A Yes sir; he has never been doubted.

Q He has enjoyed all the rights and privileges of a citizen of the Cherokee Nation?
A Yes sir; run for office, voted and served as juror; I think at one time he run for clerk.

J. H. Bowers being first duly sworn by B. P. Rasmus, Notary Public, testified as follows:

Q What is your name?   A J. H. Bowers.
Q What is your age?   A 68.
Q What is your post office address?
A Muldrow.
Q Do you know a person in the Cherokee Nation by the name of Argyle Quesenbury?
A Yes sir.
Q Are you acquainted with his wife?
A Yes sir.
Q What is her name?   A Harriett B. Wheeler.
Q How long have you known these parties?
A Since about '66.
Q Were they married at the time you first became acquainted with them?
A I suppose so; they were living in Fort Smith.
Q You understand that they were married?
A Yes sir.
Q After that time, they removed to the Cherokee Nation?
A Yes sir.
Q And was Harriett B. Quesenbury admitted to citizenship in the Cherokee Nation after they came here?
A That is my understanding.
Q After that admission, were they re-married to conform with the laws of the Cherokee Nation?
A That is what I understood.
Q It is your understanding then, that after the admission of Harriett B. Quesenbury to citizenship in the Cherokee Nation, she and her husband, Argyle Quesenbury, re-married in accordance with the laws of the Cherokee Nation?
A That was always the understanding.
Q You know of your own personal knowledge that since that time, Argyle Quesenbury has been recognized as an intermarried citizen and enjoyed all the rights and privileges of that class of citizens?
A Yes sir; and know he was candidate for district clerk.
Q You were not present at this second marriage?
A No sir.
Q You didn't see the license?
A No sir.
Q But you have every reason to believe that he did conform with the law of the Cherokee Nation relative to intermarriage and that they were married in accordance with the law?
A Yes sir; I have been on the jury with him in the Cherokee Courts.

The undersigned being first duly sworn states that as stenographer to the Commission to the Five Civilized Tribes, she recorded the testimony taken in this case and that the foregoing is a full, true and correct transcript of her stenographic notes thereof.

Myrtle Hill

Subscribed and sworn to before me this the 19th day of January, 1907.

John E. Tidwell
Notary Public.

◇◇◇◇◇

F.R.   Cherokee 960.

DEPARTMENT OF THE INTERIOR,

COMMISSIONER TO THE FIVE CIVILIZED TRIBES.

In the matter of the application for the enrollment of ARGYLE QUESENBURY as a citizen by intermarriage of the Cherokee Nation.

D E C I S I O N

THE RECORDS OF THIS OFFICE SHOW: That on August 6, 1900, application was received by the Commission to the Five Civilized Tribes for the enrollment of Argyle Quesenbury as a citizen by intermarriage of the Cherokee Nation. Further proceedings in the matter of said application were had at Muskogee, Indian Territory, October 7, 1902, and January 3 and 14, 1907.

THE EVIDENCE IN THIS CASE SHOWS: That the applicant herein, Argyle Quesenbury, a white man, was married in the State of Arkansas in the year 1866 to his wife, Harriett B. Quesenbury, nee Wheeler, a Cherokee by blood, that subsequent to said marriage said applicant and his wife removed to the Cherokee Nation, where the said Harriett (or Hariet) B. Quesenbury was admitted to citizenship as a citizen by blood of said Nation December 12, 1870, by the Cherokee National Council, by an Act entitled "An Act to re-admit to citizenship the persons therein names." It is further shown that after the time of the admission of Harriett B. Quesenbury to citizenship in the Cherokee Nation in the year 1870, the applicant herein and his said wife were remarried, in accordance with the laws of the Cherokee Nation. Said Harriett B. Quesenbury is identified on the Cherokee authenticated tribal roll of 1880, Sequoyah District, No. 1015, and her name is included in the approved partial roll of citizens by blood of the Cherokee Nation, opposite No. 2589. It is further shown that the said applicant, Argyle Quesenbury, and Harriett B. Quesenbury resided together as husband and wife, and continuously lived in the Cherokee Nation from the date of their marriage in accordance with the laws of the Cherokee Nation in 1870 up to and including September 1, 1902. Said applicant is identified on the Cherokee authenticated tribal roll of 1880, and the Cherokee census roll of 1896, as an intermarried citizen of the Cherokee Nation.

IT IS, THEREFORE, ORDERED AND ADJUDGED: That in accordance with the decision of the Supreme Court of the United States, dated November 5, 1906, in the cases of Daniel Red Bird et al. vs. the United States, Nos. 125, 126, 127 and 128, the said applicant, Argyle Quesenbury, is entitled, under the provisions of Section twenty-one, of the Act of Congress approved June 28, 1898 (30 Stats., 495), to enrollment as a citizen by intermarriage of the Cherokee Nation, and his application for enrollment as such is accordingly granted.

Tams Bixby
Commissioner.

Dated at Muskogee, Indian Territory,
this   JAN 30 1907

◇◇◇◇◇

Cherokee 960

Muskogee, Indian Territory, January 30, 1907.

W. W. Hastings,
    Attorney for the Cherokee Nation,
        Muskogee, Indian Territory.

Dear Sir:

There is enclosed herewith copy of the decision of the Commissioner to the Five Civilized Tribes, dated January 30, 1907, granting the application for the enrollment of Argyle Quesenbury as a citizen by intermarriage of the Cherokee Nation.

Respectfully,

Enc I-37.   Commissioner.

RPI

◇◇◇◇◇

Cherokee 960

Muskogee, Indian Territory, January 30, 1907.

The Commissioner to the Five Civilized Tribes,
Muskogee, Indian Territory.

Sir:

Receipt is acknowledged of the testimony and of your decision enrolling Argyle Quesenbury as a citizen by intermarriage of the Cherokee Nation. Time for protesting said decision is waived and I consent that said person may be placed upon the schedule immediately.

Respectfully,

W. W. Hastings
Attorney for the Cherokee Nation.

◇◇◇◇◇

Cherokee 960

Muskogee, Indian Territory, January 30, 1907.

Argyle Quesenbury,
Sallisaw, Indian Territory.

Dear Sir:

There is enclosed herewith copy of the decision of the Commissioner to the Five Civilized Tribes, dated January 30, 1907, granting the application for your enrollment as a citizen by intermarriage of the Cherokee Nation.

You will be advised when your name has been placed upon a schedule of citizens of the Cherokee Nation and approved by the Secretary of the Interior.

Respectfully,

Enc I-38   Commissioner.

RPI

317

320

www.ingramcontent.com/pod-product-compliance
Lightning Source LLC
Chambersburg PA
CBHW020244030426
42336CB00010B/613

* 9 7 8 1 6 4 9 6 8 0 7 3 0 *